Praise for *Fathers, Sons and Football*:

'Unusual but excellent . . . Compelling stuff. The football book of the year, perhaps'   *The Times*

'A fascinating study into footballing life and an interesting social comment on the impact of the sport as a whole'
Sunday Express

'The erudition of the author shines through . . . Enjoyable and informative'   *Sunday Telegraph*

'Brilliantly written and outstandingly researched . . . Surely the best book written about the beautiful game this year'
Yorkshire Evening Post

'Evocative and atmospheric, it serves as a mordant reminder that the Glory Game can also be a deeply tawdry game'
Independent

'Riveting . . . a cult classic'   *Sentinel*

Colin Shindler was born and raised in Manchester. After graduating from Cambridge University, where he is now a part-time lecturer in history, he completed his PhD thesis on Hollywood and the Great Depression. He wrote the screenplay for the movie *Buster*, and has written and produced television series such as *Lovejoy*, *Madson* and *Wish Me Luck*. He won a BAFTA for his production of *A Little Princess*.

His first book, *Manchester United Ruined My Life*, was published by Headline in 1998 and became an immediate bestseller. It was shortlisted for the William Hill Sports Book of the Year Prize. His first novel was *High on a Cliff*, also published by Headline.

Charge Sheet

Name: COLIN SHINDLER
Address: Maine Road, Manchester 14
Date of birth: Bert Trautmann's debut
Occupation: Manchester City fan
Previous offences: See separate sheet
Ethnic origin: Enough of this already

You are charged with the following offences:

1. That between the dates of 20 August 1965 and 13 June 1975 you revered Michael George Summerbee 'on this side of idolatry' and that anything you have written about the said outside-right/centre-forward should be read with the accompaniment of nine pounds of coarse sea salt.

2. That between the dates of 24 June 1994 and 14 November 1997 in the vicinity of Greater Manchester and beyond you saw many of the games played by Nicholas John Summerbee with your own son to whom you muttered the words 'He's nothing like as good as his father' in excess of one thousand times.

3. That on 6 May 1998 you did cause to be published a best-selling memoir entitled *Manchester United Ruined My Life* which made fun of a very rich merchandising operation thereby greatly offending the population of Scandinavia and the People's Republic of China in which you took an inordinate delight.

4. That on 2 January 2000 you began work on *Fathers, Sons and Football* with malice aforethought and the intention of bringing into disrepute vindictive football authorities, venal Football League chairmen, incompetent football managers, dirty and stupid football players, blinkered and bigoted football fans, the Conservative & Unionist Party of Great Britain and Northern Ireland and David Beckham.

Plea entered: Guilty
Verdict: Sent for trial by readers

Also by Colin Shindler

Manchester United Ruined My Life
High on a Cliff

Fathers,
Sons
and
Football

Colin Shindler

headline

First published in 2001
by HEADLINE BOOK PUBLISHING

First published in paperback in 2002
by HEADLINE BOOK PUBLISHING

10 9 8 7 6 5 4 3 2

ISBN 0 7472 3225 3

Typeset by
Letterpart Limited, Reigate, Surrey

Printed and bound in Great Britain by
Mackays of Chatham PLC, Chatham, Kent

Text design by Ben Cracknell

HEADLINE BOOK PUBLISHING
A division of Hodder Headline
338 Euston Road
London NW1 3BH

www.headline.co.uk
www.hodderheadline.com

To the memory of George Morley Summerbee
1914–55
The first of the line

Contents

Acknowledgements   xi
Sunderland   1
Winchester   9
Preston   21
Preston II   40
Portsmouth   61
Chester and Barrow   77
Cheltenham   98
Bristol and Swindon   125
Swindon to Manchester   145
Manchester – the Glory Years   167
Manchester – Cups and Cock-ups   194
Around Lancashire   215
Budapest to Swindon   237
Manchester – the Inglorious Years   262
Sunderland – Paradise Lost   289
Coda   317

Acknowledgements

My primary debt of gratitude is to the Summerbees themselves, particularly to Mike who flattered me enormously by asking me to write this book in the first place, and then for the sheer enjoyment of his company on our travels both geographical and historical. Tina has been constantly helpful and good-natured as I pried my way into her past, and both their children, Rachel and Nick, have been as honest and forthcoming as any biographer could possibly have wished.

Dulcie Summerbee gave me a full and illuminating picture of the life she led with George and it is her view of the reality of a life in professional football that colours this book. Her other son John provided vital information on their life together in Cheltenham and Nick's fiancée Leonie clearly shares the family trait of emotional honesty.

Mike's cousin Raymond and his mother Ruby Summerbee were particularly helpful in recalling their memories of George and his brother during the 1940s and 1950s. Heather and David Milne gave me vital help in researching the early history of the Summerbee family.

At Preston, I am grateful to Ian Rigby for information on George's difficult days at Deepdale and the club itself generously provided Mike and me with the hard evidence contained in the original documents of the time. Jack Rollin and Brian Glanville helped to guide me through the war years. At Portsmouth, Richard Owen not only gave me statistics but the key to

George's life by loaning me his rare copy of Jimmy Guthrie's autobiography and by introducing me to Bert Barlow who played alongside George at Fratton Park.

At Barrow, I am particularly indebted to John Bassett and Wilf Livingstone at the club and to Norma Lock for her reminiscences of George when he was a player there. At Cheltenham, I remain grateful to Ron Coltman and Ken Elliott for their memories of life with George in the early 1950s.

Everyone behind the scenes at Manchester City has been extremely helpful but I must mention in particular David Bernstein, Chris Bird and Sara Billington. Peter Brophy's knowledge of the Blues and his ability to navigate his way effortlessly along the electronic highway was greatly appreciated. I was delighted to listen to Francis Lee, George Best and Frank Clark as they shared their memories of Mike and his family as did nextdoor neighbours Peter and Mary Cobb. Ian Marshall, my much valued editor at Headline, proved a staunch and constant champion of this book, despite labouring under the handicap of being a Manchester United supporter.

At Sunderland, Niall Quinn and Chris Makin both helped to clarify situations that were not always apparent to an outsider.

Alastair Campbell was particularly helpful in our correspondence on Mike's days at Burnley.

As ever, my own family, Lynn, Amy and David, remain the best 'three at the back' in the history of the world.

CHAPTER ONE

Sunderland

History, Karl Marx tells us, repeats itself, first as tragedy then as farce. It isn't necessary to be a Marxist to appreciate the truth of this observation. Supporting Manchester City leads to much the same conclusion.

When Mike Summerbee played for Manchester City in the late 1960s there was a song in everyone's heart (well, there was in mine), every day was like the first day of spring, there was a chicken in every pot, a car in every garage and you could still get change from a £5 note. It cost six shillings to stand on the Kippax and watch Joe Mercer's aces fill the heart with gladness. Nobody had ever heard of the Spice Girls or Virgin West Coast trains.

If Mercer and Malcolm Allison were the brains of that glorious Manchester City team and Colin Bell was its heart, then Mike Summerbee was its soul. I loved them all in one way or another but I loved him best. He was not only brave, strong and skilful, he was also demonstrably human. He had, in the memorable phrase of that sage of Moss Side, former chairman Peter Swales, repartee with the crowd. In fact, he had not only repartee with the crowd (which Swales didn't mean) but rapport with them as well (which he presumably did, although since Swales was handicapped by an inability to speak English it is hard to be sure). Summerbee's flashes of merriment that were wont to set the Kippax on a roar included playing with a policeman's helmet on his head and kissing the referee who

1

was marching towards him with the intention of booking him or worse. For a player whose fierce competitive instinct caused sleepless nights among opposing defenders, Mike was (and is) a remarkably warm and humorous man.

Twenty-nine years after Mike made his debut at Maine Road, his son, Nicholas, followed the same path from Swindon to Moss Side. By the 1990s the economy was in a mess. The Chancellor of the Exchequer, Norman Lamont, could see the green shoots of recovery but nobody believed him because everyone was sniggering at his attempts to evict Miss Whiplash from the basement of his house and he had trouble explaining why his Access account couldn't seem to support the purchase of a bottle of Beaujolais at Threshers off licence in Paddington.

This was the England of John Major as refracted through the writings of George Orwell – not so much long shadows on county grounds (there was no one there to cast a shadow) and old maids bicycling to Evensong, more rush-hour gridlock and the disintegration of the National Health Service, and the editor of the *Sun* threatening to dump a bucket of shit over the Prime Minister after Black Wednesday ('Ha ha, Kelvin, very funny,' said the Prime Minister weakly or possibly weekly).

Nicholas Summerbee played for a Manchester City side that had become a national joke. In the *Guardian* there were calls for Ann Widdecombe to take on the job of manager since the previous incumbents had failed so spectacularly. For anyone who had recently seen City beaten in both legs of a League Cup tie by Lincoln City, the prospect of Ann Widdecombe putting the fear of God into Eddie McGoldrick and Gerry Creaney wasn't such a bad idea.

In this national and local atmosphere of fear and loathing, Nick played out his time at Maine Road. He played in the No. 7 shirt as his father had done, and he looked and ran like his dad. The fans wanted success so badly we could taste it, and because of all that, Nick Summerbee came to symbolise both the chimera of achievement and the reality of the humiliation.

2

The crowd turned on Nick and vented its fury on him because every week he was visible for 90 minutes. When they announced his name it was invariably booed.

At the start of the 1997–98 season, Nick had been dropped from the starting line-up and made only sporadic appearances from the bench. After a particularly disastrous and spineless home defeat by bottom of the table Huddersfield Town, Frank Clark – the manager of the month in November 1997 – decided he had to do something to save his job and the sanity of 30,000 supporters. He transferred Nicky to Sunderland in a straight swap for Craig Russell known briefly and erroneously as 'The Jarrow Arrow'. Each player was allegedly worth £1 million. It seemed like the end of the long connection between the Summerbees and Maine Road but, of course, nothing in football is that straightforward.

Two months later, Nick returned to Maine Road in a red and white striped shirt, a key player in a side that was threatening to storm to promotion. City were also threatening to leave Division One – through the trapdoor. The stage was set for some kind of crowd reaction because it wasn't just Nick who was returning for the day but the former City manager Peter Reid and his centre-forward, local hero Niall Quinn. We all knew something was going to happen but none of us knew exactly what.

In the Main Stand, near his friend the chairman Francis Lee, sat Mike Summerbee, who worked in the club's commercial department on match days, and Tina, his wife of 30 years. Mike was winding himself up to a fine fury, defending his son against the abuse of the crowd. If he could, he would have taken them all on. Tina sat quietly by his side hoping that the crowd would behave, that Nick wouldn't provoke anyone, that Mike wouldn't wade into the idiots sitting 20 yards away, that both sides could win. In a box at the top of the Kippax sat Mike's 77-year-old mother, Dulcie, who would happily have sprinted across the pitch to help Mike take on the crowd if they started on her grandson. In the Platt Lane stand I sat, stood, sat, stood, sat, stood in concert with the rest of the crowd as they prepared to show Nick Summerbee how they really felt about him – as if he didn't know.

In the City dugout, Frank Clark wasn't too sure what they might do, although he anticipated, as we all did, that the immutable law of the former player would operate against City yet again. 'You can never tell how crowds will react to players coming back. I was certainly worried about him turning it on, scoring two goals, but I was quite surprised at what happened.'

When the teams emerged at five to three, the true nature of the hostility was immediately revealed. The names of the players were read out over the public address system. Craig Russell's name was greeted with cheers from City fans hoping he might be 'the one' (football fans believe in the imminent arrival of the Messiah more fervently than the most devout Hassidic Jew) and loud applause from the Sunderland contingent who had retained their warm memories of a willing local player. Niall Quinn was greeted with rapturous applause, being a folk hero in both cities, but the name of Summerbee brought forth a tidal wave of discordant sound from City fans that drowned the token cheers of Sunderland supporters. I was wondering how Nick was feeling at that moment. Two and a half years later I found out:

At the start of the match, I was standing in the middle of the pitch and they announced the two teams. When Craig Russell's name was mentioned he got a standing ovation from the Sunderland fans because they liked him up there. When Niall Quinn's name was announced he got a standing ovation from the City fans and I got booed. I thought I'd get a bit of boo, I kind of like it, but nothing like what I heard. I looked across at Quinny but he didn't say anything. I never felt so lonely in my life.

4

Early in the second half, Quinn nodded the ball down to Lee Clark who put Summerbee away down the right-hand side. From Nick's cross, Kevin Phillips beat Wiekens in the air and the ball skewed off the back of Wiekens's neck past Wright in the City goal. It all seemed so inevitable. It was the seventh match in succession in which Phillips had scored, a Sunderland record. As they had against Huddersfield Town, City understood their role in this dumb show. It was to play the victim, which they did with great conviction, not surprisingly since they had been rehearsing for a very long time.

As City looked a despondent, defeated bunch, so Sunderland moved around Maine Road with the air of men who had come to do a professional job and were surprised to find how cooperative their opponents were. Nick had been under instructions from his father to wind up the crowd at every opportunity. There is one winger's trick that gains instant response from any crowd. Merely placing the ball inches outside the designated area from which a corner kick is supposed to be taken is usually enough to provoke a response from the most even-tempered spectators. It is regarded as scandalous cheating. Kicking an opponent in an attempt to cripple him rarely arouses the same degree of antagonism. Malicious wounding, aggravated bodily harm, assault with a deadly weapon, none of these arouses the ire of a crowd like placing a football nine inches beyond a white line. The mild-mannered Nicky doesn't usually bother with this sort of provocative behaviour but this day was different.

'Dad told me to put the ball outside the D but I didn't do it too much – it's not me and besides I've got to live in Manchester. When I did, everyone was shouting, calling me a wanker. These are grown men going berserk. The ref came over and I apologised and put the ball back inside the D but as he went back to the middle I put it out again.'

It happened just yards from where I was sitting so I can attest to the crowd's collective lunacy. The storming of the Bastille and the attack on the Winter Palace must have started with just such a moment. If someone had told them they could get hold of Nicky Summerbee because he had been spotted in Warsaw, they would have invaded Poland.

As City's performance on the field declined still further, Nick Summerbee became the principal target for the crowd's impotent fury. Frank Clark, who was sacked a month later, was spared the vitriol that day, and Francis Lee, who was forced out a few weeks after that, was ignored in favour of the Sunderland winger. The City team amounted to a collection of spineless, untalented individuals who were heading inexorably for the relegation that overwhelmed them on the last day of the season.

Nick Summerbee had escaped that fate. By some unfair stroke of fortune, Nick had leapt overboard and found refuge on a lifeboat that was travelling in the opposite direction. It seemed to us that Reid and Quinn and Summerbee were still umbilically linked to City. What right had they to go swanning up the A1 to Wearside while we were left watching Ged Brannan and Tony Vaughan? Reid was sitting in the dugout; Quinn had the inestimable advantage of having been a one-time City hero; the crowd redoubled the fury and spite it hurled at Summerbee.

The result was never in doubt. City played like condemned men who had anticipated defeat since the moment they trotted out of the tunnel. In the Main Stand, Mike sat smouldering, his own emotions clearly in turmoil. He couldn't help remembering the day he had returned to Maine Road a few months after his transfer to Burnley – he had received a standing ovation. Mike's instinctive loyalty has been to City since the day he signed in August 1965 but he is a father as well as an old City hero and his son had been suffering from the crowd's abuse for years. On the other hand, his close friend and former playing colleague Francis Lee was the embattled chairman of a failing club. Francis Lee knew well enough the consequences of this sort of home defeat and that Mike's son should be the one providing the nail for Phillips to hammer into the coffin was not much consolation. Francis had always told Mike to cool it when on the receiving end of criticism of his son. Mike took as much notice of such advice as he had when confronted with the unwelcome attentions of defenders during his playing days.

Tina Summerbee was shaken by what she encountered that day. She had married a City hero, her life was punctuated by a mixture of deep respect from City followers and gentle sarcasm from those of different persuasions, particularly United supporters. Life had been difficult during Nicholas's time at Maine Road but she had hoped that with his transfer the crowd might have learned to forgive and forget. The only way the crowd would have forgiven Nick that day was if he had scored three own goals in a 6–0 defeat and been sent off for picking his nose – and 'forgive' still isn't the right word.

Nick's sister Rachel didn't go to the game. She simply couldn't face it. She knew, perhaps better than any of the others, the depth of the antagonism. She worked in retail in Manchester and had been confronted with the reality of what the crowd thought about her brother too often to kid herself that today was going to be any different. She knew how passionately they hated Nick and she wasn't going to be there to witness its apotheosis.

Her grandmother was, though. Dulcie Summerbee had married a professional footballer, given birth to another and now was about to watch the third generation of her family in action. She knew how difficult a footballer's life could be. She had watched helplessly as her husband was forced out of the game he loved and delighted in her younger son's triumphs, but now, instead of enjoying her role as the grandmother of a Premiership player whose financial future was assured, she found life even harder.

It was as if all the anxieties that had gripped her since she met George Summerbee on a Preston bus in 1937 had been redoubled. Her twilight years were blighted as she sat in front of the television every Saturday afternoon, waiting for news of

Nicholas. Was he dropped? On the bench? Did the manager like him? Did the crowd like him? Would he get injured? Lose form? Lose his money? Lose his livelihood? Dulcie knew the lot from personal experience.

At the end of the match, Dulcie stayed in the box at the top of the Kippax, seething with anger at the way the fans had treated her grandson. If someone had given her a shotgun she would have emptied both barrels into the hostile crowd below her. Mike and Tina walked across from the Main Stand and into the lift that took them to the top of the Kippax where Dulcie sat waiting for them.

They talked quietly until Nicholas, freshly showered and smiling, came to join them all. They had planned to go home together but nobody was much in the mood for celebration. The only comfort they could take was that Nick had played well, crossed the ball for the winning goal and he was on course for a triumphant return to the Premiership. The sustained hostility of the crowd, however, had left its mark. The Summerbees drifted away into the cold unwelcoming January night as Frank Clark and his lieutenants shook their heads and wondered how they could stop this great tanker of a football club from breaking up on the rocks. Answer: they couldn't.

Mike drove his mother back to her little cottage in the Peak District. She has lived alone for some years, both her husbands having died. Despite her proximity to the game, Dulcie has never cared too much for football. The fate of the men close to her who were so adversely affected by it made sure of that. It might arouse crowds to peaks of ecstasy but all she knows is that it can destroy the lives of those who play it for a living. For 65 years she has been involved with it, ever since that day when she caught the same bus as two young men who had climbed aboard at the stop closest to Deepdale.

CHAPTER TWO

Winchester

On 1 August 1914, Germany declared war on Russia in response to Russia's mobilisation of its armies. Within days Britain and France had declared war on Germany and the First World War had begun. The *Hampshire Chronicle* reported the grave facts with appropriate solemnity, not on its front page which was, in the style of the day, devoted to classified ads, but on page three which had an entirely different connotation in 1914 than it does today. As Asquith's government made valiant efforts to preserve the integrity of gallant little Belgium, the first contribution of a Summerbee to the war effort was noted on the back page. Playing for Winchester College Servants against New College Oxford Servants at the College Meads, Bert Summerbee made the third top score of 12 as his team crushed the opposition by 17 runs. Somehow it seems appropriate that as the war clouds gathered over Europe, a Summerbee was playing sport. A few weeks later Bert Summerbee's nephew, George Morley Summerbee, was born in Winchester.

George was the son of Harriet Mary Ann Bell and Charles Edward Summerbee, the first product of the Summerbee/Bell connection. Besides Charles and Bert, there were five other Summerbee siblings, their Christian names a testimony to the moral certainties of Victorian England – Fred, William, Ethel, Rose and Edith. There is evidence of Summerbees in that part of Hampshire for many generations. Mike's belief is that the

Summerbee nose is a consequence of a romantic liaison between Oliver Cromwell and a Winchester floosie during the six-day siege of the castle by Cromwell's army in 1645. Sadly, no historical records exist to prove his thesis and it is difficult to imagine the dour and humourless Lord Protector of England blowing his nose, whatever its size, on the corner flag at Old Trafford as his putative descendant was to do. 'They used to hate me when I did that.' Mike smiles at the recollection. Oliver Cromwell would have called it God's will.

George Summerbee was born on 22 October 1914 into a solidly working-class family, the third of four children. His older sister, Vi, was born in 1906 and his brother Gordon in 1913. Another sister, Joan, was born in 1916. For generations, the Summerbees had been builders, bricklayers and publicans and had a particular association with a public house called The Bricklayers' Arms. However, Charles began his working life as a gas fitter and ended it as a motor mechanic. The fact that Bert played for the Winchester College Servants is a clue to the place of the Summerbees in a strictly ordered hierarchical society. The Servants were allowed to play on College Meads only after the young gentlemen had concluded the summer term.

Jane Austen, who died in the town in 1817, could have picked up the *Hampshire Chronicle* of 1 August 1914 and found little to surprise her, apart from the annual wage paid to a cook which had reached £28. A farmhand earned 14 shillings a week and a three-bedroomed house could be rented for ten shillings a week. There were weekly auctions of cattle, lamb and pigs and much attention was given to the Hospital Fête and the Romsey Horse Show. The local amateur light opera society was replacing its traditional production of *The Mikado* by Gilbert and Sullivan with a daring new production of *The Gondoliers* by Gilbert and Sullivan. Just to make everyone feel that nothing in the world would ever change, the letters column was filled with local correspondents complaining bitterly that the weather was too hot.

George and his siblings grew up in a landscape that had altered little over the centuries. Much is written today of the prosperous south-eastern corner of England. However, from the middle of the 18th century to the middle of the 20th things were different. If you drew a horizontal line across the country through the Potteries, north of what is now the Keele services on the M6 was the land of the industrial revolution and radical change. Below it lay an England that, with the exception of London and to a lesser extent Birmingham, was principally pastoral, farmland studded with ancient market towns one of which was Winchester.

The hills around Winchester are low and sedate, their fields presenting a spectacle that has remained untouched since the common land was enclosed. In George's day, the streams by the water meadows were so clear that the children could reach out and touch the trout, which were there in abundance. To the east, west and south of the city lay open country with sloping downs. Beyond Black Bridge and College Walk, the rural landscape spread out in front of them so that the youngsters were in the country yet still within a mile of the flat where they all lived in City Road near the railway station.

Although the power of the local rivers had been harnessed to the needs of production since mediaeval times, it was to drive flour or corn mills. In the industrial north, the rivers were the repository of the effluence of factories. Hobnailed boots couldn't survive in them, never mind the fish. The first major road in the area, the Winchester bypass, was built in the 1930s and that was probably the first time the air of the region was polluted by the coming of the industrial age. As late as 1933, J.B. Priestley wrote in his innovative travel book, *English Journey*, that the countryside surrounding Winchester was 'so empty and lovely, so apparently incapable of earning its exquisite living, that people ought to pay just to have a glimpse of it, as one of the last few luxuries in the world for the ranging eye.' Priestley was from Yorkshire and he couldn't help but note the difference between the gentle, welcoming beauty of the rolling Hampshire downs and the stark, unwelcoming grandeur of the Pennines, which he would have regarded as 'the country' when he was growing up in Bradford.

For most people, however, this was no pastoral idyll – four children and two parents in a two-bedroomed flat made sure of that for the Summerbees – but rural society in the south was slow to change when compared to the industrial north. The people were not necessarily more contented than their radical working-class counterparts in the north but they were less likely to turn to political action as a means of redressing their grievances. When I asked John Summerbee, Mike's brother, about his father his very first words were, 'My dad was a Communist.' I think what he meant by this somewhat startling statement was that George was a union man, not a Marxist revolutionary. He was a pioneer of the Professional Footballers Association at a time when the clubs wished that organisation had been strangled at birth. Even joining the PFA may not have occurred to George had he remained among his ain folk in Winchester.

Wealth in the north of England was based on industry. The workers fraternised with the bosses (without lessening their resentment of them). In the south, wealth was traditionally derived from the possession of land, which placed a different kind of barrier between rich and poor. Winchester belonged to a conservative England, to say nothing of a Conservative England. The nonconformist chapels made few inroads in this part of Hampshire where the Established Church still held sway.

A mile away from where George Summerbee's family lived lay Winchester College, the public school founded in 1382 by William of Wykeham to act as a feeder school for New College, which he had already endowed at Oxford University.

The fact that the young boys of privilege who boarded there lived lives of wretched deprivation and physical abuse would not have impacted much on the Summerbee boys. Their paths never crossed. Even their football was different. Winchester Football is the college's equivalent of the Eton Wall Game. It is doubtful if George or Gordon ever played it.

Instead, they played the game the rest of us know and clearly they played it well. The Summerbee boys moved swiftly through the ranks of the Hampshire League, George at Totten and Gordon at Basingstoke, until they were both signed by Aldershot Town in the Third Division (South) when George was still only 19 years old.

George and Gordon were close but as competitive as you might imagine two sports-obsessed brothers to be. Their niece Heather recalls that the rest of the family was inordinately proud of them, making sure that, if food was scarce, the brothers had the meat. The relationship between the two men is significant.

There is almost seven years between my brother and myself, so I grew up grateful to have the mysteries of leg spin or the offside laws imparted to me by a 13-year-old who clearly knew everything there was to know about the art of spinning a cricket ball and the rules of Association Football. My brother took some pleasure in his willing if not particularly gifted pupil. But as the age gap narrows between brothers, and particularly if they move into the same profession, the tension must inevitably rise. What must have galled both Gordon and George was the habit that everyone had of lumping them together.

The 99 boys who entered their first year at Bury Grammar School with me after the 11 Plus exams were initially divided into three classrooms according to alphabetical order. This came as a great relief to Rogers (G) and Rogers (A), a pair of twins so identical I wondered how their parents could ever tell them apart, or indeed how they knew, without touching the other one, that they weren't constantly looking into a mirror. There was no chance that I or any of their classmates or teachers could tell one from the other, so they always played on the same football side and were referred to jointly as Rogers, whether (G) or (A). Nobody dared separate them in case they either melted down instantly into a molten liquid or else spontaneously combusted like Monty Python's Mrs Niggerbaiter. They are probably living together today like the Bedser twins. (Cue two outraged letters from the North and South Poles.)

I mention the Rogers brothers because I am sure that if ever they felt they no longer needed the protection of each other's presence they must surely have started to find the encumbrance of a shared identity a major obstacle in life. So must it have been for the Summerbees, known to the newspapers as Summerbee (G.C.) and Summerbee (G.). The former was Gordon Charles but we shall now call him Bunt since that was how he was always addressed by the rest of the family – a corruption of the phrase 'Baby Bunting', which was presumably coined for him at an age younger than when he made his Football League debut.

Neither Bunt nor George could force his way into the Aldershot first team at the start of the 1934–35 season. The *Aldershot News* carried a photograph of the brothers taken at the pre-season trial game. George looks hauntingly young, an irony because he was shortly to age considerably and look older than his years for the rest of his life. Instead, both brothers played for Aldershot Town Reserves against Folkestone and were instrumental in a 3–2 victory.

Two weeks later, on 15 September 1934, they were both picked for the first team, George at right-half, Bunt at left-half. Their opponents were Swindon Town and Robins supporters reading this will be glad to note that the Summerbees' first encounter with their team ended in a 3–2 victory for the home team at the County Ground.

For the match against Northampton Town the following week, which ended in a 2–0 victory, the *Aldershot News* began its tradition of referring to George and Bunt jointly:

> The brothers Summerbee tackled quickly and 'feeding' well were very effective in the first half but failed to shine in the second period. Whether or not the ground was too heavy for them I cannot say but they were slow and uncertain and too often out of position.

I find it difficult to imagine how they could both be out of position all the time, and only in the second half, as if this had been a deliberate plan with the brothers communicating with each other as they had done at the age of eight via cocoa tins linked with a piece of string. They were now yoked together in the mind of the local football reporter like a pair of oxen.

And thus, as late summer turned to autumn and autumn to winter, Bunt and George settled down to become regular members of the Aldershot Town first team. The club had been admitted to the Football League in time for the start of the 1932–33 season and since then had struggled to avoid having to apply for re-election. With no tradition of success or anything in the way of financial reserves, unearthing promising youngsters at little cost was their main hope of survival. The Summerbees fitted the bill and even the occasional nightmare result and performance produced the sort of respect now accorded the Neville brothers. After a 3–0 drubbing at Brighton we learn that 'The brothers Summerbee were not as successful as their opposite numbers but came through a trying ordeal with credit' – which reads exactly like the *Manchester Evening News* reporting on England's eviction from Euro 2000 courtesy of Phil Neville.

In December 1934 and January 1935, George Summerbee played the best football he would manage in the next 13 years. Despite the absence of Bunt, he played a blinder in a 2–0 defeat at Bristol City: 'Summerbee at right-half played perfect football during much of the game and was very nearly the best man on the field.' The next week he starred again as Aldershot crushed Bournemouth 4–0 in the first round of the FA Cup. When Bunt rejoined the first team for the trip to Barrow in the second round, they performed mightily in a 2–0 triumph at Holker Street on a ground where George was to experience his happiest days as a professional footballer. Sitting in the stand that day was James Taylor, the key figure on the board of directors of Preston North End, whose malign influence was to cast such a heavy shadow over George's future life. He admired George's play and took steps to ensure that it benefited Preston North End.

For a club such as Aldershot Town a good Cup run produced much-needed revenue so it was with some dismay that the newspaper saw how it was frittered away. An attendance of 6,472 produced receipts in excess of £300 but since it cost £2 6s 6d per player to take the team to the north-west coast of Lancashire and since, profligacy piled upon profligacy, they stayed in a hotel on Friday night and Saturday night, the profits from the enterprise, the local paper muttered, were considerably less than had been anticipated. The idea that treating the players well and investing money in the train fare instead of making them walk the 250 miles from Aldershot with their boots round their necks might have had something to do with their victory seems not to have occurred to the writer.

It was a matter of some pride that the brothers Summerbee had established themselves as professional footballers. It gave them status in a society that still respected such professionals as schoolteachers and policemen and in which the rule of law held sway in an atmosphere unimaginable today. We can only shudder at the fate that befell Charles Cooper who was hauled before the hanging JPs of Winchester. Facing a charge of drunkenness he pleaded in mitigation that he 'only had eight pints, your worships'. Since Mr Cooper was thought not to be in training to become the Leader of the Conservative Party in the near future, the plea fell on deaf ears. Mr Cooper left the dock ten shillings poorer but grateful that transportation to Australia was no longer an option.

The larger clubs were already aware of the Summerbee wing-halves and, according to Bunt's son Raymond, they were being watched by a scout from Arsenal, by far the biggest club in the land at that time. In 1934, Arsenal provided seven of the England team that beat Italy 3–2 in the notorious Battle of Highbury. To sign for the Arsenal was the dream of every football-obsessed young man in the country.

The scout was in the stand, checking on Bunt, when George got involved with one of the opposing forwards. The skirmishing looked like it might develop into something more serious so Bunt sprinted across the field with the intention of saving his temperamental younger brother from any possible grief at the hands of the opposition or the referee. By the time he arrived, the skirmish had developed into a mêlée of angry players. Bunt, in attempting to drag George away from trouble, was instantly caught up in it and when the referee restored order Bunt, the would-be peacemaker, was the only player to be sent off. The scout from Arsenal watching from the stand must have concluded that any player who steamed 50 yards to join in a fight and get himself sent off was not the sort of player to be walking through the hallowed Highbury portals on a daily basis. Bunt never heard anything more from the marble halls and indeed he never moved out of the Third Division (South).

For George, though, the beckoning finger of fame loomed larger. First Division clubs Huddersfield Town and Blackpool were both allegedly interested in the Aldershot right-half. When the much anticipated third-round tie against Reading finally got under way, George gave yet another impressive display, scoring, if contemporary reports are to be believed, direct from a free kick 'forty to fifty yards out'. It was Aldershot's only goal in a 3–1 defeat in front of 17,666 people who paid the grand sum of £1,163. Being thus knocked out of the Cup left the club free to concentrate on the fight against having to apply for re-election to the Football League. In April 1935 they managed it by the slenderest possible margin, finishing second from bottom after losing their final game of the season 8–1 at Exeter.

George played no further part in the campaign. By the time the game at Reading had finished, George Summerbee was no longer an Aldershot player. After the Barrow game, Angus Seed, the Aldershot manager, had followed Jim Taylor back to Preston where he signed a contract giving Preston North End an option on George's services from the moment Aldershot's Cup run ended. According to the Preston North End minute books, 'On 3 January 1935, Mr Jas Taylor reported on player Summerbee of Aldershot F.C. and stated he had an interest in George Summerbee the right half-back for whom Aldershot required £650 when dismissed from the Cup. Mr Taylor was granted power to secure this player if still satisfied.' Five days later Mr Taylor reported to the committee that he had confirmed the transfer fee at £650, providing the player was physically sound. Two weeks later, Mr Taylor reported that action would be taken regarding the signing of George Summerbee in the next few days.

On his way south to watch Preston play a fourth-round Cup-tie at Swindon in the last week of January 1935, Jim Taylor met George Summerbee and Angus Seed at a hotel in Cheltenham. George signed for Preston. It is quite extraordinary how certain towns crop up time and again in the life story of the Summerbees – Barrow, Swindon, Cheltenham, in particular – as if some divine hand were so ordering it. Just to add to the pile of coincidences, the Aldershot team included, besides Summerbee G. and Summerbee G.C., two players by the name of Lee and Oakes (names familiar to Manchester

City fans of a certain age), giving it a somewhat eerie appearance.

Aldershot were sad to see George go, particularly the *Aldershot News* reporter, who would be forced from now on to write about Bunt as an individual player rather than as the back half of a pantomime horse:

> [George Summerbee] has developed well as a right-half and has shown a liking for the pivotal position. If, with the experience and training he will receive at Preston, he does not develop into a first-class centre-half, I shall be surprised. It is a pity the directors are forced to sell such a brilliant player but unfortunately the position was forced on them by their financial liabilities.

A mere few weeks earlier, this brilliant player was being recommended for reserve-team duties by this self-same commentator in his reports. It was an early lesson for George that the local football reporter shares the prerogative of the newspaper baron and the harlot down the ages – power without responsibility. On this occasion, he benefited from this edgy and uncertain relationship, but he soon discovered the other side.

George was undoubtedly excited to be leaving Winchester, for all its superficial charms. According to J.B. Priestley, the place 'looked more old than new. I never pass through these smaller cathedral cities, on a fine day,' he wrote, 'without imagining I could spend a few happy years there, and never find myself compelled to spend a morning and afternoon in one without wishing the day was over and I was moving on.'

As the smartly dressed George Summerbee climbed aboard the train that would take him from the pastoral south to the industrial north, from the security and familiarity of the family flat in City Road, Winchester, to the cold strangeness of digs near Deepdale in Preston, perhaps he felt something of Priestley's impatience. Writing his story 65 years later, I feel like one of the audience watching a Hitchcock thriller – you know the identity of the killer and look on as the heroine unwittingly places her life in his evil hands. 'Don't do it, George!' I want to cry out. 'Stay in Winchester! Go back to Aldershot!' Too late. The train lumbers forward with a jolt. He is leaning out of the window, waving goodbye to Mum and Dad through a dense cloud of steam, to his sisters Vi and Joan, and above all to Bunt who is presumably feeling a weird mixture of great fraternal pride and intense professional jealousy. George is 20 years old and he believes his future could not be brighter. Preston and a lifetime of soul-destroying obscurity beckons.

CHAPTER THREE

Preston

George Summerbee signed for Preston North End on standard terms – £5 a week during the season and £4 a week during the summer which ran from the first week in May until the last week in August. If he played in the first team he would receive a further £1. Until the outbreak of war when his wages, like those of all other players whose contracts were suspended, were reduced to 30 shillings per match, George Summerbee's income remained more or less unchanged. From 1922 to 1946 the maximum wage permissible for a professional footballer was £8 a week.

To put this ostensibly derisory amount into perspective, the average working man's wage in the mid 1930s was £3 for a 46-hour week. The secretarial support staff at Preston earned £1 10s a week. The average price of admission to the ground was one shilling. Depending on your perspective, you could argue that footballers were well paid. A miner, if he was working for 12 months, which was unusual, earned just over £100 in a year. At Preston, George Summerbee was on about £250, while a provincial bank manager earned around £350.

Twelve months after George Summerbee arrived in Preston, the left-wing publisher Victor Gollancz commissioned George Orwell to write another in the genre of books begun by William Cobbett and Thomas Carlyle in the 19th century, which described the social and economic health of England. Orwell was shocked by the conditions he found in

Wigan, Barnsley and Sheffield, and his unforgettable depiction of working-class life in the north of England in 1936 was published under the title *The Road to Wigan Pier*.

Twenty miles from Deepdale, George Orwell discovered families living in one-up, one-down slums. The lavatory was sited 50 yards away. The rent for this 'home' was 7s 3d a week. In such houses there were usually two beds for the whole family. The father slept with his sons, the mother with her daughters, although clearly the custom was occasionally breached otherwise there wouldn't have been quite so many sons and daughters. The total income for a family of six of this nature, assuming the man to be on the dole, was 32s 6d a week. A single man was awarded 15 shillings; a husband and wife who were both unemployed had to make do on £1 4s.

One man who was seen carrying firewood lost his dole entitlement. Carrying firewood was regarded as a job. In vain did the man plead that the 'firewood' was his furniture and he had been seen doing a midnight flit because he couldn't afford to pay the rent. His dole money was stopped regardless.

The humiliations heaped upon the poor by these conditions spread out like ripples on a pond. An ageing parent could not afford to live with his children and their families. He would be regarded as a lodger and his children's dole would be reduced accordingly. Many such parents were forced to move into lodgings and hand over the pension to a lodging housekeeper. They were reduced to a scarcely imaginable existence on the verge of starvation.

George Summerbee spent 30 shillings of his weekly £5 on lodgings, breakfast and probably dinner included. Down the A6, Orwell found families living on 30 shillings in total. The man, his wife and two small children spent nine of those 30 shillings on rent, leaving 21 shillings to spend on food, clothes, heat and light. What must their diet have been like – a loaf of white bread, some margarine, corned beef, sugared tea and potatoes? There would have been no money for fruit or any other vegetables.

While George, Bill Shankly and the O'Donnell brothers were playing one-touch five-a-sides, a few miles away dumpy, shawled women with their sacking aprons and their heavy black clogs were kneeling in the cindery mud and the bitter wind searching for tiny chips of coal on the slagheaps. Every so often the coal company hauled them off and prosecuted them for stealing. The mines were privately owned and the slag belonged to the company.

Ironically, Preston suffered less acutely during the Depression than most of the other cotton towns in Lancashire because the local economy had weaned itself off total reliance on the cotton trade. Cotton had been king in Lancashire for over 100 years. Manchester was known as Cottonopolis and the towns around the city, from Burnley in the north to Preston in the west and Oldham on the eastern edge of the county, grew to service the industry and its workers. The cotton mills dominated the skyline then as the tall skyscrapers built to house the all-pervasive financial services sector do today. The low houses that lined the streets of Rochdale and Bolton and Bury were built for the workers who toiled in the mills.

If you walk along the pedestrianised precincts and through the shopping malls that disfigure their centres today, each marked by its ubiquitous Marks & Spencer, British Home Stores and W.H. Smith, it is hard to grasp the historical importance of such towns. Until the outbreak of the First World War, these places were commonly regarded as 'the workshop of the world', the centre of its trade and the heart of its manufacturing base. The air was permanently polluted by the constantly smoking chimneys. As late as 1956, just before the first effects of the Clean Air Act became evident, my mother had to take me to Blackpool to recover from an attack of sinusitis brought on by inhaling the soot and grime that hung in the air we breathed. The front of Manchester town hall in Albert Square is now a completely different colour from the grim black façade I remember when I was growing up.

The contraction of the textile industry decimated Lancashire during the interwar years. Preston's economic difficulties were well advanced before the Depression made film stars out of Gracie Fields and George Formby, but although unemployment affected about 10,000 workers, other employment opportunities arose as the cotton industry collapsed. In 1929, 50 per cent of the adult insured population of the Preston employment area was employed in textiles. By 1939, this figure had fallen to 25 per cent and after the war it dropped as low as 13 per cent.

What happened in Preston in the 1930s is what happened throughout British industry in the postwar years – namely, the replacement of the heavy industries that had fuelled the great export boom of the 19th century by the consumer and service industries required to feed the increasing home demand. In December 1937 when Oldham registered 11,000 unemployed, Burnley 8,000 and Blackburn a catastrophic 14,000, Preston had just over 6,000. As the train carrying George Summerbee to his new life in the north pulled into Preston station, he saw the building work just started on the Courtauld's rayon plant, a huge symbol of the future for the traditional textile industry.

In 1933, J.B. Priestley saw Preston in the way that everyone who grew up in Manchester always saw Preston before the building of the motorways – as a staging post on the way to Blackpool:

Beyond Preston, in a flat and characterless countryside, all the roads suddenly become very straight and wide and display large cheerfully vulgar advertisements. This is because they, like you, are going to Blackpool. Even if you did not intend to go to Blackpool, once you had got beyond Preston you would have to go there. These roads would suck you into Blackpool. That is what they are there for. There is no escape.

More succinct is the comment of Zuckerman, the bespectacled Jewish kid of primary school age in Jack Rosenthal's delectable television film, *The Evacuees*. He attempts to lead his party of three in a mass breakout from the tyranny of evacuation to an unwelcoming house in Blackpool by roller-skating back to Manchester (four skates to be divided by six feet). Asked by the youngest, 'Are we nearly there yet?' when in fact they are still skating slowly along the promenade on the south shore, Zuckerman replies to the point – 'We're not even in Preston yet.'

What saves Preston from anonymity is what saves dozens of other towns across the country from a similar fate – the local football team. It seems unlikely that Hartlepool or Scunthorpe or Gillingham would impose themselves on the conscious mind of the nation if it were not for the fact that their names are heard and seen in the weekly football results. Even today, 40 years after their demise as a Football League club, Accrington evokes a smile of recognition as the home of Accrington Stanley while neighbouring Bacup and Haslingden can make no such claim to spurious fame.

Preston North End, however, are a considerable cut above those teams and always were. They were founder members of the Football League in 1888 and won it for the first two years of its existence, finishing as runners-up in the next three seasons. In 1888 they also reached the FA Cup final after an infamous 26–0 win against Hyde United. Defeat in the final by West Bromwich Albion stunned the town but it was quickly attributed to players having 'got cold' while sightseeing in London, nobody being quick enough off the mark to complain about the colour of their shirts.

On 31 March 1889, North End beat Wolverhampton Wanderers at The Oval to win the FA Cup without having conceded a goal in the competition. Having also won the first league championship earlier in the year without losing a game, they set a record that is unlikely ever to be equalled.

No video, CD or replica strip crowned these remarkable triumphs, merely the nickname the Invincibles. Preston North End were the best team in the country.

The 20th century, however, proved less successful and in 1925 they were relegated to the Second Division. The arrival of two people heralded the start of better things for the club. In 1932 the manager, Lincoln Hayes, departed after one season in charge and the board of directors decided they could do better themselves. The club was run by a committee from 1932 to 1949, with the exception of the 1936–37 season when Tommy Muirhead was nominally in charge. In effect, though, the committee was a device by which the aforementioned redoubtable Jim Taylor imposed his personality on the club. Then at the start of the 1933–34 season, Preston signed the Scottish right-half Bill Shankly from Carlisle United. As the first team floundered as usual in the middle of the Second Division, Shankly was playing in the reserves. After a 2–1 defeat at Gigg Lane at the beginning of December, it was decided to give Shankly his debut. The result was a convincing 5–0 home win over Hull City. Shankly played every remaining match that year in a settled half-back line with Bill Tremelling, the North End captain, and Jimmy Milne at left-half. Holding off the challenge of Brentford and Bolton Wanderers by a point, Preston clinched the second promotion spot, seven points behind championship winners Grimsby Town.

George Summerbee arrived in Preston in the middle of their consolidating season in the First Division. Despite a bright start in which they won five of their first seven games, the autumn had been a grim time for North End. The settled defence that had been the backbone of the promotion drive the previous season started to ship goals at an alarming rate. Bob Batey was signed from Carlisle and he replaced Jimmy Milne from the beginning of January, the month in which George Summerbee was bought from Aldershot.

Ironically, from the moment George arrived at Deepdale,

results picked up – no thanks to George, of course. The defence kept 12 clean sheets and the single goal defeat at the Hawthorns in a disappointing sixth-round tie against West Bromwich Albion was the only match Preston lost in a 15-match run. They finished the season in a respectable mid-table position with 15 wins and 15 defeats, taking 42 points from 42 games.

George began his new life in the reserves. This wasn't entirely surprising. Shankly, who was a year older than George, had followed the same pattern the previous year. If he kept his nose clean and played his heart out, his turn would come. Injuries or loss of form in the first team would see to that.

The local paper, the *Lancashire Daily Post*, reported the arrival of 'G. Summerbee' and informed its readers that Preston's latest signing was 'one of two brothers in the Aldershot side and the better player. He is five feet ten inches and weighs ten and a half stone.' I hope George didn't send that particular clipping back to Winchester. I don't suppose Bunt would have been too thrilled to see it.

George's first game in Preston colours on the Saturday after his transfer resulted in a 3–1 home win over Blackpool Reserves at Deepdale but more exciting for him and his waiting family back home was the *Post*'s report on the following midweek game at Bramall Lane:

> Summerbee, the new right-half, made a good impression in the reserves game with Sheffield United. Summerbee has a distinctive style but he plays crafty football and Kelly owed much of his opportunity to shine to this youngster's constructiveness.

Despite this good early impression, George played out the remainder of his first season at Deepdale in the reserves. When the season finished at the beginning of May, he collected his £4 a week summer wages and returned to Winchester to be with his family. Unlike George's younger son who worked during the summer, there is no memory of George or Bunt taking a job, although it is entirely possible that they helped out in the garage where their father was the chief motor mechanic. The hedonistic delights of Winchester in the summer months, with the prospect of long lazy days on the cricket field, proved overwhelmingly attractive. The remaining family members believe the boys were slightly spoiled by their proud parents. After all, not many of their neighbours could boast of two sons who played professional league football. John Summerbee, Mike's brother, believes his father was also good enough to have played Second XI cricket for Hampshire.

There is a rare photograph of George taken before a pre-season practice match played in aid of Hospital Charities at the start of the 1935–36 season. That was the day North End officially opened the new Pavilion Stand, incorporating new dressing rooms, a boardroom and offices. It is clear that, under the leadership of Jim Taylor, Preston were a club with considerable ambition – rather like the early days of Peter Swales. The first team played the reserves and in the picture George sits on the front row next to his friend Bill Shankly. Shankly wears the traditional white shirt and dark shorts of Preston while George is clad in the coloured shirt and white shorts of the nameless others. Much as he liked Shankly, it would have been only human for George to wish an injury on his friend at some time in the season. Arriving back for pre-season training, still on his summer wages of £4, George discovered that the club had signed Hugh and Frank O'Donnell from Celtic. Frank played at inside-left and Hugh at outside-left. George, not yet 21, hadn't started to panic but he was conscious of the fact that Andrew Beattie, who had arrived at the club at much the same time as him, had already made his debut on the left wing, albeit in Preston's last match of the 1934–35 season. If Andy Beattie continued in the first team, it would be at left-half or left-back and that limited George's chances still further.

The number of Scottish players on the books was soaring relentlessly. Jimmy Dougal arrived from Falkirk in 1934, the same year that James 'Bud' Maxwell signed from Kilmarnock. Maxwell was an instant success, scoring 25 league and Cup goals, and Dougal proved to be a goalscoring stalwart for the next 12 years. The O'Donnells immediately settled into the first team, scoring 28 goals between them over the season. Their success makes it easier to understand Jim Taylor's predilection for collecting Scotsmen, but as the team continued to prosper in the second half of the decade, it also confirmed his prejudice that only players born north of Carlisle could play. Tom Finney later recalled, 'We were taught to play the Scottish way with short passes.' This made sense since the forward line was made up of goalscorers who were rarely taller than 5 feet 7 inches. It should have been good news for George whose strength, by all accounts, lay in the accuracy of his passing, but still he remained solidly out of favour.

If Taylor remained the most significant presence in the club, he was happy to leave the training to Bill Scott and his assistant Jimmy Metcalfe. Perhaps on account of the Scottish influence, the training did not emphasise, as so much traditional English training did at this time, monotonous lapping of the pitch and endless cross-country runs. Peter Doherty wrote later of his experience of training: 'Players lope aimlessly round the track in small groups, talking to relieve their boredom and wondering whether they can drop out inconspicuously. They regard perpetual lapping as a form of slow torture.' While it certainly didn't anticipate the current beliefs in weight training, rigorous attention to diet and scientific gym work, the philosophy in force at Preston North End was innovative for the time in its emphasis on five-a-side and three-a-side games. It was a system Shankly was to take with him to Liverpool in the 1960s.

The ball was in constant use, in direct contradiction to the traditional belief held in English football in the 1930s that if you denied footballers the chance to work with the ball during the week, it would increase their appetite for it on Saturday afternoons. There is a flaw in this argument. If you've spotted it, you would have been in line to coach the England side of the 1930s, had they bothered with anything as namby pamby as a coach. If you were a true international player, it was felt at that time that all you needed was a letter from the FA informing you of your selection and a second-class rail warrant to Wembley Park.

In the pre-season of 1971–72, I trained with Manchester City in the belief that it would help me to write about footballers with more understanding. (In fact, I could probably have made the same observations from the touchline but I was 22 years old and obsessed with the players.) Despite the hard training of the morning – and it was genuinely hard – I was surprised by the amount of free time that footballers had, and presumably always had and still do. I understand perfectly well that the body cannot operate for 40 hours a week as it does during the 90 minutes of a match or even the two and a half gruelling hours we used to spend at Wythenshawe Park on a Monday morning. Of course players need time to wind down both physically and mentally, otherwise they end up like Roy Keane, but frankly as someone who had the Judeo-Christian work ethic implanted the same day they took away my foreskin (well, maybe not precisely the same day) the shock of the 'afternoons off' never diminished. Why do most of us who work for a living fail to experience a sense of amazement when Alex Ferguson tells us that Beckham sometimes stays behind in the afternoon to work on his dead-ball kicking? In preference to what exactly? More shopping? Internet share dealing?

What did footballers do back in the 1930s? Eddie Hapgood, captain of Arsenal and England during that decade wrote about his own working routine in his autobiography, *Football Ambassador*. Sunday was treatment day when players who had suffered a knock during Saturday's match spent the morning on the treatment table while the rest of the team sat in the bath in the next room. For the rest of the week they had to sign the arrival book, which was a marginally more acceptable version of clocking on. Monday was light training, lapping the ground with some head tennis. Tuesday was harder training with eight to 12 laps of the ground followed by skipping and shooting while wearing canvas shoes. What a relief that flip-flops hadn't been invented then. On Wednesday and Thursday the work got increasingly harder, with more concentrated running and some gym work. On Friday they really went at it with very heavy gym work, including the punch bag and skipping as if a heavyweight world boxing title were at stake. Then came baths and the big moment of the week – the announcement of first and reserve teams for the following day, which was always made at noon. Afterwards the players went into the boardroom for a conference about the next day's match. At Blackpool, the players would report to a local hotel on Friday afternoon if they were playing at home the following day. The manager would thus be sure that the players were tucked up in bed by 10 p.m. Any player permitted to remain in digs could expect a visit from the trainer at 9.45 p.m.

Thirty years later Malcolm Allison reversed this idea almost completely. Instead of building up to the game by making the work increasingly onerous he made Monday morning the worst day of the week so that by the time Friday came the players were bursting to play instead of being so tired they could scarcely pick up their legs as was the case on a Tuesday morning. On Friday afternoons Stan Gibson, the City grounds-man, generously allowed the players to run on the pitch but it was a light training session only.

So now we know what they did during the day and we can see how attractive the Preston training sessions must have seemed to players whose previous experience of training was restricted to the boring mechanical routines of even Eddie Hapgood's successful Arsenal. But what else did they do? They didn't pose for adverts or help their wives sell records – unless George spent time in Dulcie's grandparents' shop selling gramophones, which isn't quite the same idea as David Beckham flogging his wife's latest CD in the Oldham branch of Woolworth.

It is not possible to argue from the lack of newspaper tittle tattle that professional footballers in the 1930s were better behaved than they are today. It is simply that any indiscretion committed in the 1930s would never find its way into the popular press. Nevertheless, from all reports, it seems that the Preston players of George's era probably were pretty well behaved. Bill Scott, interviewed about them shortly before their appearance in the 1937 FA Cup final, remarked, 'Players today take the game more seriously than in the old days and regard it as a profession rather than a gay life that will go on for ever. Nine of our first team do not smoke and all are well-behaved fellows.' It may well be, of course, that this exemplary behaviour stemmed from the lack of an alternative.

These were the days when golf clubs didn't welcome working-class oiks, although no doubt some of them got in somewhere, so when they weren't either playing football or training to play football, they spent a lot of time in cinemas, pubs, snooker halls and the local palais de danse. There really wasn't much else on offer, particularly in the 1930s in Preston; and by the time Mike started out on his career, almost nothing had changed. Life for Mike Summerbee in Swindon in the 1950s was not a whole lot different from the life his father led in Preston in the 1930s.

George was a skilful defender who by rights should have benefited from Preston's relatively innovative training and cultured style of play, yet throughout the 1935–36 season he barely got the sniff of a place in the first team. Bill Shankly missed just one game – at home to Portsmouth at the beginning of October. Presumably he had been hit by a meteorite because it is difficult to imagine anything of this world capable of keeping Shankly out of a match. If George entertained hopes that he might be asked to deputise, his hopes were soon dashed. The position went to Bob Batey. Ten days later, George celebrated his 21st birthday.

Whenever the team's performance warranted a change, a victory was achieved and the mood passed. Although the first team lost eight of their first nine games away from home, their form at Deepdale was so strong that they won six of their home games during the same period and avoided the need for wholesale changes. The extra £1 for a first-team appearance and the chance to pick up a win or draw bonus was as important in those times as the prestige that accompanied a regular first-team place.

A look at the social conditions of the professional footballer inevitably leads to the vexed issue of money. Money dominated their thoughts and even a cursory examination of the respectful, usually bland beyond belief autobiographies written by players whose careers were subject to the tyranny of the maximum wage, reveals a preoccupation with the fact that they all considered themselves grossly underpaid.

In *Football is my Business*, as told to his friend Roy Peskett in 1946, Tommy Lawton revealed his accounts for the year May 1938 to May 1939, in which his goals helped the Everton 'School of Science' side win the First Division by Easter.

Winter pay @ £8 per week	£266.0.0
Summer pay at £6 per week	£100.0.0
Eight internationals @ £8 per match	£64.0.0
Bonus for winning league championship	£25.0.0
Bonus @ £1 per league point	£59.0.0
Total wages	£514.0.0

Footballers didn't complain, they muttered. The power in

football rested firmly with the Football Association and the Football League at the highest level and the provincial businessmen who ran the clubs, the 'little shopkeepers who govern our destiny' as Billy Meredith contemptuously termed them. Jim Taylor was to Preston what Peter Swales was to Manchester City. They were petty tinpot dictators who ran their clubs for their own greater glory and told the fans that their unstinting efforts were dedicated only to their desire to fulfil the dreams of the supporters because they were fans at heart themselves. Professional football, for most of its existence in Britain, has been a mirror image of the class-ridden corrupt society from which it grew.

Not everyone in the history of the game can be tarred with the same brush. The great men of the game – Bill Shankly, Joe Mercer, Jock Stein, Matt Busby, Bobby Moore, Stanley Matthews, Tom Finney among others – were and remain great men because their dignity as players and, in some cases, later as managers raised them above the morass. However, they had been in the game long enough to know how to survive, to ensure that their talents were allowed to flourish, and they did that, mostly, by keeping their heads down.

It was the rebels who suffered, players like Billy Meredith, Peter Doherty and Len Shackleton. Neil Franklin and Charlie Mitten went to play in Colombia after the Second World War for what they thought was a veritable fortune. When the venture collapsed and they returned to England, cap in hand, they were driven out of the game. Matt Busby made sure that Charlie Mitten never kicked a ball for Manchester United again and that he had little opportunity to do so to any significant degree elsewhere. In 1952, Tom Finney was approached by Palermo and offered a £10,000 signing-on fee and bonuses, £100 a week, a villa, a car and free travel. Diffidently, the Preston plumber conveyed the information to Jim Taylor. 'Tha'll play for us or tha'll play for no one,' came the short answer. Finney stayed at Preston. He knew the reality of the professional footballer's position all right.

If Taylor ever felt his position of influence under threat, it must have been at the end of the 1935–36 season. Preston finished in seventh position in the First Division but went out of the FA Cup in the fourth round at Sheffield United. Tommy Muirhead, the former Scottish international, was appointed secretary–manager in April 1936, presumably with instructions from Taylor to concentrate on the first part of the job. The only other consolation for the fans at this time came as they watched their despised rivals Blackburn Rovers relegated.

George Summerbee featured as a regular in the Central League team but the extra £1 and the extra status that would have come his way from first-team selection remained tantalisingly out of reach. On 28 April 1936, he was re-signed as a Class 2 player on wages of £5 in the summer, £5 in the winter and £7 in the first team, a state of affairs that looked further away than ever. (Bill Shankly re-signed as Class 1 on wages of £8 in the season, £7 in the summer and £6 in the unlikely event of his being dropped.)

What did George say when he went home to Winchester in May this time? Last year was fine. It would have been surprising if he'd been whisked into the first team having arrived in January in time to watch the seniors embark on their strongest run of the season. He thought he was being groomed to step smoothly into the first team when the time was right, but when would the time be right? Jim Taylor and the club held all the cards. To Taylor, Summerbee was a useful sort of chappie to have around for a fiver a week. He was being played in every defensive position, which increased his usefulness while at the same time demoting him in the queue behind the specialist reserves.

Ambitious clubs such as North End were expanding their staffs, employing up to 40 or 50 professional and part-time amateur players. Unfortunately, as Manchester City discovered during the 1990s, the mere acquisition of large numbers of players is no guarantee of anything other than eventual financial meltdown. The result in the dressing room can frequently be catastrophic as fear and disillusion poison the atmosphere. Every new face is a threat to someone, a rival for a prized first-team place. Even if the face is young and the player overawed and deeply respectful of his peers, the old professionals don't necessarily like it. To many of them, the innocence and optimism of the youngsters bring back memories of how they were when they first joined the club before the social, financial and psychological reality of life as a professional footballer hit them.

As the 1936–37 season progressed, George passed from the eager optimist to the hard-bitten professional as he saw his chances of playing in the first team recede still further. Like a man on the wrong escalator, he was looking upwards even as he was moving inexorably downwards. As many as 23 players were chosen for the first team that season but George Summerbee was not one of them. There were seven debutants including Tom Smith, signed from Kilmarnock, who eventually replaced Bill Tremelling at the heart of the defence.

George played his part in one of Preston's most successful Central League campaigns but it is hard to follow the career of a reserve-team player. The local paper mentions his existence when there is space to fill and a couple of hundred words is barely enough to describe the goals with the names of the scorers. A solid reliable game was likely to produce nothing but anonymity. At some point, the realisation that he was just a reserve-team player and not a youngster awaiting his break in the first team swept over George like a tidal wave. The whole point of a professional player's existence is to appear in the first team. The reserve team has always been called 'the stiffs', a pointed reference to rigor mortis, because to be turning out in the Central League on a regular basis was to be down among the dead men. Such was George's fate.

On the last day of 1936, George was reported to have

made 'a timely tackle' in a 2–1 win over Blackburn Rovers reserves. In the middle of the following week, he reported for training at Deepdale to discover that nine of the senior squad were injured or ill, including Bill Shankly who was regarded as very doubtful to take the field at Wolverhampton on Saturday. On the Thursday, Shankly was pronounced definitely unfit to play. Maybe this time . . . but a player called Fitzsimmons was summoned to travel to the Midlands in case he was required to take Shankly's place. His services were not required. Bill Shankly dragged himself on to the pitch at Molineux, although perhaps it would have been better if he had not bothered. Preston lost 5–0 and Frank O'Donnell was sent off for head-butting Stan Cullis. I hope this humiliation gave George a slight shiver of pleasure.

There wasn't much else to be pleased about in 1937 until he caught the bus from the ground to his digs one day and his eye lit upon a tall and attractive young woman. Her name was Dulcie Ryan and it appears that the initial chat-up lines as copyrighted by footballers since the dawn of time didn't work on her.

I got on the bus and went upstairs and he was sat on the back seat with another footballer who got off, and we started to talk. He said to me, 'Would you like to go to the pictures one Saturday night?' I said, 'I don't know who you are or anything.' He said, 'I'm a footballer.' I said, 'I'll have to ask my mother.' You had to in those days. My mother was a widow and if she said be back at nine o'clock, you were back at nine o'clock. I said, 'What do you do?' and he said, 'I play football for Preston North End.' I said, 'What's that?' Anyway, I went home to my mother and told her, 'I met a boy and he wants to take me to the pictures.' She said, 'You've got to be careful. They've a terrible reputation have footballers.' I said, 'He's not like that. He's very quiet,' and she said, 'That's nothing to go by.'

Dulcie's initial impression of George reveals a love of clothes; he passed that on to his son and his grandson.

> He was well dressed and his shoes were spotlessly clean. He was like that till he died. He had a number for his shoes at Barretts shoe shop because they were made for him. When he got them he used to clean them for a month before he wore them. He was very, very particular about his shirts and ties. When I got serious with him, he asked me to wash his shirts.

I can only hazard a guess in attempting to recreate the dialogue that must have prefaced this request. I do, however, have a clear image of George arriving at Dulcie's house, immaculately groomed as he would be if he were taking her out for the evening, a bunch of flowers in one hand, a bag of dirty washing in the other.

'Oh, are those for me?' asked Dulcie rhetorically, her eyes drawn to the lavish bouquet her suitor held in front of her.

'They certainly are,' said George, his eye drawn to the trim figure he found so appealing. 'And these too.'

He lifted up the large laundry bag at his feet, which Dulcie had failed to notice as she took the flowers in her arms and inhaled their captivating scent.

'What's that?'

'It's my dirty washing.'

'Oh,' said Dulcie, colouring prettily. She knew very well the significance of the request George was about to make.

'I was wondering if you could have it back by Friday?'

Well, all right, it might not have been exactly like that but the request was made to the flummoxed Dulcie who took maternal advice.

> I knew nothing about men's clothes. I had no father. My father died when I was about seven. My mother said,

'What does he think he's doing?' and I said, 'I don't know but I'm going to do them.' He usually sent them all home to his mother.

Dulcie understood the significance of George's request. He had talked a lot about his family in Winchester. There was no point talking about football. George hadn't got a great deal to boast of during the 1936–37 season and besides, Dulcie wasn't greatly interested in it. By taking in his washing, Dulcie was slowly supplanting his mother in George's order of priority. His mother, suddenly finding that George was taking his washing elsewhere, knew she had a rival on her hands. It was to be a top-of-the-table clash with unfortunate consequences for both sides.

CHAPTER FOUR

Preston II

Apart from the arrival of romance in his life, the second half of the 1936–37 season was dominated for George by the best run the reserve team had ever made in parallel with the first team's triumphant run towards Wembley. As with so many teams who reach FA Cup semi-finals, Preston were consumed by thoughts of Wembley but still faced with a meaningless last quarter of the league programme. They weren't going to be relegated and they were a long way behind the championship leaders, including a resurgent Manchester City who were battling it out with Charlton and Arsenal. Changes were made to rest key players in preparation for the semi-final tie with West Brom at Highbury on 10 April.

George was a key player in the reserve side, which was on course to win the Central League title. Yet while fellow reserves Andy Beattie, John Batey, Bob Batey and Joe Vernon were all promoted at this time, George Summerbee was not. Andy Beattie made an immediate impact. The local reporter, 'Viator', called him 'the best back on the field' and made it clear that in his opinion Beattie 'cannot be left out'. However strong his friendship with Andy Beattie, this turn of events drove George crazy as he continued to catch the eye in matches of no significance. He 'presented a stubborn front' in a hard-earned win over Newcastle United reserves on Easter Saturday and read in the paper that he was 'a powerful back' and a 'reliable defender', which sounds rather strange considering the reserves lost 4–5.

However, the Central League title seemed destined for Leeds after Preston lost 3–1 at Elland Road in what appeared to be a title decider. It came the week after the first team had beaten West Brom 4–1 in the eagerly awaited FA Cup semi-final in front of a disappointingly small crowd of 42,000. That same day, Arsenal were playing a league game against Manchester City before 75,000 at Maine Road and lost to goals by Toseland and Doherty. City had remained unbeaten since Christmas Day and now had the momentum to take the title.

Andy Beattie had impressed not just Viator. He was chosen to play for Scotland against England in the biggest international of the year at Hampden Park. George greeted the news with disbelief. For months he and Beattie had been playing against other reserves in front of a few hundred spectators who couldn't afford to follow their team away from home. Beattie had played just a dozen games for the Preston first XI and most of those were at right-half or right-back; now he was chosen at left-back to play in front of a huge and passionate crowd of his fellow countrymen, 149,000 of them as it turned out. In fact, Beattie was given a torrid time and turned inside and out by Stanley Matthews at his brilliant best, but Scotland still avenged the massacre at Culloden with a 3–1 victory.

North End won their last league match of the season at Portsmouth to finish in 14th place. The winners of the First Division title were Manchester City who had won 16 and drawn seven of their last 23 games. They were, of course, relegated the following season; the next time City were to reach these rarefied heights was in 1968 when one of George's chromosomes played a significant part. In the meantime, however, Preston was consumed with Wembley fever and George looked on from the sidelines. His mood was hardly helped by his contract negotiations. No press conference was announced in order to 'unveil' the re-signing of George Summerbee in April 1937. He was demoted from Class 2 to

Class 3 and his wages reduced accordingly to £4 in the summer, £5 during the season and £6 in the first team. Was this recognition that he was never going to make it? Was George pathetically grateful for the offer of another contract or was he seething with anger at being treated so shabbily? Like an actor who is slowly being forced out of the business because he can't get an audition, George was not even being offered the opportunity to fail. Why did Jim Taylor bother to sign him in the first place?

The trainer, Bill Scott, knew perfectly well on which side his bread was buttered. Days before the team played Sunderland at Wembley, Scott gave his own impression of Taylor in the local paper.

> He is undoubtedly an outstanding personality in football. He loves the game for its own sake and I do not think I will ever meet anyone who understands it better or one better able to handle players. He is a father to them and no one has left Deepdale without holding him in high esteem.

George choked on his toast and marmalade reading that. The fact remained that Taylor ran Preston as his own personal fiefdom and anyone who crossed him was marked for life. It is a great pity that the universe cannot be so ordered that Taylor might find himself chairman of a club containing Benito Carbone, Pierre Van Hooijdonk, Fabrizio Ravanelli and Nicolas Anelka (and all their agents).

The Cup final was played on May Day 1937. Preston came to a standstill. Even the relentless grinding of the mills was slowed. Between 10,000 and 15,000 fans travelled to London from Preston on Friday evening and Saturday morning, many of them without tickets. Top-priced 10s tickets were being offered for sale by touts at the unheard-of price of £5. Not even the inconvenience of a public transport strike could dampen the enthusiasm of the crowds, who simply walked from Euston to Wembley. The players had left on Wednesday to stay at the Chateau de Madrid hotel near Bushey in Hertfordshire.

Despite taking an early lead through Frank O'Donnell against the previous season's league champions, Preston were unable to resist the sublime skills of Raich Carter. Sunderland scored three goals without reply in the second half and the Cup went to Wearside.

The crowd walked back to Euston, noting the start of preparations for the coronation of King George VI which was to take place 11 days later. Jim Taylor had other things on his mind. If the presence of seven Scotsmen in the first team could not win him his first FA Cup, there was clearly a flaw in the composition of the side. After much deliberation, Taylor decided that the problem was that there were not enough Scots at Deepdale, so he spent the summer months acquiring more in the shape of Bobbie Beattie, Andy's goalscoring brother, Jimmy McIntosh and George Mutch who was wasting his time in the Second Division with Manchester United. What more could George Summerbee do to attract attention, other than wear a kilt at training or arrive for reserve matches playing the bagpipes? As if to compensate for this latest Jacobite incursion, Taylor relieved himself of the need for a manager and Tommy Muirhead resigned. The committee reasserted nominal control where Taylor had previously settled for *de facto* power.

It looked like a shrewd manoeuvre when the 1937–38 season re-established Preston North End as a leading First Division club. They chased Arsenal all the way to the title, the decisive match coming three games from the end when Arsenal won a fiercely fought encounter 3–1 in front of 42,000 at Deepdale, during the course of which Jimmy Milne, the stalwart Preston left-half, was badly injured. Another Cup run meant the team was due to take the field for the final the following week and this time George had reason to hope that he might be selected . . . Not again, you say. Surely he's learned his lesson from the miserable experience the previous year. However, after three and a half years in the reserves, George Summerbee finally made his first team debut.

On Monday, 4 April, George had distinguished himself in a reserve-team defeat at home to Everton when he had proved 'more than a match for the international Gillick'. On Saturday, 9 April, Scotland travelled to meet England at Wembley with a team containing four Preston Scots – Andy Beattie, Bill Shankly, Tom Smith and George Mutch. We can only assume that Jim Taylor was suffering from some kind of brainstorm because to his astonishment George Summerbee was chosen to take the place of Bill Shankly at right-half in the match at home to Derby County.

Shankly played 41 games that season, as he did most seasons. His enthusiasm for the game never dimmed and he was a match for the most gifted of inside-forwards. Peter Doherty wrote of his debut for Manchester City when they were soundly beaten by Preston 3–1 at Maine Road:

> Bill has always been a wily tactician but that day he excelled himself. He dogged my footsteps all afternoon muttering, 'Great wee team North End, a great wee team,' and subduing me so effectively I must have been a grave disappointment to the thousands of City fans who had come along to see the club's expensive capture.

Fortunately, Doherty turned out to be more Colin Bell than Lee Bradbury.

There was only one area in which George triumphed over Shanks – George got the girl. Dulcie's mother knew Hannah Usher, Shankly's landlady. When the two of them were invited for tea one Sunday afternoon, Shankly and Dulcie were introduced to each other. One day, he asked her to go to the pictures with him.

'He was lonely, that was all,' Dulcie recalls. 'But he was so boring. He couldn't talk about anything else, only fitba' as he called it.'

On that 9 April, George must have been happier than at any time since he stepped on to the Preston-bound train in Winchester. He was a first-team player, he was in love with a wonderful girl and he was getting his laundry done every week without having to send it back to Hampshire. The team was going to Wembley in a couple of weeks, and an exotic foreign tour to France, Czechoslovakia and Romania was scheduled for the week after the final. George looked as though he was in line for inclusion in both squads.

His debut match went well. Preston were on such a roll at the time that even with four first teamers on international duty they were still too strong for Derby whom they defeated soundly 4–1. According to Viator, who made a habit of damning him with faint praise, 'Summerbee settled in well after a shaky start, his passing showing intelligence.' It wasn't much but it was a start. Three days later George was back in the reserve team which lost 1–0 at Southport and on the Saturday Bill Shankly resumed his first-team spot as George gave the latest of his 'sound displays' in a 2–0 defeat at Gigg Lane. Still, he'd done it; he'd played in the first team. They couldn't, in the words of the contemporary hit song, take that away from him.

George Summerbee travelled with the first-team squad to the now traditional hotel in Bushey, five miles from Wembley. Dulcie continued to work in her grandparents' musical instruments shop in Preston as her boyfriend trod the hallowed turf of Wembley in his best suit and posed for the photographers with the rest of the team. Mike has a copy of the photograph showing his father with the other players standing in the goalmouth and reaching up to touch the crossbar. When the photograph was printed in the local paper, George Summerbee was cropped out. 'He was twelfth man that day,' Mike tells me because that's what his dad told him. But in the days before there were substitutes, what exactly did 'twelfth man' mean? If it meant 'they would have chosen me if someone had been injured', that might apply to everyone in the squad who didn't walk out at Wembley on the Saturday afternoon. Certainly the squad of 13 players who posed for the official photograph with the FA Cup in front of them did not include Summerbee.

Any hopes George might have entertained of playing in the match itself soon vanished. Batey replaced Milne and Maxwell deputised in the forward line for the unlucky Jimmy Dougal. The match was won famously in the last minute of extra time when George Mutch, still dazed from the foul that had won a penalty, cracked the spot kick against the underside of the bar and into the net. All the Preston staff rose to their feet to acclaim this victory, the sweeter for having suffered the previous year's disappointment. Jim Taylor had invited everyone at Deepdale to share in the Wembley experience, including the groundstaff boys, 15-year-old Tom Finney among them. When I expressed surprise that Taylor had stumped up the cash for the whole club to stay in hotels, Sir Tom just smiled. The very idea! They all caught the 9 a.m. train from Preston and got the 6.30 p.m. back from Euston straight after the match.

George came home with the team on the Monday evening. Four coaches were waiting at the station to take them on their triumphal journey through Preston where a reported 80,000 people lined the streets to celebrate the successful conclusion to Preston North End's greatest season since the days of the Invincibles.

George was taken on the European tour although there is no evidence that he actually played in any of the games. The journey by ferry across the Channel and thence by train across the Continent was long and arduous but afforded the occasional surprise. The full England team, having been persuaded by their own Foreign Office to give the Nazi salute before the start of the international match in the Olympic Stadium in Berlin, had just smashed six goals past the

Germans in a manner that would not be replicated until Mike Summerbee did something similar with Sylvester Stallone's team of POWs 40 years later at the conclusion of *Escape to Victory*. The Preston party missed seeing Hitler in Munich by a single day, the Führer being more concerned with removing the Sudetenland from Czechoslovakia than with getting Bill Shankly's autograph. They went on to Oberammergau but nobody thought fit to explain the significance of the Passion Play which was taking place there as part of its ten-yearly cycle. The players were very surprised to find that the entire population of the Bavarian town was wearing beards.

Back in England, George took Dulcie to Winchester for the formal introduction. Clearly the relationship had blossomed in the 18 months they had known each other and Dulcie had eventually felt secure enough in George's affections to reveal her true age.

> For a long time I didn't tell George how old I was because I was so young. One day he said to me something like, 'Have you ever thought of getting married?' and I said, 'Not for years yet.' He said, 'Why?' and then I had to tell him. He said, 'Good Lord, they'll be having me up for going out with someone that's too young,' so I said, 'If you feel like that, you'd better clear off.'

It was, as you will have gathered, a more romantic age than ours, but the path of true love ran no straighter then than it does now. Dulcie was six years younger than George and very conscious of their age difference.

> I was frightened of telling him in case he never came back. I was getting very fond of him. I liked him a lot. He was so clean and particular. That attracted me because I'm very particular myself.

47

The prospect of the trip to Winchester terrified Dulcie.

> Oh dear me, that was a terrible ordeal. I hadn't a lot of clothes and I hadn't a lot of money and I wanted to look great. I had a Godmother who was wonderful, and Auntie Edie who was very good to me. My Godmother, Auntie Bec, said, 'I've got a lot of clothes that'll fit you.' She'd been on a cruise. So I had quite a lot of nice things to wear.

In Winchester, Dulcie shared a bedroom with George's younger sister, Joan, while George slept on the couch in the living room. By this time Bunt, who was still playing for Aldershot, had moved into a flat in the town, not far from older sister Vi who was married to a soldier in the Indian Army. Dulcie believes Vi was responsible for pointing out her inferior social status to her prospective in-laws. In fact, the social status of George's family and her own was reasonably similar but that wasn't the way it appeared to Hattie, George's mother. Dulcie's mother had her own house for a start, as opposed to the two-bedroomed flat in Winchester, but that didn't prevent them from passing judgement on her.

> I was having a bath one day and I heard his mother talking to Vi. 'She seems all right,' she said, 'but she talks so common.'

The words were like daggers plunged into Dulcie's heart. She believes Vi told them of the north-country women who lived on the army base.

> She said, 'They're all common.' I thought, 'They're talking about me.' We went for a walk, George and me, and I said to him, 'It's going to be very difficult for us to be married.' He said, 'Don't talk daft.' I said, 'Well, your

mother doesn't like me. She doesn't even like the way I talk.' He said, 'Well, you do talk different.' I said, 'I'm from Lancashire and I'm proud of it and I'm not changing.' He said, 'Well, you won't see much of them because wherever I'm playing football, you'll come and live with me.' But I never did, you know.

The north–south snobbery divide works in both directions. For all that the Summerbees of Hampshire looked down on the Ryans of Lancashire, there was (and still is) a belief in the north that 'real' people live up there. We folk who kept coal in the bathtub, raced whippets and lived on black puddings might have seemed grim and dour to them lot from London, but we were also gritty, plucky, warm-hearted and democratic (with a lot of exceptions). Them lot that lived south of the imaginary line drawn across the middle of England were conversely a bunch of lazy, effete snobs. This belief has long been ingrained in football crowds. We know that West Ham United don't enjoy being drawn away to Oldham Athletic in the third round of the FA Cup in a match to be played at Boundary Park on a vile Saturday afternoon in January with the driving rain whipping in off the moors and Heathcliff due to play as a bustling centre-forward for the Latics, all broody and mono-syllabic. The southern Jessies might as well save themselves the inconvenience of the trip.

D.H. Lawrence, leaving Harold Larwood down the coal mines of Nottinghamshire while he ran off with Frieda and wrote novels in the sunshine, conforms to our innate beliefs about north and south. The cold climate makes people hard working, the sun makes them lazy. British football clubs always feel comfortable buying players from Scandinavia. They speak English and they don't mind living in the rain in Manchester. Middlesbrough's ill-fated flirtation with Ravanelli and Emerson was bound to end in heartbreak. Besides, the peoples of the southern climes are sly, cowardly and lecherous whereas those of the north are vigorous, hard-working and moral. Didn't we instinctively know as children, when taught for the first time about the fate of the Spanish Armada, that we were going to win? Pompous and lazy, sailing enormous galleons and playing away from home without having done their homework on the British weather or the tides around our island fortress, the Spanish were doomed to defeat. The logical conclusion of all this, as George Orwell points out, is that the south of England is one enormous Brighton inhabited by lounge-lizards, whereas the most virtuous people on the planet are probably the Eskimos.

Ironically, despite being made to feel socially inferior by the Summerbee women, Dulcie got on particularly well with Charles, George's father, who was a diabetic, much given to eating all the wrong things as soon as everyone's back was turned.

He said to me, 'You mustn't take any notice of the other side of the family. They've always been snobs and there's no reason for them to be.' He told me things about them that were nothing to do with me but he was just trying to reassure me. He said, 'He's a nice lad is George.' I said, 'I know, but I'd have liked his mother to have liked me.' Anyway, I never went there again – only when the children were born.

Dulcie, Vi and Hattie were three of a kind – once their minds were made up, they never changed them. Dulcie was quite convinced that the Summerbees of Winchester looked down their noses at the working-class, north-country Ryans with their 'common' flat vowels. So if that was how they felt, she wouldn't be giving them the chance to be rude to her ever again. Conversely, they thought that if George wanted to get mixed up with that common Lancashire lass, he'd made his own bed so he could lie on it.

This split in the Summerbee family is a reflection of the divide that has run through the country since the advent of the Industrial Revolution. The BBC, that supposedly great unifier of the nation, was itself a divisive influence in this regard in the 1930s. The BBC decided there was a right way to speak and a wrong way to speak and Dulcie Ryan's accent would not be allowed on the BBC unless as part of a documentary about the northern working class. It took a world war for the BBC to allow Wilfred Pickles to read the news. Lord Reith would not have been happy about it. He once banned one of his newsreaders from delivering the Epilogue. The newsreader, Reith discovered, was divorced.

Dulcie came home and broke the news of her disastrous trip to her mother who remarked tartly, 'Don't worry. You're not marrying his mother.' It wasn't much consolation. Dulcie brooded about it while George, probably with some relief, returned to his digs and to Deepdale for pre-season training and a big shock. He was on the list.

The official records of Preston North End do not state whether George had applied for a transfer, although we can imagine that he might have welcomed the prospect of a merciful release from the torture of the past three and a half years. On 11 July 1938, it was 'Resolved on the proposition of Councillor J. Blackburn, seconded by Mr Alderman W. Omdo that the player Summerbee be transferred at a fee to be agreed by the Chairman.' Two weeks later the matter was laid to rest when 'the Chairman stated that the negotiations regarding our player Summerbee had been dropped'. The vision of the blue sky outside his Preston cell was just a mirage. George Summerbee had been denied parole and was condemned to serve his full sentence.

Dulcie remembers a time when Preston placed a large fee on George's head. Logic suggests that this might be it. It was larger than the fee that Preston had paid for him and there was no earthly reason why any club would pay that amount. George spent the next two weeks sitting on the doorstep of the Football League offices, begging them to intercede and ask Preston to lower his fee. Clearly, if the club responded, it was not to any effect. Maybe they had taken fright because Tom Smith, who had been such a decisive influence at the heart of the defence during the successful 1937–38 season, had been injured more seriously than they had previously suspected on the close-season European tour. George was a 'useful' player to have in reserve. As it turned out, Smith played just one match all season.

George began the season in the familiar surroundings of the reserve team but he gave 'a sound display' at centre-half in a convincing 3–0 win at home to Liverpool. At the same time the first team was getting badly beaten at Leeds United and so, for the midweek game at Chelsea, on 21 August 1938, for the second time in his life, George Summerbee trotted out with the stars he had envied for so long. The defence read: Holdcroft; Gallimore, A. Beattie; Shankly, Summerbee, Milne. He rolled the names over his tongue a dozen times. It must have sounded like music.

I can see George in the dressing room at Stamford Bridge, picking up the programme and finding his name emblazoned there as if for all time. This was a major chance. Tom Smith would be out for a while. Clearly Bob Batey wasn't pulling up any trees as his replacement and if Taylor had turned to George so early in the season, there must have been a strong possibility that he could make the centre-half spot his own for the year. If Preston performed anything like they did the previous season, he would soon be playing Ted Drake and Tommy Lawton off the park so the England selectors would be bound to notice him. Shankly had played the last six league games of the 1937–38 season but, stretching a point, George could tell himself that he had played in two of the last nine league games, which made him a first-team player with an inconsistent record of appearances rather than the reserve-team player he had been for three and a half years.

Perhaps his head was still full of such absurd thoughts when they kicked off. At half-time Preston returned to the dressing room with a fortunate single goal lead but by the end of the game Chelsea had scored three times without reply and Preston trooped off a well-beaten side. The *Lancashire Daily Post* was ruthless in its analysis:

> Summerbee tried hard to fill the gap [left by Smith]. He is not without composure and some of his tackles were as skilfully timed as they were effective. Even so, he failed to block the middle path to goal completely and the fact that [Chelsea's centre-forward] Mills had a share in all Chelsea's goals shows where North End's defensive weakness lay. Summerbee was keen enough to shine but he did not look robust enough to withstand the forceful challenges of Mills.

As newspaper criticism went in the 1930s, this was a crushing indictment. It would have caused a mixture of embarrassment and outrage in the dressing room. No friend of George would have appreciated this kind of public humiliation and words would have been spoken about Viator. Others would simply have recognised that George had indeed had a poor game and got what he deserved while being profoundly grateful that they themselves had escaped such censure. Either way, it did for George.

Everyone read the local paper, fans and Jim Taylor alike, and George must have known its impact. The prediction of the *Aldershot News* four years before, that George would make his mark as a centre-half, proved to be without foundation. The best case one could put forward for George that day at Stamford Bridge was that he was being played out of position. As a skilful wing-half whose principal gifts were that he could read the game and pass the ball accurately, he would not have enjoyed the physical buffeting that was frequently the sole tactic employed by a strong aggressive centre-forward. Whatever the excuses or explanations, George's fate was never in doubt.

Batey was restored for the home game against Liverpool which Preston won 1–0 and George returned to life with the reserves. On 3 September 1938, George picked up his largest ever wage packet from Preston North End – £8. It was the last wage packet to be inflated by the first-team appearance bonus for a long time. George Summerbee was not a first-team player who made occasional appearances; George Summerbee was a reserve. The acceptance of this lowly status hurt.

It would have been hard, in such circumstances, to have wanted to go to war with Germany because of trouble in 'a faraway country of which we know little' as the Prime Minister so thoughtfully worded it. At the end of this month the Munich Agreement was signed and Chamberlain returned to England a temporary hero, waving his infamous 'scrap of paper'. Footballers, more than most professional people, tend towards self-absorption because of the intensity with which their careers are conducted. Placing George and Dulcie in an historical and social context makes it easier to understand why appeasement was popular in the country as a whole in September 1938.

Nevertheless, 1939 turned out to be a good year for marriages as couples realised that this might be the last year of peace. On Friday, 27 January 1939, George Summerbee married Dulcie Ryan in Preston, paving the way for the conception of Manchester City's greatest outside-right. George's best man was the reserve-team goalkeeper Jack Fairbrother. George and Jack found themselves in similar circumstances – like Shankly, Harry Holdcroft, the first-team goalkeeper, clocked up an infuriating number of consecutive first-team appearances and, unlike Shankly, his international days were over. Groom and best man suffered and empathised together. However, Fairbrother did displace Holdcroft soon after the wedding. Holdcroft eventually opened a butcher's shop on Liverpool Road where he spent the rest of his working life.

The war clouds that were gathering over Europe in 1939 were as nothing compared to the war that had already broken out in the midst of the Summerbees. George got married without a single member of his family being present. He had clearly decided that his future lay with Dulcie and if that meant upsetting his parents and siblings so be it. As a mitigating circumstance, the journey from Hampshire to Lancashire in deepest winter was a difficult one to make. It was snowing heavily that Friday, although the first-team match went ahead the following day at Deepdale as an unchanged Preston North End gave George Summerbee a dubious wedding present by beating Birmingham City 5–0.

George moved out of digs and into the marital home – his mother-in-law's house – in Argyll Road, quite close to Deepdale. It all sounds uncomfortably reminiscent of the film version of Stan Barstow's *A Kind of Loving.*

Dulcie's father was in the Artillery during the Great War. He had been injured when one of the large field guns exploded and he returned to Preston with one leg shorter than the other. His health never recovered. Since leaving school at the age of 14, Dulcie had been working in the family shop in the centre of Preston. It was a large double-fronted store selling gramophones and wirelesses. Even with George's £5 there wasn't the money to spare to move into their own place. It was to be another 11 years before that happy day arrived. Meanwhile Dulcie's mother, Lillian Ryan, continued to be a constant presence in their lives. Dulcie recognises this wasn't an ideal start to married life.

I used to take my wages home. I started at ten bob a week and she would give me what I needed. It was usually about half a crown. It didn't go far, even then. She was only a little woman, not five feet tall but very, very strict. Young people today would never stand for it.

There wasn't much in the way of relief at the club. Shankly missed two matches all year but his place on both occasions was taken by debutant Jackie Cox. Jimmy Milne at left-half missed three games all season and his place was also filled by Jackie Cox. George wasn't even first reserve for the half-back positions any more. Perhaps it was during this bleak midwinter that thoughts of communism started to infiltrate his mind. Certainly he must have been in favour of any political philosophy that incorporated the hanging of Jim Taylor from the nearest lamp post to the players' entrance at Deepdale. Throughout the 1938–39 season, George continued to waste his life in the reserve team as they finished bottom of the Central League. To cap it all, over Easter he was sent off.

However, in the last game, away to third-placed Charlton at the Valley, George Summerbee made his third and final official appearance in a first-team shirt. Andy Beattie, who had otherwise missed just one game all year, was suddenly indisposed and George featured at left-back in a meaningless game that ended in a 3–1 defeat. There was no mention throughout the week that Beattie was struggling to be fit but if this was a carefully conceived plan by Andy and George, it failed. George's old nemesis on the *Lancashire Daily Post* reported coldly:

Summerbee who deputised for Andrew Beattie had not enough speed and took up too square a position and when it came to a race for the ball the North End left-back was rarely in it.

Still, on 9 May 1939, George picked up an enormous £7 10s in his wage packet. On that same day, the minute book notes dryly: 'It has been reported that our player Summerbee has been fined three guineas by the FA and suspended for seven days from 26th August.' The Summerbee temper had reasserted itself. All the evidence tells us that George was not verbally abusive. We can therefore only assume that he was sent off for a bad tackle or, more in keeping with family tradition, retaliating against one.

It is interesting to note that although the players' wages were paid in pounds the fine was levied in guineas. The Football Association clearly saw themselves as professional gentlemen and therefore entitled to add the extra 5 per cent to the bill. The players were plebs and stumped up the cash.

Being fined most of your week's pay and then being without wages at all when the suspension took place was a serious affair for a professional player in 1939. It may well have been that Andy Beattie decided to help his friend George with a little bonus of the first-team appearance money. Either way, in the last week of August, as Hitler prepared to march into Poland, George Summerbee was sitting out his suspension.

The men who ran football acted with a decisiveness rarely apparent in times of peace. On that blissfully sunny Sunday morning in September, while the country basked in the last days of glorious summer, everyone was listening to the wireless as the Prime Minister addressed the nation from the Cabinet Room at 10 Downing Street. Scarcely had Neville Chamberlain pronounced the fateful words, 'and consequently this country is now at war with Germany', than they snapped into action. They suspended the contract of every professional footballer.

More precisely, players ceased to be paid on 6 September. Most players were paid fortnightly. By paying off contracts smartly, directors were able to save the wages that would have been due for the week ending 9 September. In addition, clubs retained the registrations of their players and therefore the feudal hold over them that they had held since the birth of the professional game. When games were played, it was reluctantly accepted that the players would have to be paid something. A fee of 30s per match was painfully agreed, but no bonuses would be on offer.

For professional footballers who had no savings and a family to support, the declaration of war meant the future was bleak indeed. George would have heard Chamberlain's message with all the other players who made a habit of going into the ground on a Sunday morning for a massage. You might have thought that they would have had enough of each other's company on the other six days of the week but this probably tells us something about the home life of professional footballers. Dulcie remembers George coming home after learning that he no longer had a job at Preston.

'When war broke out, George came in and said, "My contract's finished and we've no money." ' The phrase 'we've no money' was one that was to be repeated any number of times over the next 15 years.

Peter Doherty drew the same conclusions as the rest of his colleagues who, by 7 September, were probably all communists.

'It was a grim lesson for the professionals and one that some of us took to heart very seriously. Without a scrap of consideration or sentiment, our means of livelihood were simply jettisoned and we were left to find fresh ones as best we could.'

Andy Beattie found himself in severe financial difficulties during the war. Embarrassed, no doubt, he wrote to Preston North End requesting help. The relevant minute of the Finance Committee is dated 12 November 1940:

A letter was read from Andrew Beattie asking for further financial assistance. After discussion, it was agreed he be informed that owing to the position of football at the moment it was impossible to do anything for him.

In other words, 'Thank you and good night, you stupid improvident Scotch git.'

When war broke out, Doherty applied for work with Leyland Motors and Vickers Armstrong in Manchester but he was refused employment. Eventually he found manual work in Greenock and wrote to the Manchester City chairman to inform him of the fact. The chairman wrote back to remind him that, since City still held his registration, he was banned from playing for anyone in Scotland. Any infraction of this ruling would result in Doherty jeopardising his future benefit. For the British Empire and its Commonwealth, this was not their finest hour. A mutinous Doherty came back to Lancashire, acquired a job as a chauffeur which lasted precisely one day and was eventually employed in an ordnance factory near Warrington.

In Preston, Jimmy Milne, Jack Fairbrother and Willie Hamilton all joined the police, and Bill Shankly worked as a riveter at the recently opened English Electric factory before opting for life in the RAF. Stan Mortensen worked variously in a garage, a butcher's shop, a woodyard, a shipyard and a biscuit factory before also joining the RAF. He was badly hurt when the bomber in which he was flying crashed. Anybody with a useful trade was desperately needed to contribute to the war effort. Professional footballers who joined their clubs straight from school rarely had such skills to offer. Tom Finney, the Preston Plumber, was a notable exception.

Encouraged by Stanley Rous, the secretary of the FA, top footballers joined the Army Physical Training Corps. For a time the Aldershot team boasted the services of Frank Swift, Matt Busby, Stan Cullis, Tommy Lawton, Jimmy Hagan and Joe Mercer as well as that old Aldershot favourite, G.C. Summerbee. His brother, George, was not asked for. The acquisition of a reserve-team player from Preston North End was not much of a feather in anyone's cap.

George wanted to fight for his country. Even if Jim Taylor

could afford to be choosy, the King probably couldn't, and you didn't need to have been born in Scotland to die for England. Unfortunately, George had fallen off a chair when he was a small boy and broken his arm in five places. It had had no impact on his career as a professional footballer but the armed forces were a different matter. They just didn't want him – any of them. His elder son, John Summerbee, recalls, 'He was so upset because he couldn't go in the army. He tried everything, air force, rear gunner, everything, but they didn't want him. In those days a lot of rear gunners never came back. He always felt very guilty not being able to fight.' Rejection by the armed forces who were crying out for volunteers just about summed up George Summerbee's life so far.

CHAPTER FIVE

Portsmouth

For the last three months of 1939, George devoted his time to the ultimately unrewarding task of finding a way to fight for his country. When his country decided they could deal with the Axis powers without his help, George started writing to every contact he had in the game in the hope of getting away from Preston. Early in the new year he received a letter from a director at Portsmouth who told George that he could secure a job for him at Follands, the aircraft factory just outside Southampton, if George would agree to play for Portsmouth.

George needed no second bidding. His young wife, on the other hand, was refused permission to follow him down to the south coast, not by the War Office but by her mother, a much more fearsome proposition altogether. Lillian Ryan realised that the dockyards at Portsmouth would become regular targets for German bombers and she was in no mood to let her 19-year-old daughter anywhere near the Luftwaffe. George was surplus to her own requirements and she was quite happy to wish him luck as she waved him goodbye. Lillian kept her seasonal work, helping to manufacture Christmas cards in a workshop in Preston, and Dulcie continued to work for the jeweller Percy Goldberg in the arcade in the centre of town.

The Portsmouth director, aware of the proprietorial attitude taken by clubs towards their players, must have suggested to George that he inform Preston North End that he would be playing for the works team. The relevant minute for

13 February 1940 reads: 'The Chairman reported that G. Summerbee had gone home to work and that permission had been granted for him to play for Folland Aircraft FC.' It wasn't untrue. His home was down south and initially George went back to Winchester to live with his parents in the two-bedroomed flat above the grocer's shop in City Road. It was wartime and because of the widespread disruption, there wasn't the same sense of frustration and embarrassment he felt during the long close seasons in the mid to late 1930s.

The minute accurately reflected the fact that he probably would turn out for the factory team; he just omitted to mention Portsmouth FC. Presumably, at some point permission was granted; clubs could be feudal in seeking to retain control over their players, just as Operation Sea Lion was attempting to ensure that even the Football League and the Football Association would be ruled from Berlin. (Mind you, I'd like to see them try. I am intrigued by the idea of countless Nazis being hauled over the coals by the FA disciplinary committee for attempting to reclaim sixpence on an expenses chit for a bun and a cup of tea bought on Carlisle station while changing trains, as Stanley Matthews once did, to his everlasting shame.)

Portsmouth managed to retain the services of the majority of their 1939 Cup-winning team throughout the war years although the backstage staff were reduced to three – the superstitious secretary–manager Jack Tinn, a groundsman and the tea lady whose duties ranged from polishing the FA Cup to fire-watching. Towards the end of the war, wing-halves Jimmy Dickinson and Jimmy Scoular joined the England centre-half Reg Flewin to form the half-back line that would be the basis of Portsmouth's league championship winning glory years in the late 1940s. But by that time, George had returned to Preston and so once again all he could do was to look from afar as his friends won medals and glory.

George made his debut for Portsmouth in front of 6,012 spectators in March 1940 in a 2–1 home defeat against

Tottenham Hotspur. He went on to make 122 league and 27 Cup appearances for Pompey at full-back or left-half which meant that his goal tally was even less impressive than that of his son and grandson. He even failed to score in the 16–1 victory over Clapton Orient.

Once down on the south coast, George soon came under the influence of Jimmy Guthrie, the Portsmouth captain who had lifted the FA Cup after beating Wolverhampton Wanderers 4–1 in the last final before the war and who was to have a major impact on the rest of his life. Guthrie was one of those fierce wing-halves whom Scotland used to export in droves. He had made his way south from Dundee to become the driving force of that Portsmouth team. He was also a tough negotiator with a passionate hatred of club officials who exploited their employees (i.e. everyone). Unlike others who thought similarly, he was prepared to do something about it, and in the face of the widespread apathy exhibited by his fellow professionals he soon rose to pre-eminence in the players' union.

Bert Barlow, who scored the first goal in that 1939 Wembley triumph, remembered the unseemly backstage negotiations that preceded the showpiece occasion.

'They offered us four Cup final tickets to buy and gave us one free for the wife. Guthrie said, "You can stick them!" The lads said, "What's the good of playing if the relations can't come and see us?" Every Tom, Dick and Harry was getting tickets bar the players and Guthrie said to the directors, we were playing at Derby that day, "Right, we're not bloody playing today." We finished up with sixteen each to buy – half-crown ones.'

In the days of the maximum wage and illegal under-the-counter payments, Cup final tickets were a recognised way for players to earn extra cash by selling them on the black market, whatever the demands of friends and relatives. Unfortunately, the practice is now endemic in the game so that players on £8,000 a week behave in much the same manner as their predecessors who were earning £8 a week. Portsmouth supporters will be glad to learn that Guthrie's threatened strike produced not just 16 tickets for each of the players, but also a 1–0 win at the Baseball Ground.

Guthrie's successful threatened strike encouraged him to believe he could win this game every time he played at Wembley. In 1942, he tried it again. This time Guthrie's *casus belli* was the wages paid to players in the first week of September 1939. Yes, it was nearly three years previously but Guthrie was a man who never forgot a grudge. Indeed, it would appear he lovingly nurtured them.

On 30 May 1942, Portsmouth were due to play Brentford in the London War Cup final. In the dressing room at 2 p.m., Guthrie informed the manager and the directors that all the players who were on Portsmouth's books in the 1939–40 season wanted their wages for the week ending 9 September 1939; otherwise they would leave the 72,000 people who had gathered in the stadium outside to spend the 90 minutes after three o'clock playing I Spy or, worse still, community singing 'Cherry Ripe' with Arthur Caiger, the old man in the white coat. At 2.52 p.m., the directors, with evident bad grace, surrendered, muttering darkly that Guthrie would never kick a ball in English football again. Given that it was 1942 and the U-boat campaign was effectively starving Britain into defeat, none of the players took the threat seriously. Eight quid now meant more than the possibility of suspension at some time in the uncertain future. Unfortunately, this time Guthrie won only one of the two battles. He miskicked a penalty that would have brought an equaliser and the ball rolled slowly into the arms of the grateful Brentford goalkeeper. The second and conclusive Brentford goal went in off his head. It was a performance of which Jamie Pollock would have been proud, as City fans know to their cost.

George Summerbee watched this match from the bench in a mood of black resignation. He had played most of the season at left-half but because this was such a prestigious match it was felt that an attempt had to be made to recruit as many of the original Portsmouth team as possible. Summerbee was what was known as a guest player, albeit one who made 149 league and Cup appearances for Pompey, which was 146 more than he would achieve for Preston North End who held his registration for 11 years. So, after the frustrations of the missed Cup finals of 1937 and 1938 George was forced to endure further torture as once again he watched his team-mates playing for glory. His name appears on the programme as one of three official reserves.

He wasn't alone in being thus discriminated against. The following season Arsenal reached the League South Cup final and Bill Shankly, who had been guesting for the Gunners for most of the season, was ignominiously dropped for the Wembley showpiece in favour of a regular Arsenal player whose release from the services had been secured for the match. Shankly's language was so intemperate that it positively shocked Joe Mercer. 'He was most indignant and his language was awful,' Mercer later recalled. Arsenal won 7–1, which probably didn't do much to widen Shankly's vocabulary.

If life in Preston had been stressful for George because of his lack of first-team action, life on the south coast during the war years was considerably more exciting. As Lillian had surmised, the concentration of dockyards and aircraft factories made Portsmouth and Southampton constant targets for raids by the Luftwaffe. In September 1939, the Supermarine works at Woolston alongside the Itchen was the sole source of Spitfire production. Follands at Hamble, for whom George, Jimmy Guthrie, Bert Barlow and seemingly hundreds of professional footballers worked, were sub-contractors for Supermarine. Hamble was a focus of the aviation industry. Fairey at Hamble Point did much the same as Follands and the nearby Armstrong Whitworth factory produced the Albemarle light bomber.

Bert Barlow recalls how footballers found jobs in wartime: 'I had a job working on the roads in a village just outside Barnsley when I got a letter saying there was a job going at Follands. I said, "What about the wife?" and they said, "If you come down here, you can get a furnished place or something." When I got to Follands, I found George was there and Rochford and Guthrie and Morgan. Other players were down there 'n' all – Dickie Foss, the future Southampton manager Ted Bates, he was there, Jack Scott who was the trainer for them, Peter Buchanan. Full of footballers it was. You could get anybody a job there because it was run by [the manager of Portsmouth] Jack Tinn's pal. That's how all the jobs came along. I got jobs for three of them.'

When George arrived at Follands in February 1940, rationing for butter, bacon and sugar had already started but during the phoney war nobody was sure what Hitler's next move would be. In May and June, however, the blitzkrieg demolished the defences of Belgium, Holland and France. It was only a matter of time before Great Britain felt the full force of the Luftwaffe if not the Wehrmacht.

The Battle of Britain began in July 1940, fought in the skies over Kent and the approach to London. A couple of months later, the citizens of Southampton discovered for themselves the impact caused by aerial bombardment. On 24 September a daylight raid was made on the large Supermarine works in Woolston. The devastation was enormous. The raiders came in low, following the line of the Itchen, and virtually demolished the main centre of Spitfire production, killing over 90 people in the process.

It was the first indication to George and his footballing colleagues that this was a civilian war and they were now in the front line. Disruption became a way of life. The footballers at Follands moved house regularly. They would come home from the factory to find that the flat they were living in had been bombed out or that the people who owned it had unexpectedly returned because the house they had gone to had been destroyed in a bombing raid. After the Battle of Britain had been won by the home side, daytime raids gave way to night attacks with the prospect of still further devastation.

Dulcie decided that waiting in Preston for Hitler to get bored and call off the war was pointless. She was 20 years old and she wanted to be with her husband so she made her way to Southampton where she arrived in time for the intensification of night-time bombing. On the night of 30 November 1940, 800 high-explosive bombs and 9,000 incendiaries virtually obliterated the town centre of Southampton. Ruby Summerbee, who married Bunt in 1942, still has crystal clear memories of those nights of terror.

> Whenever we went down to see [George and Dulcie] we invariably spent the night in the shelter because we were bombed. We were there the night the town was fire bombed right the way down to the High Street. Dulcie was tough then. One night we got there just as the siren went and she was asleep in the house alone. George was at work – he had to work nights – and Dulcie had just gone off to bed. The rest of the town was in the air-raid shelter.

John Summerbee recalls that one of the few war stories his father ever told him was of the trauma of the blitz on Southampton.

> He told me he was on firewatch at Follands and he was running to put out an incendiary bomb when he fell into a ditch and the bloke who took his place to deal with it got blown up in front of him.

Both Southampton and Portsmouth were under siege. What 30 November 1940 had been to Southampton, 10 January

1941 was to Portsmouth – 171 people were killed and 430 badly injured in that night's bombardment. The night attacks on the two towns continued until the bulk of the Luftwaffe was diverted to the Eastern front to help with the invasion of Soviet Russia in June 1941. Fratton Park, despite being surrounded by munitions works and a railway yard, and being close to a major port, amazingly suffered no damage.

Food shortages, power cuts, cold and damp were accepted as normal features of everyday life. George and Dulcie took comfort in one of the few activities for which the government had not issued wartime regulations and in August 1941, Dulcie returned to Preston to give birth to their first child, John. Like his younger brother, who arrived 16 months later, John was born in St Joseph's Hospital in Preston.

> I'm not a Catholic but they were the only people who would take me in. There was a war on. I wrote to my mother and told her I was having a baby and I had to be evacuated. She said, 'Come back home. You can't have the baby here but you can live here.'

Dulcie returned to Southampton with the baby as soon as she could. George was besotted with his first-born child. 'John was John before he was born,' says Dulcie, which sounds like A.A. Milne. I suspect George had merely fallen prey to the disease that afflicts many new fathers and their dreams of achieving immortality through their children. John would carry his father's hopes through childhood until they were destroyed in the cruellest possible way.

While Dulcie was back in Preston, George moved in with Guthrie and his education began in earnest. For a start, Guthrie's temperament found an immediate echo in George's approach to the game. According to Bert Barlow, 'Guthrie was a hard man. They used to have tin cups in the Portsmouth dressing room because if we went in at half-time and we were losing, he used to sweep the china ones off the table in one go. You'd have to get out of his way. If he went to the toilet and you were in his way, he'd just knock you down. He'd kick things or kick the door as he went by.' An outbreak of diarrhoea in the Portsmouth dressing room must have induced more than the conventional discomfort.

George was a quiet man off the field but on it he clearly hated losing and approved of Guthrie's approach to the game. Appropriately, just before Dulcie went home for the birth of their second child, George managed to accomplish something no other Portsmouth player, not even the great Guthrie himself, matched throughout six years of total warfare. On 12 September 1942, in a League South game at Stamford Bridge that ended in a 2–1 victory for Chelsea, George Summerbee was sent off.

Nowadays players are sent off with such regularity that it is quite surprising to find 22 players on the field at the conclusion of the game. Players who are sent off for such offences as 'walking towards the referee in an aggressive manner' (Manchester City's Irish genius Kevin Horlock at Bournemouth, February 1999) or attempting to French kiss Stan Collymore in a built-up area during the hours of daylight (Manchester City's redoubtable Yorkshire defensive linchpin Andy Morrison at Fulham, August 1999) cannot fully appreciate the seriousness of being sent off in ancient times. Managers didn't take the easy way out by claiming to be fortuitously unsighted, or launch scathing attacks on the competence of referees, whatever their private reservations. It was a matter of financial hardship and some social disgrace to be sent off in those days. George, by all accounts, didn't say boo to a goose in the dressing room, which makes his behaviour all the more interesting.

Guthrie and Summerbee got along famously and they were regular players in the seven-a-side matches Portsmouth played during factory dinner breaks to entertain the workers.

The spectators paid sixpence for admission and the money raised went to war charities. As a notorious hard man himself, Guthrie would have appreciated George's commitment. It was Guthrie who made a 'Communist' out of him. Within the business of football, the Professional Footballers Association has traditionally been seen as a weak union, rather as Equity, the actors union, has been one of the weakest in the entertainment industry, and for the same reason of supply and demand. There is no shortage of young men who want to become professional footballers or young men and women who want to become professional actors. It would be hard to throw an empty crushed lager can into the toilets of a nightclub without hitting half a dozen of each variety. On the other hand, the post of chargehand electrician on a low-budget British feature film doesn't carry quite the same component of glamour; until the impact of Thatcher's union-busting activities, the technicians unions held enough power to impose their will on the broadcasters and film companies. Most players in George's day paid their shilling sub and regarded it as a tax they couldn't do much about. Football was run by and frequently for the Jim Taylors of the world. During his time living with Guthrie, the barrack-room lawyer, George Summerbee started to see that things didn't always have to be like that.

There were two distinctly different influences acting on Guthrie and Summerbee. One was the increasing clamour for fundamental social change to be enshrined in legislation; the other originated more specifically from the conditions prevailing in football. Every footballer had a story of personal humiliation but there wasn't much he could do about it as long as the clubs maintained a feudal hold over their playing serfs. The PFA failed to convince anyone of the justice of its case for more than half a century. In 1909 it signed an agreement with the FA not to affiliate to the General Federation of Trades Unions and its fate was sealed. The PFA became nothing more than a tame poodle. Until 1939, the players knew that professional football was a mirror image of British society, class-ridden, greedy, spiteful, introverted and protective of its own. Of course the players wanted Cup final tickets to sell on the black market; of course they demanded money to turn out in testimonials and benefit matches; of course they looked after their own careers first and regarded bright talented youngsters as a threat. Why wouldn't they? Who had ever helped them? Not the PFA, that was for sure.

The players also knew that the bosses had no right to lecture them on honesty when the game they ran had been corrupted by deceit and greed from its inception. In 1915, Manchester United were caught match fixing on a scale that Hansie Cronje and Mohammed Azharuddin could never match. They bought a 2–0 win off Liverpool (cash only, no leather jackets unwanted by the wife were needed as added inducement) and thereby avoided relegation. Given Liverpool's constant failed attempts to beat United throughout the 1990s the thought occurs that perhaps Roy Evans and Graeme Souness would have been better off withdrawing money from the cashpoint machine and handing it to the United forwards rather than wasting it on inept defenders who didn't know how to mark them.

United had a good war – apart from the minor inconvenience of having their ground bombed to rubble (by Uwe Rosler's grandad, according to a popular song heard in the environs of Maine Road) – but in 1940 they took part in a match that has passed into history as one of the more ludicrous of wartime spectacles. They were playing Blackburn Rovers at Stockport County's ground. Blackburn could raise just seven players and had to advertise for the four needed for a full team. The only criterion was that the players' feet had to fit the sizes of the available boots. One of the volunteers had the correct sized feet but lacked any discernible ability to play football, regularly miskicking, and was periodically flattened by the United players as if he were a cartoon character. The name of this volunteer was not recorded but rumours have since arisen that he might have been called Edghill (or Frontzeck or Gomersall or McGoldrick).

The wartime disruptions exacerbated the strained relations between players and clubs. The players who in peacetime made no trouble reacted to the slights and deprivations with similar resignation, periodically thanking God and the FA that they had been spared to play football when their contemporaries were dying by land, sea and air in the struggle to preserve democracy. Others, including Guthrie and Summerbee, continued to cause aggravation to the noble burghers who still so unselfishly ran football for the popular good. Peter Doherty's memoir, *Spotlight on Football*, is a catalogue of thoughtless actions committed by a club Doherty couldn't wait to leave, particularly in view of their inflexible response to the guest-player system. One week Doherty agreed to a request from Walsall to play for them because he was on a course that took place just a few miles from their ground. City knew he was temporarily located in the west Midlands and took the trouble to loan him out to West Bromwich Albion. When Doherty applied to City for formal permission to play for his friend at Walsall he was told to report to the Hawthorns – 'In spite of the fact that all contracts had been cancelled, I was still receiving orders as if I were a full-time player getting a normal weekly wage.' As soon as the war was over, Doherty was transferred to Derby County.

The greatest bone of contention between players and management was over the benefit system, which was designed to reward loyalty. These days it has become such a joke that players demand and receive thousands of pounds in 'loyalty' bonuses to leave clubs while demanding equally large signing-on fees elsewhere. In George Summerbee's day, however, those loyalty bonuses were usually all a professional player could expect when his club deemed him surplus to requirements.

The basic idea was that players who had been with a club for five years received a loyalty bonus of £500. Players who remained with one club for longer than five years received £650. In theory it was perfectly clear. In practice almost everyone had to fight for what he was owed because the club would find some reason why in that particular case the bonus wasn't due. Stanley Matthews, a model professional if ever there was one, had to go on strike to get his money from Stoke City, and although he was eventually awarded the £650, he had to go without wages for three months in order to get it: 'As far as I was concerned, I'd shown great loyalty and it had not been reciprocated. What's more, the belligerent attitude and hard line taken by the club put a dent in the implicit trust I had in those running the club.' If a 'good boy' such as Matthews, who kept his head down and his mouth firmly shut, felt that way, how do you suppose players such as Guthrie and George felt?

As the tide of battle turned and it became apparent that at some point in the future the Allies would win, the thoughts of all men turned to the kind of world they could expect to return to after demobilisation. The unemployment problem that had so paralysed the country during the 1930s had been cured by the need for wartime production and there was a growing conviction that after this war, unlike in 1918, they were not going back to the bad old days. The desire for change produced a landslide for Clement Attlee's Labour party and a humiliating rejection of Churchill and the forces of Conservatism. The vast majority of people had not fought for six years to return to power a Conservative government whose foreign secretary went hunting with Goering. They had not suffered injury and privation to return to the England in which *The Times* altered the reports from its correspondent in Berlin for fear of offending the Nazis, or to the England of Kingsley Wood who opposed the bombing of the Krupps munitions factories because they were private property.

In 1943, Beveridge produced the prototype of the welfare state. In 1944, R.A. Butler guided his Education Bill through parliament, creating the possibility of social mobility through the 11+ examinations – the downside of the secondary modern schools took a little while to register. High on the list of priorities were full employment and decent housing. The Luftwaffe had done England a favour by initiating a major programme of urban slum clearance across the country.

The war changed Great Britain in significant ways. Working-class men, who in the Depression of the 1930s never amounted to anything more than dole recipients or factory fodder, had fought for their country, seen their friends killed, travelled the world and knew they were just as good as the toffs who gave them orders. The impact of the war on football professionals was the same as on other working-class people looking for the end of social deference.

Of course, the idea that travel broadens the mind doesn't always hold with professional footballers. In the mid 1970s, a television documentary crew accompanied West Bromwich Albion on their close-season tour of China, in the days when China restricted western visitors to Richard Nixon and his media advisers. It was a rare privilege. It gave British television audiences one of their first chances to see the Great Wall of China. When asked why he couldn't be bothered to visit it and preferred to stay in the hotel, John Trewick, the Albion defender, replied pithily, 'Yer seen one wall, yer seen the lot.'

Tommy Lawton who, to judge from his book *Football Is My Business*, seemed to have spent the war scoring goals for one representative side after another, was touring Italy when the Germans signed the treaty of unconditional surrender. By 19 May 1945 he had reached Florence where he noted in his diary, 'Shopping occupied our attention in the afternoon and a visit to a church the name of which I've forgotten (I believe it was called the Dome). It had mosaic decorations on the outside but was very plain inside, a strange and disappointing contrast.' Thus is Brunelleschi's Renaissance masterpiece, the Duomo, the city's majestic Cathedral of Santa Maria del Fiore, dismissed by England's wartime centre-forward in critical terms Niklaus Pevsner could not have equalled.

However, it is indisputable that working men gained political strength from their wartime experiences. The Professional Footballers Association was infected with a spirit of optimism and change. Guthrie was forever writing to Jimmy Fay, the union's secretary, with his ideas for the players' future welfare. As early as 27 November 1943, a Beveridge-type scheme was proposed by the players' union to include such radical innovations as the abolition of the maximum wage, the introduction of a £4 a week minimum wage, the establishment of a superannuation scheme and increased bonuses for FA Cup semi-finals, finals and representative games. Players' contracts were to run for 12 months without the demeaning lesser summer wage, there was to be compensation for injured players, and the iniquities of the transfer system were to be resolved. The Football League Management Committee rejected it out of hand until the war was won, after which, of course, the committee tried to pretend it had no idea what the union was referring to. In November 1945, the players eventually threatened to strike unless they got their way. With extreme reluctance the Football League coughed up an increase of £1 a match and a peacetime bonus of £1 a point.

Needless to say, in the euphoria of peace and victory in Europe and victory in Japan, players willingly returned to their clubs as indentured serfs. The crowds happily paid their shilling entrance money and poured back into the ramshackle grounds with their unsafe terracing and three urinals to serve the needs of 38,000 people. In the face of this overwhelming vote of confidence in their management techniques, why should the football authorities care what the players wanted?

In the country at large, the promised radical changes of the post-war Labour government – the nationalisation of the mines and the railways, the introduction of a national insurance scheme and a National Health Service – heralded a new dawn in social affairs. Yet football returned not to this new era of 1945 but to the complacency of 1939, to its traditional world of bitterness and greed, to a world in which Jim Taylor was still the king of his Preston castle and where professional footballers continued their Faustian pact in which, in return for being underpaid for playing the game they loved, they suffered the old series of petty humiliations and crass exploitation.

George Summerbee believed that he was returning to Preston North End a different man from the one who had left in February 1940. He was certainly no longer the nervous insecure youngster with stars in his eyes who had stepped off the Winchester train in January 1935. He had learned from Jimmy Guthrie that footballers who stood up to the bosses could sometimes win if they presented a united front. However, he had now given hostages to fortune. He had been married for six years and was the father of two pre-school aged children. He was also 31 years old and facing the unwelcome realisation that the end of his playing career was in sight.

CHAPTER SIX

Chester and Barrow

George and Dulcie returned to Preston to live in Dulcie's mother's newly acquired house in Penwortham on the south-western side of the town. Mike's first memories are of this house, a solidly built semi-detached on a new estate in West End. Round the corner was the local redbrick primary school on Crookings Lane which both Mike and John attended, although the principal feature of the neighbourhood and the focus of both boys' attention for the next few years was the recreation ground ('the rec') which abutted the back of the house.

George Mutch lived round the corner and his kids and the Summerbees played endless Scotland v. England matches, which were occasionally augmented by the arrival of real Scottish internationals. When they were not available, other methods were employed to bring the sides up to strength. Norma Lock first met the Summerbees in 1948 in Barrow, where she and her husband used to live before moving to Penwortham. She recently wrote to Mike with her recollections of the boys.

I lived from March 1950 in a house in Crookings Lane which backed onto the 'Rec' as did yours. At that time my husband played for Preston Post Office and there were many times when a timid tap on the door announced the Summerbee boys, asking if Reg was coming out to play. Obviously they were a man short. Reg invariably obliged.

At the time, Mike was seven years old; Reg was 28.

None of these families had much money and in the deprived, austere world of post-war Britain there wasn't much alternative to the endless games of football and cricket that dominated the boys' lives. Both parents worked so it was Lillian who stayed at home to look after them. The naturally high-spirited boys didn't conform to her notions of social propriety and she reacted to what she considered their provocative behaviour with a somewhat Victorian response. John recalls the experience with both a smile and a shudder. 'My grandma and my mum used to have a strap. My dad didn't. He just used to lose his temper. He didn't mean it probably but he had a quick temper and he did lose control.'

George's last game for Portsmouth was in a public trial game at the start of the 1945–46 season. He returned to Preston to find that the club had 15 players still serving overseas, including the Beattie brothers and Tom Finney, and a further 22 in Britain not yet demobbed from the Services. George thought he must be in with a chance of a game now. He was, but although the FA Cup competition was back, albeit on a two-legged basis, Preston were still playing their league matches in the wartime League North so the matches were not regarded as official. It was perhaps as well, for Preston, missing their established stars, could manage only 19th place out of 22 clubs.

One reason for Preston's poor performance was that Taylor had decided to give the local youngsters a chance. Preston's future lay with Tom Finney and his contemporaries, not George Summerbee or the guest players, a system that Taylor felt strongly had been open to abuse during the war years. Even with all those first-team regulars missing, George soon found himself back in the miserably familiar environment of the Preston North End reserve team, his sole consolation being that his wages had risen to the giddy heights of £8 a week. Shankly and the top men at the club were now on £10 so the differential had been maintained.

George had never felt exactly welcomed by the management at Preston; now he suffered another humiliation. John Summerbee remembers his father telling him of the day a director tried to prevent him from getting on the team bus just as he was about to board it.

'What the hell do you think you're doing?' demanded the director, assuming George was some kind of interloper.

'I'm getting on the bus.'

'Why? Who are you?'

'I'm George Summerbee.'

'Are you a player here or what?'

'I've been at this club for eleven years.'

The director was not impressed and George slumped into his seat on the charabanc, red in the face with a combination of embarrassment and anger.

By Christmas, George was at his lowest ebb. He had never been quick but at 31 he knew he was getting slower and consequently he felt more frustrated and bitter. He decided to have it out with Taylor. On 3 January 1946, the chairman informed the board of directors that at his own request George Summerbee was being placed on the transfer list. There wasn't much of an outcry from the board who would have looked forward to offloading a player who was the wrong side of 30 and saving £8 a week into the bargain.

Not wanted at Deepdale and struggling to find an identity for himself in his mother-in-law's house, even the five-year-old John was aware that his father was suffering.

'It was hard living with my grandma. It did my dad's head in. They didn't get on. Not one little bit. Maybe that's why he took us to the cinema a lot.' John goes on to recall George taking him and Mike to see *Lassie*, which reduced the two boys to tears. After that, Mike spent hours rummaging for pennies in various coat pockets so he could go to the cinema without his parents.

A fortnight after agreeing to George's request for a transfer, Taylor changed his mind. The club was short of players and they needed even George Summerbee. Three weeks later, Taylor's caution was justified. George was summoned to first-team action for the first leg of the fifth-round FA Cup tie at Charlton. For some reason not immediately apparent, George played at left-back, even though he was right-footed, and Andy Beattie played at right-back even though he was left-footed. The team did not play well and although six years of total war had passed since George had last come under scrutiny, the local paper maintained its unforgiving stance. George was dismissed as being 'hesitant and lacking confidence at left-back'. He was dropped for the second leg at Deepdale. Preston were hammered 6–0 by the eventual finalists.

This was to become the pattern for his last few months at Preston. A couple of weeks later, George was picked again, this time at centre-half against Blackburn Rovers. Preston won the local derby 2–0 and George retained his place for the next match at Bradford which Preston lost 3–1. George was dropped and Williams reinstated.

On Easter Saturday, 22 April 1946, George played his last first-team match for Preston as centre-half in a 2–0 win at Huddersfield in front of fewer than 10,000 spectators. It was obvious to all and sundry that the present Preston side was not remotely good enough to compete successfully in proper First Division football, which would re-start in August 1946. On Easter Monday, George played in the reserves where his 'experience was an inspiration'. The paper obviously rated him as a reserve-team player. That night the board met to discuss the retained list for the following season. When the club published it in the local paper the next day, George Summerbee's name was not on it. It really was over.

On 24 May, the chairman reported to the board that Summerbee had been transferred to Chester for £600. Chester were a perennially impoverished team in the Third Division (North) of the Football League. For them, £600 was an enormous outlay and great hopes were invested in this record signing. The *Chester Chronicle* recorded: 'The Chester manager, Mr Frank Brown, has been impressed by his displays as a full-back and signed him for that position. He is five feet eleven inches and weighs eleven stone.'

Although he was dropping down two divisions, George must have looked forward to this new beginning with great eagerness. He was signing for a manager who really wanted him, they were paying a lot of money for him so he would be bound to be well treated by the club. It might be a small pond but he was going to be the biggest fish in it. In addition, he was finally free of both Jim Taylor and his mother-in-law. Perhaps more important than all this was the fact that he left Preston, according to the minute book, with £350, which must have represented his loyalty bonus.

The odd thing is that Dulcie can remember nothing about it even though it was more money than either of them had ever seen in a lump sum. Dulcie thinks that she would have regarded it as belonging to George rather than to the two of them as a married couple. She continued to work in Preston, the boys went to school in Penwortham and George moved, possibly with a tinge of relief, into digs in Chester, although even that was not straightforward.

The *Chester Chronicle*'s sports reporter clearly believed that his duties extended into more socially responsible areas than would be the case today. Five days before the season began, after informing his readers that the Chester staff now comprised 12 full-time and nine part-time professionals, he added a plea from the Chester manager, Frank Brown, who 'is experiencing difficulty in finding accommodation for one or two players and would be glad of assistance in this matter.

Summerbee is now doing his training with Blackburn Rovers.'

It wouldn't have been impossible to commute from Preston but clearly George enjoyed visiting the red sandstone cathedral which had formerly been a Benedictine monastery and the fine collection of Roman coins in the Grosvenor museum in this ancient walled city north of the River Dee. It was certainly preferable to returning each day to Preston, his mother-in-law and two small kids.

He began his first match for Chester playing right-back away at York. It wasn't exactly a masterclass in the art of defensive organisation but his new team came away with a point in a 4–4 draw. Eleven and a half years earlier, the local paper had spotted a classy, thoughtful player and this latest debut produced much the same reaction, along with his photograph as the potential new star of the side: 'Summerbee, the newcomer from Preston, played well within himself and struck me as being thoroughly competent to look after himself in Northern Section football.'

Unfortunately that was probably the highlight of his entire career at Chester; things began to deteriorate quickly. The next match ended in a 3–1 defeat at home to Doncaster Rovers. The local reporter turned on George who, he alleged, 'allowed himself to be rattled by the diminutive Nettleton whom he found awkward to tackle'. He concluded ominously that Summerbee 'will have to play better'.

George would not have been pleased to be singled out in this manner but almost immediately the team's form picked up. After 11 games they had scored 33 goals, amassed a total of 18 points (two points for a win in those days) and were equal first in the table. But at the end of September, George sustained a serious injury that kept him on the sidelines for a month, and Chester's successful run showed no sign of ending with their star player incapacitated. In November, the manager announced that George would return to first-team duty for the vital local derby match with

Crewe Alexandra, but when the teams took the field George was nowhere to be seen. George's place at right-back had been taken by a young lad called Reg Butcher, a part-timer from South Liverpool who trained in his home town and met the rest of the team on match days. The local reporter remarked that young Butcher was going 'from strength to strength' and that 'Summerbee must bide his time before returning to the first team'. The paper was basically a mouthpiece for Frank Brown who had been in charge since 1938 and was to remain there until 1953. He seems to have decided early in the season that George was an expensive mistake. By the end of this miserable year, George was a regular player in the Chester reserves where it was noted that it was 'encouraging to know he played a splendid game at centre-half'. How topping. That was just the sort of triumph worth sticking in the scrapbook.

Chester's fine run of league form continued into the FA Cup competition where they reached the fourth round and were drawn at home to play Stoke City, then riding high in the First Division. It was arguably the biggest game Chester had played since they joined the Football League 15 years earlier. It was exactly the sort of game George Summerbee hoped would come his way. Now at last Chester would benefit from his experience and knowledge of the game at the higher levels. The Chester club was buzzing. Thoughts of an improbable double – a Wembley appearance and a first-ever promotion to the Second Division – raced through the minds of the local citizens, unchecked by reality.

Frank Brown not only did not pick George for the Stoke game, he was not even part of the squad from whom the final 11 were chosen. Eighteen thousand people packed Sealand Road to watch a typical Cup-tie which ended scoreless. High-flying Stoke were relieved to take Chester back to the Victoria Ground where, after 70 minutes of the replay, they were winning comfortably 3–0 in front of a crowd of 42,000.

Chester rallied, scored twice and with minutes to go forced the ball over the line to send the match into extra time – as they thought. Unfortunately, the referee, as referees have done from time immemorial, shrugged off the protests of the little team and waved play on so that the big boys could have their place in the snow.

Chester were so upset by this cruel reversal that their league form declined as well and then young Reg Butcher was injured. However, scrutiny of the Chester first teams and reserve teams for the month of March 1947 reveals no sign of a recall for George Summerbee. He was restored to the reserves for the match at Runcorn on Good Friday, which ended in a calamitous 4–0 defeat. For the match the following day, George was dropped. A month later his name appeared on the 'Open to Transfer' list released by the club – so much for the fond hopes of August 1946.

Observing George's career at this time is rather like watching Manchester City in recent years – just when you think you've hit rock bottom somebody finds the location of the trapdoor and you go hurtling ever downwards. In addition to his loss of form, there seems to have been a major breakdown in relations with Frank Brown, exacerbated by George's union activities. It came to a head when Andy Beattie persuaded George to go to a union meeting in Manchester. Dulcie recalls the time.

It was about membership. A lot of clubs didn't want their players to join. Anyway, he went to this thing and he couldn't train for two days because it took quite a long time to get it all together. When he came back he was called into the office and they asked him where he'd been. He said, 'I've been getting all the men here to join the union,' and they said, 'Oh no, you're not!' He came back to me and said, 'I don't know what I'm going to do because I believe in it and the lads believe in it.' Eventually, we had no money for six weeks . . .

After that it led to the transfer list because they wouldn't let him play. They treated him very badly.

Both Dulcie and John Summerbee have clear memories of those six weeks in which George was suspended by Chester and had his wages stopped. The financial hardship was so great that John remembers his parents, in tears, taking the piggy banks from both boys and breaking them open. The coppers in there would have to be enough to get them through to the end of the week. It was obviously traumatic with all the emotional turmoil such a situation would inflict on all parties. For John, the horror of the experience remains undimmed by the passing of the years, but it is his belief that George was financially irresponsible. Even in the hardest of times, George refused to compromise on clothes. He always had handmade Daks suits hanging in the wardrobe and those well-polished, handmade shoes from Barretts. It wasn't just that he took an admirable pride in his appearance – he insisted on it even when the money might have been better spent elsewhere. George retained some of the childlike attitudes typical of professional footballers who are shielded by their clubs from the irritations of real life. Dulcie recalls ruefully, 'When they were little, we would go out walking and the boys would climb trees to see if there were any eggs in a nest, and someone once said to me, "You don't need any more children, you've got three." '

None of this, however, can alter the pain that George obviously felt throughout that terrible time at Chester. He had been greatly influenced by Jimmy Guthrie's talk of the players' need for a strong union and in May 1946 he was transfer-listed by Preston, in May 1947 by Chester. Neither club could wait to see the back of him.

The *Chester Chronicle*, privy as ever to the manager's most intimate thoughts, printed the news that came as no surprise to George or Dulcie, just before the retained list was announced:

> Summerbee, who was bought from Preston last season, may join Barrow, now managed by former clubmate Andy Beattie. Barrow have made a tentative enquiry for this player and as Chester are not likely to be asking for a big fee, it is not improbable that he will go.

Amidst the double negatives is the clear indication that the deal was already done and that Brown wanted to be shot of George whether the club got a penny for him or not. In the event, they didn't.

The first six months of 1947 were probably the worst of George's career. In dispute with an unsympathetic management, in and out of a Third Division club's reserve team, suspended without pay for six long weeks, he was close to breaking point. Andy Beattie had promised George that as soon as he got his first job as a manager he would make sure George was his first signing, but when Beattie arrived at Barrow in the spring of 1947, he didn't call straightaway. It seemed to the family that, in the midst of George's great crisis, one of his best friends in the game had gone missing. Dulcie felt this was a betrayal and held it close to her heart for many years, even going so far as to berate Beattie eight years later for his pusillanimous behaviour. It was the last time she ever saw him. George had to endure the final three months of humiliation at Chester in full before Beattie's call finally came.

George himself rarely complained. He turned his disappointment inwards. Sometimes Dulcie wished her husband would speak out and tell people when he thought they were taking advantage of him, but that wasn't George Summerbee's way and it isn't his grandson's way either. Mike, however, is a different character. Nobody in the northern hemisphere can be unaware when Mike is upset.

If the circumstances surrounding his transfer were unpropitious, happily the three seasons George Summerbee spent at Barrow were the most rewarding of his playing career. Barrow-in-Furness, to give the town its full name, is, despite its proximity to Morecambe Bay and the Lake District, a mainly industrial town and shipbuilding activities had inevitably attracted the attention of the Luftwaffe. Apparently, the authorities there were strong on law and order – the week George signed for the club a 19-year-old bus conductress appeared in court, charged with the crime of ringing her bell too soon and causing a woman carrying a shopping bag to fall off the platform of the bus.

When George arrived in 1947, shipbuilders Vickers-Armstrong were by far the largest employer in the town, and many of the team had jobs there. For the part-timers, therefore, training sessions had to be scheduled for after the 7.30 a.m. to 5 p.m. shifts. George was brought in by Andy Beattie because his experience would be invaluable in the rebuilding of the team; for George it was a chance to play under a manager who liked and respected him as a man and as a player. It had never happened to him before and he was now almost 33 years old. Inevitably, he immediately became the club's representative to the players' union. Guthrie would have expected no less.

Andy Beattie had left Preston as the great pre-war side finally broke up. George Mutch, the hero of the 1938 Cup final, goalkeeper Jack Fairbrother who had been George's best man in 1939, and Jimmy Dougal, the long-serving goalscoring forward, as well as Andy Beattie, all played their last games for Preston in the 1946–47 season. The following year, Bobbie Beattie departed.

Andy Beattie was determined to adopt some of the good management habits he had observed during his time at Preston. He arrived at Barrow towards the end of the 1946–47 season and made an immediate impact, guiding the unfashionable Lancashire club to ninth position in the Third Division (North), 15 points adrift of Chester; without the help of George Summerbee, Chester had finished an impressive third, 16 points behind the promoted champions, Doncaster Rovers.

Barrow faced the same financial problems that confronted nearly all the teams in this division. The 1945–46 season had begun with Barrow possessing no strip for the team to wear. This particular problem was rather dwarfed by the discovery that the club possessed no players. The two problems together give a new meaning to the contemporary chant of disaffected spectators, 'You're not fit to wear the shirt.' The latter problem was partly solved by inserting an advert in the *Evening Mail* requesting pre-war players to contact the club.

The week George signed for Barrow, Andy Beattie told the club's Annual General Meeting, 'If a manager is in negotiation for a player who is married, he finds his task much easier if he can offer accommodation. Particularly is this the case with Barrow, which it must be admitted is rather off the beaten track.' A housing fund was set up to which a certain Mrs Barker contributed ten shillings. Mr Craven, however, could spare five shillings only. This wasn't going to solve the accommodation problem. Andy Beattie passed on to other matters, pleading for volunteers to help with some of the menial jobs that the groundstaff boys would normally do – Barrow couldn't afford any groundstaff boys.

George eventually found digs with an old couple who lived in Chatsworth Street, around the corner from the ground in Holker Street. Dulcie remembers that the man cooked fried eggs for George's breakfast and was so spectacularly successful at it that 'he never once broke an egg'. Presumably he broke the shell otherwise it wasn't much of an accomplishment.

Barrow was only an hour or 90 minutes away from Preston by train. It would surely have been possible to commute, even with the change of trains at Carnforth (the railway station that featured so heavily in David Lean's contemporary hit film *Brief Encounter*) but, as he had at Chester, George opted to remain at the ground, travelling home on Saturday nights. Dulcie says he was allowed to come home only if they won, which, given Barrow's record of success, seems a little harsh.

If George's arrival on Saturday nights or Sunday mornings, to say nothing of the extent of the week's income, were dictated by the football results, it is not difficult to imagine the tension in the house when the boys gathered round the wireless to listen to 'Sports Report' (which started in January 1948) and the reading of the classified football results.

Dulcie used George's arrival as an inducement to the boys to demonstrate what they had learned during the week. The tasks included the tying of shoelaces, the telling of time and the riding of bikes. John, the older and the apple of his father's eye, was bright and quick and he accomplished them all with ease. Mike struggled with all three, his mother suffering with the humiliation almost as much as he did.

When he wanted to ride a bicycle, he just got on and rode. It took Michael longer. I had to run with him. John learned to tell the time just like that, but Michael took ages. George said to him, 'When I come home at the weekend, you must know how to tell the time.' I said, 'Don't talk to him like that, he never will.' I said that some people learn things quickly. It takes others longer. George said, 'Come on, what's the time?' and there was so much crying and I was cross. Michael came to me and said, 'I can't do it with him asking me like that.' So I said to his father, 'You go outside and let him stay in with me.' The moment his father had gone away he said the time, you see. It was the same with fastening his shoelaces. He tried so hard and just couldn't get it right and yet I used to sit with him and teach him how to do it and he did quite well for me, but he wanted to prove to his father that he could do it and he couldn't.

It was obvious to everyone which of his sons George favoured. Dulcie delivers her opinion with blunt Lancastrian honesty.

George loved John but he took very little notice of Michael. He used to pluck at his jumper because he was so nervous of his dad. That's why I leaned towards Michael and I always have.

Mike is equally blunt, proclaiming that his very conception was probably a mistake. 'I was a shot in the dark,' he tells everyone mischievously and, considering the Summerbee family life in the maelstrom of wartime Britain, Dulcie and George separated for long periods, Dulcie struggling with the demands of a toddler and a job, it seems unlikely that in 1942 with the outcome of the Battle of the Atlantic so uncertain she and George would have wanted another baby so close in age to their first. Mike is nowhere near as self-confident a person as appearances may suggest; perhaps his self-doubts were inculcated at an early age, exacerbated by the awkward relationship with George. Did the additional responsibility of another child colour George's reaction to Mike? It is clear he only had eyes for one of his sons and it wasn't the one who went on to play football for his country. George's hopes for Mike were dashed by the inability of the future tormentor of First Division defenders to tie his own shoelaces or ride his bicycle.

Andy Beattie had many of the same characteristics as George, rather quiet, self-contained, very professional, more like Busby than the vociferous, exuberant Shankly, and George was quick to grasp the offer of administrative experience that Beattie shortly made him. Not only did it increase his wages but it convinced George that if a managerial opportunity did crop up, he would be well placed to accept it.

One of George's tasks was to go to the post office each week to buy the National Insurance stamps for the club. It was there he first met Norma Lock, whose husband Reg played with the boys on the rec. She says his handwriting 'was a joy, at a time when our generation had just discovered Biros and the result was a lazy scrawl'. Norma remembers George with enormous affection as 'the brother I always wished I had – thoughtful, well-mannered, protective and gentlemanly'.

Barrovians took him to their hearts immediately and one look at the team sheets over the seasons George played there reveals why. The man who had played exactly ten first-class games since the beginning of 1935 set a new record for Barrow for consecutive first-team appearances. In season 1947–48 he appeared in all 42 league games, as he did the following year. In 1949–50 he missed just four but he had already become the first player in Barrow's history to make 100 consecutive first-team appearances.

George's arrival to take up the left-half position coincided with the emergence of right-half Billy Lee. These two wing-halves together with the club captain George Forbes provided a half-back line of such strength and consistency that for Barrovians of a certain age the three names roll off the tongue as easily as Barnes, Ewing and Paul, or Lee, Bell and Whatsisname.

The 2–1 win at home to Halifax Town on Boxing Day 1947 took the club to the top of Division Three (North). They had already beaten Carlisle United 3–2 in the first round of the FA Cup, attracting a record 14,801 spectators to the tiny Holker Street ground. One goal scored by Wilf Livingstone brought a hard-won victory away to non-league Runcorn in the second round, and produced a mouth-watering tie away to Chelsea in the third round and hopes of a classic giant-killing. Unfortunately, that was where that particular dream came to an end. Chelsea were in no mood to play the sacrificial victim and Barrow returned north on the wrong end of a 5–0 scoreline. At least there was the satisfaction of a share of the gate money provided by the 44,336 who watched the match.

Barrow's league form fell away slightly and they finished seventh, but no defence in their division conceded fewer goals than Barrow's; it must have been a source of some satisfaction to George that one of the three teams that failed to score against them either home or away was Chester. The club that had given him such a hard time the previous year finished a humiliating three places from the bottom.

For the first time in his professional career, George Summerbee was a happy man. Norma Lock confirms that her memory of George at this time was of a man at peace with himself. Mike and John recall this season only as the time of the great freeze, the worst winter in living memory. John remembers his father dragging firewood along the cinder track towards the house in West End – they had run out of fuel and George had gone out to scavenge wood like the poor man just before his legendary meeting with Good King Wenceslas. They have no memory of the death of their paternal grandfather who died in Winchester that year at the age of 70.

During the close season the money earned during the Cup run was spent on re-constructing the terracing, raising the capacity to 20,000, and Barrow supporters had every expectation of building on the success of the previous season. It must therefore have come as a rude shock to learn, two weeks before the first match of the season was due to be played, that Andy Beattie had resigned as manager. Apparently, differences between the chairman and the manager were so great that the manager was compelled to tender his resignation. More surprisingly, the board of directors refused to accept it and, in an almost unprecedented move, forced the resignation of the chairman instead. However, this was not the end of the problem and Beattie had clearly become disillusioned with the job at Barrow. A first victory in the league eluded Barrow until the 12th game of the season and by the time the clocks went forward again, Andy Beattie had successfully terminated his contract in order to take up a similar position at Stockport County.

It would have been logical had Beattie nominated George as his chosen successor. After all, it seems likely that part of the attraction of Barrow for George (aside from the fact that it wasn't Chester) was the chance to apprentice himself to the trade of football management. It is something of a tradition in football that the senior professional wanting his first break in management succeeds to his mentor's vacant position. Peter Reid got his break when Howard Kendall unexpectedly returned to Everton in 1990, and David O'Leary was so much the logical successor to George Graham when the latter returned to north London that everyone has now forgotten how keen Leeds seemed to be to entice Martin O'Neill from Leicester City.

George later told the *Gloucestershire Echo* that he had turned down the job because he wished to move south, but since the move south didn't materialise for another 15 months that seems unlikely. However, if George was expecting the call from the chairman of Barrow after Beattie's departure, it never came. Instead, Barrow brought in Jack Hacking from Accrington Stanley. Results picked up slightly and Barrow finished 13th in the table, still five places clear of Chester but five below Beattie's new club. Again the problem was the attack – Barrow scored fewer goals than any other team. The defence remained as secure as ever but the club gained the dubious honour of becoming the worst supported team in the Football League. Barrow was ever a rugby league town.

The immediate post-war years have long been regarded as football's boom time. When Moscow Dynamo brought their magnetic and exotic mixture of skill and cheating to Britain in 1945, they attracted huge crowds – 82,000 crammed into Stamford Bridge to see a 3–3 draw with Chelsea, 54,000 went to Highbury to watch a ludicrous match played in thick fog. It finished 4–3 to the Russians but nobody could be sure because none of the crowd could see the whole pitch. They beat Cardiff 10–1 and played out a 2–2 draw in front of 90,000 at Ibrox.

Annual attendances at league matches rose from 35.4 million in 1946–47 to over 40 million in each of the next three seasons. In the season 1947–48 gross receipts rose to over £4 million for the first time. In 1946–47 all but six of the professional clubs made a profit, an unparalleled state of prosperity. The players, of course, continued to see very little of it. The popularity of football was part of a much broader social picture as the people of Britain returned to their traditional pleasures on an unprecedented scale. The glorious summer months of 1947 enticed three million people to watch county cricket.

Barrow, however, seemed a town apart. After the disastrous attendances of 1948–49, the following season showed no improvement. Crowds averaged less than 6,000 and they had little to cheer as the club dropped a further two places to finish below Chester and Beattie's Stockport County, who beat them 1–0 at Holker Street in the final home game of the season. A week later, George went to Lincoln to play his very last match in the Football League as a full-time professional. Barrow were beaten 4–0 and George gave away a penalty.

It must have been with a mixture of relief and regret that George symbolically hung up his boots, at least as a full-time player. The regret would have been much greater if he had thought he had no future in football. But he had just had three full and successful seasons at Barrow where he had found the public recognition that had been denied him for so long in Preston. The local paper bade him the sort of fond farewell he had never experienced at any of his previous clubs:

While there are no great surprises in the retained list which was issued by Barrow A.F.C. yesterday, there are few who will not regret the parting of veteran half-back George Summerbee . . . Not even his most severe critic can deny the quality of his football. His positional football and distribution are such that I would recommend all young players who have watched him to model themselves on his style.

He couldn't say in the words of the well-known cliché that football had been good to him because it certainly hadn't. Football had spent a long time elbowing him in the face and when he refused to crumple to the floor, it had brought him down from behind – but still he couldn't give it up. Jack Hacking had given George permission to apply for the manager's job at Cheltenham Town, then in the Southern League, and wrote on his behalf to George's prospective new employers:

> His football ability is beyond question, and he would be a most suitable person to fill the position of player–manager with any club. His knowledge of the game and his experience will be a great asset on and off the field of play.
>
> The pleasant way he goes about his work will greatly help the coaching which I know is necessary with your club, and for this he is quite capable to demonstrate on any part of the game.

Cheltenham couldn't afford a player of George's experience and a new manager so it was in their interest to find a player–manager. George was perfect for them and in July 1950, to his great joy, George was offered a two-year contract. He was on the first step of the managerial ladder. His old Preston colleagues Andy Beattie and Bill Shankly (now at Carlisle) had started just before him but everyone had to start somewhere and Cheltenham was a more than respectable place for George to put into practice all the ideas he had been thinking about during his playing career.

Cheltenham Town was a non-league set-up admittedly but it would mean a return to the south and, finally, a club house. The Summerbees would be together as a family in a house of their own, effectively for the first time. He and Dulcie had been married for 11 years. The boys would get to know their father as a constant presence in their lives instead of as the man who arrived occasionally with presents. John and Mike had grown up with their mother and grandmother. Their father had dedicated himself to his career and, as so many footballers have to do during their relatively short professional lives, he had been forced to place the demands of the club before those of his family. In 1950 the man was expected to be the main breadwinner. Dulcie had always worked it is true; in Preston in the 1930s, if you had a job you kept it because you never knew when the next one might arrive. But the woman's job was always of secondary importance. Dulcie would move to Cheltenham and find something there. If she had to change professions it didn't much matter. It was the man's profession that dictated the family's circumstances.

Dulcie was a little fearful of the move. For a start, it meant she would be leaving the security of her Lancashire roots and she knew from experience the cultural differences that existed between Lancashire folk and southerners. More specifically, she knew just how insecure football was as a profession. George might be full of hope and expectation now but she wondered what would happen to them if things went wrong down south. It wasn't just the two of them now. They had the boys to consider.

The boys, however, could scarcely wait to get there, they were so excited. Cheltenham in Gloucestershire was the land of the recently retired England cricket captain, Wally Hammond, and it was a relatively exotic place compared to the bleak streets of the Lancashire asphalt jungle. It was a wonderful opportunity for all the Summerbees to play at happy nuclear families.

At Barrow they said goodbye to George with regret. He was popular and well respected by players and supporters. Wilf Livingstone couldn't help noticing as he shook George's hand that George looked a funny colour. He looked, if truth were told, rather ill. No one said anything. This was 1950 and you didn't make personal remarks like that. George never mentioned feeling ill and nobody suspected that inside that athletic body vital functions were already starting to seize up. As far as everyone was concerned, the Summerbees were off on an exciting adventure.

CHAPTER SEVEN

Cheltenham

If Dulcie Summerbee needed a portent, she received it just before the family was due to move from Preston to Cheltenham. She was on her knees cleaning the carpet of the house in West End when her forefinger was torn open by an unseen needle buried in the carpet. The wound refused to heal and by the time moving day arrived the finger had swollen badly and she was in considerable pain.

The four of them caught the train from Preston and changed at Crewe. During the wait for the next southbound service, Dulcie found a chemist's shop and showed the finger to the pharmacist who advised an immediate trip to the hospital. How could she? They were moving house and she had two little boys to look after. She got back on the train but the journey became increasingly difficult to bear. When they arrived in Cheltenham, she discovered that the infection had turned septic. The first month in her new home was spent with her finger strapped up until the swelling could be lanced.

The Summerbees moved into a flat above a grocer's shop in Great Norwood Street until the club house in Oakland Avenue was ready. It was the same month that the Cheltenham-based First Battalion of the Gloucestershire Regiment sailed for Korea from Southampton on board the now infamous *Empire Windrush*. John remembers the time with great affection:

It was just down the road from a sports shop and our dad used to take us in there all the time. I remember there was a brilliant smell of leather. The shop's gone now. The man who owned it taught me how to lace a ball.

Mike's first memory of Cheltenham is of the Promenade, the wide and spacious street in the centre of town with its splendid Regency houses, leafy trees and impressive statues, such a contrast to the mean streets of Preston. Unfortunately, he found his first days at Naunton Park Junior School much less rewarding:

When we first went to school in Cheltenham, the other kids thought the Summerbees were French because they couldn't understand a word we were saying.

Even when the language problem had been dealt with, Mike's academic career still didn't get out of the starting blocks. He struggled so badly to learn his times tables that he was taken out of his regular classroom and sent off to an annexe down the road from the main part of the school. This was where the backward children were taught in case they managed to transmit the virus of mathematical incompetence to the rest of the school. Yet at an early age he joined the local library and was eagerly devouring *The Coral Island* by R.M. Ballantyne at the age of nine. His appetite for books grew over the years – his collection is now housed in floor to ceiling bookcases.

Mike wilfully ignored the possibilities created by R.A. Butler and his Education Act of 1944 – when the 11+ examinations came along he decided that he couldn't be bothered working for them. John was already in Naunton Park Senior School and was enjoying the sport there. Since that was all that Mike lived for, it seemed pointless worrying about the square root of 144 or the date of the Battle of Bosworth. Mike duly joined John and discovered the benefits of a school with three sports masters, Mr Whittaker, Mr Wills and Mr Parry. Mr Whittaker was a classic sports master, always wearing shorts and, in summer, an athletics vest. He was a good-looking man with some of Malcolm Allison's charisma and, not surprisingly, he excited Mike's admiration. Mr Whittaker soon recognised Mike's natural talents and by the age of 11½ Mike was captain of his house football, cricket and athletics teams.

As every gifted athlete discovers at school, spectacular prowess on the field leads to privileges off it and Mike duly exploited the tolerance the teachers extended to the undersized sporting hero. The redoubtable Miss Holdenhurst, Naunton Park's toughest teacher, sent Summerbee minor to the headmaster to be caned for miserably failing yet another mental arithmetic test. In the middle of the 20th century, it was still believed that the violent application of the cane to the unprotected bottom was a brilliantly successful educational tool. Anything, from a list of world capitals to a belief in the existence of God, could be instilled by this method. In this, one of his earliest confrontations with a disciplinary committee, something that was to feature so frequently in his future professional career, Summerbee was the victor. The headmaster administered three light taps of the cane and returned him to the classroom with an admonition to score on Saturday.

The only teacher who appeared to be immune to the Summerbee charm was Jimmy Crowe, the metalwork master. In my experience it is always the metalwork or woodwork masters who desire to inflict on generations of terrified schoolboys the same contempt that society has heaped on them for their choice of career. A regiment of psychotically disturbed woodwork masters would have brought (an admittedly uneasy) peace to the Middle East years ago. Even the most bigoted of youths would think twice about joining the fundamentalists if he were faced with the prospect of spending any time in an apron being supervised by a man standing behind him tapping a two-foot ruler into his open palm with menacing intent. 'You'll never amount to anything, Summerbee,' was Crowe's line. 'They'll bury you under a football pitch.' Five years later, Mike Summerbee, star forward in Swindon Town's young side, returned to Naunton Park for an open day in an MGB convertible sports car. It did little to improve the self-image of the metalwork master but it felt wonderful to Mike.

The whole point of coming to Cheltenham, however, was to advance George's career and for the four of them to be together as a family. Initially at least, John thought this was successful.

> I liked coming to Cheltenham because Dad took us to the ground a lot and he was with us all the time. He included us in the training. When he got there, he found it was all terrible – there was no kit, nothing, and he tried to make it into a proper professional club. He did a great job.

Councillor Leslie Smith, the club chairman, declared that the appointment of George Summerbee would lead to a 'complete rejuvenation of the club's life. In Summerbee, we have the man who can put the club in the position in which we would like to see it. The board was unanimous in his appointment, although we had applications from men of very high repute.' Later, Councillor Smith turned into the Ken Bates of Cheltenham Town but in July 1950, George went through the ritual of telling the local paper how, after the first training session with his new charges, he appreciated that he had some 'very good material to work on'.

Despite, or perhaps because of, this boardroom bravado, the players must have been a little worried by the arrival of a man of whom it was unlikely any of them had ever heard unless they had relatives in Barrow. The man George was replacing as manager, the former Aston Villa, Reading and Southampton player Cyril Dean, was to remain with Cheltenham Town as secretary of the club and inside-right in the first team, and George was well aware that this was a situation fraught with potential political tension. Ron Coltman was the 19-year-old reserve goalkeeper when George took his first training session in July 1950:

> We heard there was someone coming down from the north. I turned up for training on the Tuesday night and George was there. Training started that night in July 1950. We used to go for these bloody runs – heartbreaking it was – pounding them bloody streets. I could never run distances, I was good at sprinting, so I really suffered. But fair enough, it got you fit.

Cheltenham Town had finished the 1949–50 season near the bottom in 20th position in the Southern League Premier Division. The chairman had given George the job as player–manager with the traditional but still ominous warning that there was no money available to strengthen the team, although George did succeed in persuading the club to sign right-half Ted Rigby from Barrow in time for the first match at the end of August. After three games, George could see why the warning had been issued. His 'very good material' lost the first match 1–0 away to Kidderminster Harriers, George playing at left-back, then lost at home 0–2 to Guildford City and by the same score to Kettering Town. At this point, George's brand new career was in danger of disintegrating before it had begun as his new charges found themselves rooted firmly to the bottom of the Southern League.

There must have been a temptation to adopt the Alan Ball theory of management, to lecture his part-timers with telling references to his long years as a professional, the glory days mixing with the Beatties, the O'Donnells, Mutch and Shankly, but to his credit George kept his cool. Ron

Coltman, whose sterling displays for the reserves soon earned him a promotion to the first team, was grateful for George's sensitivity.

> He was a likeable man, he really was. I was learning the trade then. Everybody made mistakes but George never used to blast you in front of a group. There was a wholesale bollocking if we played bad but no individual was ever sorted out. He'd take you on the side and say, 'Know what you did wrong today, Ron? Think back to that third minute and what happened.' He had all the information in his head and he was really good at it.

One can imagine the early dressing room discussions as George tried to explain what would be required of the players. In any organisation there is always an element of resistance to change. 'Show us your medals' is the traditional cry of sceptical footballers when faced with a new manager. Failure to impose his influence on the squad inevitably creates a subversive faction and the first three matches gave George his first major crisis as a manager. Slowly his influence told and Cheltenham began to climb the table. The players began to recognise that George was offering something different from what they had been used to. The training under Bill Scott at Preston and the brief apprenticeship under Andy Beattie at Barrow helped. The Preston training had been a significant factor in his appointment, as the Cheltenham chairman later revealed:

> One of the things that impressed the board, knowing our past weakness, was his declared policy of following the method adopted at Preston, whereby training was carried out to a rigid schedule and with a definite playing plan to be adopted by first and reserve-team players.

George may have been appointed as player–manager but, whether on grounds of age or increasing medical problems, he rarely picked himself. One exception came in November 1950 when Cheltenham played Yeovil for a coveted place in the first round of the FA Cup competition. The day was one of high drama. It began when the brakes of the coach carrying the team and the directors to Yeovil failed and the coach embedded itself in the back of a petrol tanker. Shaken but unhurt, all the passengers walked the three miles to Shepton Mallet where they managed to hire a replacement bus. They got to the Yeovil ground ten minutes before kick-off. Lunch, which was normally a fairly substantial affair, was reduced to a cup of tea and a piece of toast. Perhaps this unwitting adoption of the Arsene Wenger diet gave Cheltenham the added running power to overturn a two-goal deficit and return home safely with a famous 4–2 victory. Their reward was to be drawn away to Reading in the next round.

Cheltenham was soon in the grip of Cup fever. A thousand supporters, pretty much half of the regular crowd at Southern League fixtures, made the journey to Elm Park. The match, played in front of the highest attendance in Cheltenham's history, turned out to be the last time George picked himself to start a game. It brought back bitter-sweet memories of his final game for Aldershot in 1935 when he scored in the 3–1 defeat before leaving for obscurity in Lancashire. The result was identical 16 years later and George's performance that day convinced him that, at the age of 36, the first half of his player–manager job description had to be regarded as purely nominal. It seems unlikely that even at this stage George had confided his anxieties about his deteriorating physical condition to anyone. If he was getting slower, it was just age. In fact, it is a miracle that he managed to play for as long as he did.

That first season as a whole, however, contained far more

successes than failures. Two players in particular stood out –
Peter Rushworth, although suffering from the twin handicaps
of being slight of build and the son of the man who was
shortly to take over as the chairman, flourished at left-half;
Roy Shiner, the centre-forward, embarked on a prodigious
run of goalscoring which was mostly responsible for Cheltenham's steady rise up the table. They finished that first season
under George's management an impressive sixth in the
League. George reflected on it with great satisfaction. Some
of the hurt inflicted by the disappointments of his playing
career was already starting to fade. Shankly and Beattie
weren't doing much better at Carlisle United and Stockport
County respectively in the relatively glamorous world of the
Third Division (North). Maybe all the tribulations he had
suffered were just a painful preparation for a glorious future
career as a manager.

The family had reacted to the move south in the best
possible way. George was happy to be back in the south.
Although some way from Winchester, Cheltenham was close
enough to prompt the occasional visit from Bunt and Ruby.
Ironically, in view of Dulcie's belief that the Summerbees
looked down on her because she was 'common', Ruby
remembers being impressed by Dulcie's refinement and
George's ostensible affluence.

The family was anti-Dulcie. They just didn't get on with
her but I remember she had beautiful skin, and lovely
hands with lovely nails. I remember going to Cheltenham
to stay with them when Dulcie worked in the chemist's
shop. She used to sit with her nails in olive oil. I used to
think she was lovely. I was more of the sporty type.
George was quite slight and he had lovely polished shoes.
He was always cleaning his shoes – they were spotless.

By contrast Bunt never bought new clothes until the ones he

was wearing were so old and worn they were almost falling off his back.

Dulcie, as well as looking after her family and holding down a full-time job, still found time to make tea and sandwiches on matchdays, and to wash the kit after games and training sessions at the ground: 'Cheltenham Town had no money. We used to help to clean the stands, George and I, underneath, where all the paper blows. Then when visitors were coming I used to make all the sandwiches and cakes and tea for nothing. Just to help. He tried so hard, it was awful.'

The boys, of course, could imagine nothing better than getting out of school, cycling to the ground and playing football. In the summer holidays, there was plenty to do. The boys and their friends Kenny Skeen and David Shakespeare would go to a place called Wainlows. Mike recalls:

It was about halfway between Cheltenham and Tewkesbury, a little hamlet right on the river and we would cycle there. It was where the Avon joins up with the Severn and it was lovely. You could fish for trout and we camped out behind the pub. We used to call the landlady the Black Widow because we thought she was a witch. We used to play football on the river bank. One day my mother came to see us, after a primus stove blew up and burned Kenny. I think she came with my dad and she went berserk. She didn't realise we were right on the bank with the river going past at 100 m.p.h. If we'd fallen in when we were fishing, we'd have disappeared. We were never allowed to go again.

George had more time for the boys now that he was working in the same town as they were living. By Christmas 1950, the Summerbee family had moved into the pleasant Victorian terraced house owned by the club at 36 Oakland Avenue, a five-minute bike ride from the ground. Mike and John regarded the Whaddon Road ground as their own playing field and they had a bunch of semi-professional footballers to play with them.

As the consort of a significant figure in Cheltenham public life, Dulcie was interviewed by the local paper and although she made ritual obeisance to the idea that the manager's wife uncomplainingly packs up the household contents and follows her husband round the country, she managed to convey a couple of ideas that rarely appeared in print in 1951:

> She points out that being a footballer under contract is by no means 'all beer and skittles'. She watches her husband's team whenever possible, if they have a home match, and admits by now she has not only a good knowledge of the game but also of the backstage intricacies of football – 'the less pleasant side which the ordinary public knows very little about'.

The summer of 1951 was probably the pinnacle of the Summerbees' lives as a happy family. The events of the 1951–52 season tested George to the full. Cheltenham Town were caught, as so many financially embarrassed teams are, on the horns of a dilemma. To survive, these teams have to sell their best players. If they sell their best players, they usually replace them with worse ones. If they have worse players, results will be poor. If the team's results are poor, the crowds diminish producing less revenue and those who remain become restless and because the core supporters are restless the directors become anxious. Invariably, the board feels it necessary to appease the wrath of the supporters by sacking the manager because of bad results, blithely ignoring its own culpability by setting this whole train of events in motion in the first place.

George's last season in football began with one of the highlights of his life. Keith Rushworth, who had been appointed to the position of vice-chairman shortly after George started, now took over the reins from Councillor Smith. When George proposed a series of floodlit matches at Whaddon Road, Rushworth was delighted and publicly proclaimed his manager to be 'a man of foresight'.

The floodlights were a homespun affair, the lights perched on top of larch poles like street lamp posts, but the enterprise was greeted with enthusiasm by the players and the supporters. Everyone helped and it must have looked like the barn-raising sequence from *Seven Brides for Seven Brothers*. Most of the players had skills as chippies or similar and those who didn't simply contributed their labour. The wiring was supervised by an official from the Midlands Electricity Board who later joined the board of directors.

The first team to play against Cheltenham under lights were Wolverhampton Wanderers who sent their reserves, including future England international Ron Flowers at right-half. The match was played on 17 October 1951 and a crowd of 4,153 paid to get in. Several hundred others managed to find ways into the ground without passing through the two official turnstiles. The club grossed £314 in gate money and were delighted when Wolves declined their £140 share. John, however, remembers that his father was concerned because he thought it should have been more after such a triumphant night.

'My dad thought someone in the club was fiddling. He knew what the gate was for that match against Wolves and there was still no money so he thought there was a fiddle going on somewhere.'

That night lived long in the memory of all Cheltenham fans who were there to witness the exciting 3–3 draw. The Mayor of the town declared the new boardroom officially open and then went on to the pitch to be introduced to the two teams, like royalty before the Cup final. With ten minutes to go in the game, the Central League side was leading 3–1 but a great individual

108

goal by Cyril Dean initiated a series of furious attacks by the home side and in the very last minute, Cheltenham equalised to send the crowd home happy.

Over the next six months, Cheltenham Town played seven more matches under lights, attracting over 20,000 people to the ground. The experiment was rated highly successful, despite the lights being only 20 or so feet from the ground and the moment the ball was kicked higher than that it disappeared into a black void. Play halted momentarily as everyone waited expectantly for it to descend into the lighted area again. The only people less than enchanted by this innovative series of matches were the residents of the houses in and around Whaddon Road. As soon as the floodlights were turned on, all the residents lost power. Electric toasters failed to pop, electric kettles refused to boil and television pictures slowly faded from view. The man from the Midlands Electricity Board earned his promotion to the board of directors as more power lines were installed to cope with the problem.

The other downside of the floodlit matches was that they brought scouts to Whaddon Road. Still strapped for cash, the Cheltenham Town board listened eagerly to their blandishments even as the manager drummed his fingers on the rickety table in his office. Predictably, the two players they wanted were Roy Shiner and Peter Rushworth. In November 1951, after two successive and impressive victories, 2–1 away at Chelmsford and 5–1 at home to Bath City, Peter Rushworth was transferred to Leicester City for £1,350.

The following month, Cheltenham played another successful friendly match under floodlights. Cyril Spiers brought his Cardiff City side, which was heading for promotion to the First Division at the end of the season. In the crowd this time was Alf Young who had played at centre-half for Huddersfield Town against Preston when George was 12th man at Wembley in 1938. Once George saw Alf, he knew what was going on. Young was his club's chief scout. Four days before Christmas, the free-scoring centre-forward Roy Shiner signed for Huddersfield Town for £1,250, with a further £250 to follow after ten first-team appearances. George watched the break-up of his team with a heavy heart.

There was a comic corollary to this transfer. Huddersfield discovered that Shiner was older than Young had told them he was, and manager George Stephenson telephoned Keith Rushworth, effectively demanding his money back. Rushworth, by all accounts a true gentleman and probably still conscious that his manager had only agreed to the transfer through gritted teeth, replied calmly that if he felt like that he must persuade the Huddersfield chairman to write to him officially. The deal would be called off and the money would be returned to Huddersfield Town. The Huddersfield chairman wrote the letter, copied the address out of the *FA Handbook* as 'Cheltenham, Gloucs.' and tossed it into the Christmas post. Deep in the bowels of the post office a temporary sorter decided that Cheltenham Town played in the city of Gloucester rather than in Cheltenham in the county of Gloucestershire. Successive attempts to deliver the letter in the city of Gloucester proved unsuccessful.

Meanwhile, hit by unseasonable injuries, Huddersfield Town were forced to draft Shiner straight into the first team where, over the Christmas and New Year period, he scored vital goals. The day before the original letter demanding their money back arrived at Whaddon Road, Rushworth confusingly received another letter telling of Huddersfield's intention to stick to the original deal. Two months later, Shiner clocked up his tenth appearance for the Yorkshire side and they quickly despatched a cheque for £250 to the right address. After leaving Huddersfield, Shiner continued to score freely for Sheffield Wednesday and Hull City.

After the transfer fiasco the rot set in for George's side and the second half of the season was a catalogue of disasters culminating in a humiliating 10–1 defeat away at Merthyr Tydfil, although in mitigation it should be pointed out that

Merthyr were the strongest side in the League and were champions for three successive years from 1950 to 1952. The local reporter wrote sorrowfully: 'At half-time, losing 5–0, they had no hope. At full time they had no heart.' It's a long way home from Merthyr Tydfil to Cheltenham at the best of times but it seems even longer when you've just lost 10–1.

On the Monday, the directors summoned the team and the manager to a meeting. It lasted two and a half hours. Six changes were made for the next match. George Summerbee's name was not mentioned in the local newspaper's reporting of the crisis. It is a moot point whether he made the changes or they were made for him. Ted Rigby, the right-half whom George had brought down from Barrow, was dropped and immediately asked to be placed on the transfer list. His request was granted. George's team was coming apart at the seams. Five consecutive defeats in March and April left Cheltenham Town in 18th position in the table after the crucial Easter games.

A 4–0 hammering by local rivals Gloucester, whose football team was clearly more efficient than its post office, was the final nail in the coffin. It seemed like a miserable repeat of the last rites at Preston in the spring of 1946 and Chester a year later when George's career at those two clubs was drawing to an untimely close. It was publicly announced that George Summerbee's two-year contract at Cheltenham Town would not be renewed when it expired in July 1952. Despite the results, Ron Coltman maintains that the players were surprised. 'There were no rumours or nothing,' he says. 'One day I came down to training and George had gone.'

Dulcie believes that there was a power struggle between the courteous Rushworth, who had been George's supporter, and the previous chairman Councillor Smith, who was attempting to wrest control back from Rushworth. A Scotsman called Raiside, who had been coaching in South America, was announced as George's replacement.

The day he lost his job at Cheltenham he came home and said he felt let down by the players as much as by the club. The new chairman Smith ran a factory that made things for the fire brigade. He was the one that pushed George out. I was always phlegmatic. George apologised for the volatility of the business but I said he'd get something else.

The official reason for George's departure given by the club was that he resigned on the grounds of ill-health. It is undoubtedly true that George's physical stamina seemed to drain from him rapidly as soon as he left full-time football. His former goalkeeper concedes that after the transfer of his two best players and the subsequent downturn in results, George started to accept that his career in football was nearing its end.

To tell you the truth, when I saw him after that he didn't look very well. He was very tired at the end. He never came out training with us. He used to watch us, standing by the fence down there. Ernie Williams used to take the training, and Cyril Dean did a bit.

Reeling from increasing infirmity as well as the blow to his pride, George faced a struggle to keep a roof over his family's heads. The moment George ceased to be the manager of the club, he had no legal claim to the house. While Rushworth disapproved of Smith's actions, he was unable to prevent the club from issuing the Summerbees with an eviction notice.

Some months before, George and Dulcie had decided that Cheltenham was going to be their home for a while and that they needed the security of their own house. Accordingly, they had paid a deposit on a new house that was being built as part of a row of semi-detached houses on Pennsylvania Avenue. Dulcie thinks the money for the house came from the lump sum George supposedly received when he left Preston North End. When George lost his job and his income, the house was far from completed and they had nowhere else to go. They could have gone to George's family in Winchester or, at a pinch, back to Dulcie's mother in Preston, but they were in their 30s now with two children at school, not newlyweds needing a helping hand from their parents. Besides, relations between Dulcie and George's family had not improved over the years.

Cheltenham Town didn't care about the Summerbees' problems. The club just wanted the Oakland Avenue house back and took them to court to enforce its legal claim to the property. George was too ill to attend the court hearing so Dulcie had to go by herself.

I was terrified. It had been a bad winter and the house in Pennsylvania Avenue was behind schedule. The weather was too bad for them to get the roof on. The judge was wonderful towards me. 'I'm not going to hang you,' he said, because I must have been as white as a sheet. 'You're going to stay in the house till the roof's put on.' They gave us another three months. But by then the new manager had come and he wanted to get into the Oakland Avenue house. They were paying for him to stay in a hotel. They had no money. Then the judge had me in his office and said, 'I can't give you much longer.' I said, 'It's not me, it's the builder.'

Despite the judge's lenience, eviction from 36 Oakland Avenue could not be delayed indefinitely and with the Pennsylvania Avenue house still uninhabitable, George and Dulcie were facing catastrophe until a kind neighbour came to the rescue. The woman who lived at 27 Oakland Avenue owned a shop at the end of the road above which was a small flat and she let the Summerbees stay there for a few months until they could move into 6 Pennsylvania Avenue. Mike remembers these months as a time of acute domestic disharmony. His parents, cooped up in this flat, were unhappy and fearful of the future. Not surprisingly, they argued constantly. George was a difficult man to live with at the best of times – and this, of course, was the worst of times. The temper that got him sent off on a number of occasions was always liable to flare up at home on the slightest provocation.

The gap between George and his siblings now became a chasm. He and Dulcie were in such financial straits that they were forced to ask his family for a loan. The facts are not easy to discern from beneath the layers of emotional pain that have covered them ever since. It seems that George borrowed £500 from Bunt, reminding him that he had paid for Bunt's first car, an MG roadster. Shortly afterwards, perhaps a few months later, Bunt asked for the loan to be repaid. George's financial situation had not significantly altered; he didn't have the money. How could he when he had only just borrowed it? The only solution was for Dulcie to sell her engagement ring, which she did with reluctance and in extreme emotional turmoil. The memory causes Dulcie pain to this day. John remembers it, too, as the *casus belli* of relations between Dulcie and George's family plummeting to an all-time low.

There is usually more than one side to the story of family disagreements, but Ruby, who still lives just outside Bournemouth, has no memory of the incident and, according to her son Raymond, there is nobody left alive who can substantiate the claim that George bought Bunt a car. It would have been extremely difficult for Bunt to have come up with £500 in cash just like that. He worked in a newsagent's shop owned by their older sister Vi's wealthy second husband, Bob Reed. It is possible that Bob Reed might have lent the money to Bunt and then changed his mind and demanded the money back. The instant reactions of Dulcie and John to the Summerbee Ring Cycle, however, leave me in no doubt that the bare facts of the narrative are true.

Oakland Avenue was, in the end, an unhappy sojourn for the Summerbees. In March 2000, Mike revisited the street he had left nearly 50 years earlier. He stopped the car outside number 36 and recalled some of the trauma of those weeks in 1952. Across the road, a woman, unloading her shopping from the rear of an estate car, looked at the middle-aged Mike.

'Hello,' said Mike. 'I used to live here,' he added, in case stopping in the middle of the street and staring at the house had aroused the woman's sense of civic duty, if not the neighbourhood watch. The woman looked at him briefly.

'I know,' she said flatly. 'I recognise you.' She continued to unload the shopping. 'You still look the same. Still ugly.' Somehow Mike invites this kind of riposte.

Unemployed and broke, George desperately needed a job but he also needed to regain his health. Dulcie tried to get him down to the surgery:

> When we first went to live in Cheltenham there was a gate at the end of the drive, not very high, but when he went to work in the mornings he used to run down the path and jump over the gate and think nothing about it. I noticed that gradually he couldn't do that any more. I said he ought to go the doctor because he must have rheumatism or arthritis and he said, 'It's not that, Dulcie. There's something wrong with me. I don't know what it is but I haven't got the power.'

In a small town like Cheltenham, the manager of a football team has status and his family has their own version of it. By contrast an ex-manager has none. George was fortunate that an offer of work came from Dowty Equipment Ltd, one of the town's biggest employers, courtesy of its owner Sir George Dowty. The company manufactured fuel systems, hydraulic units and mining equipment. It employed hundreds of draughtsmen, fitters, clerks and skilled machinists. Generally speaking, it had no use for a utility defender at the end of his career who could pass accurately and understood the game of football. But in the winter of 1952, George Summerbee, former professional footballer, unemployed football manager, went to work as a warehouse storeman at Dowty Equipment Ltd on the outskirts of Cheltenham.

The job had one advantage – he could get time off when he wanted and the network of former colleagues gave George something to cling to. Pat Beasley, who had become the manager of Bristol City at the same time as George started at Whaddon Road, asked him to do some scouting for the Ashton Gate club. It meant that George still had a toe-hold in the game but the mundane nine to five existence in Dowty's warehouse was hastening the decline in his spirits, making him feel claustrophobic.

Since his time at Barrow, George had looked ill, almost tubercular with his eyes seemingly receding into their sockets and his complexion different from everyone else's. When the sun came out, his new workmates would say, 'Run out, George, and get sunburned.' He used to change colour in the sun. Along with the change in complexion came an all-pervasive feeling of cold. Dulcie says:

Every winter we had to have big fires but he got cold so easily. His hands were dark inside – black people have lighter pigmentation on the palms, he was the exact opposite. I remember once he was in the bath and he asked me to come and have a look at him. His back had turned completely black. I started to laugh. I said, 'You look as though you've been on the Continent and you're all brown.' I can remember massaging his back and the colour changed. From his bottom to his waist it was yellow and up the back it was deep brown in patches.

Dulcie is unflinchingly honest, too, about George's impotence which stemmed from the same medical condition.

> I always remember him saying to me in bed he loved me and as far as sex was concerned he couldn't do anything. About a month before he died, it must have been two o'clock in the morning, he turned to me and said, 'I would love to love you, Dulcie, but I can't.' I said to him, 'Don't be so silly. It's nothing to worry about. You'll soon be all right like that.' But he wasn't.

The family staggered on through 1953 and 1954. They bought a television 'to watch the Coronation' but of course it was really to watch the Cup final, a month earlier. The Summerbee household were captivated by the famous FA Cup final known to posterity as the Matthews final in which Blackpool beat Bolton Wanderers 4–3. It was the first Cup final to be televised live to the nation. Both boys remember watching the game on the smallest television screen in the world with the lounge curtains drawn against the invading sun – otherwise the picture could not be seen at all.

George continued to work in the warehouse at Dowty Equipment Ltd but although the money he earned helped to feed and clothe his family, it served also to confirm the sickening fact that his career in full-time professional football was over. He lived for the days when he could leave early, with the boss's permission, to travel to matches and compile his reports on likely players for Pat Beasley at Bristol City.

John was his constant travelling companion. John and his father became extremely close during these years and there was no doubting to whom George expected to pass the torch. In his older son, George saw all his own youthful talent and fiery determination to succeed. His younger son was only allowed to travel with him once, to a match played at Kidderminster. Mike recalls sitting in the directors' box with his father, watching the Kidderminster centre-forward, Gerry Hitchens. The 11-year-old was distinctly unimpressed. 'He's useless, Dad,' stated Mike firmly, in the hearing of a collection of VIPs. 'He can't play. We should be at home. This is crap, this is rubbish, this is. None of these can play.' Gerry Hitchens went on to play for Aston Villa, Inter Milan and England. Mike was never taken to matches by his father again. This came as no surprise to his mother who saw quite clearly how George responded to the two boys: 'He loved those boys so much, even though he didn't love Michael as much as John.'

It is hard now to imagine the 1950s unless it is refracted through a John Major (stolen from George Orwell) prism. Yet it would be foolish to deny that those of us who grew up in that decade were conscious (if only because we were so often reminded of the fact by grown-ups) that we were living in the best of all possible worlds. It was a world free of Hitler for sure, and the maps stuck on every primary schoolroom wall showed it was a world with vast proportions of its surface still coloured pink, indicating the extent of the slowly fading British Empire. The age of austerity, along with Attlee's Labour government, was consigned to the dustbin of history. As the shelves of the shops were replenished with goods, rationing ceased. The economy boomed without the artificial impetus given to it by war and the spectre of a return to the days of the Depression was banished by the advent of virtually full employment. Britain in the 1950s was, by today's standards, racist, homophobic, repressed and authoritarian. However, the National Health Service meant that everyone could afford to go to the doctor, public transport made ownership of a car a luxury not a necessity, and children could play outside in the street and in the park without being knocked down by a car or abducted by a paedophile. The coronation of Queen Elizabeth II appeared to symbolise how the country could harness the traditions of the glorious past to the promise of a prosperous future.

In Cheltenham, the Glorious Gloucesters came home from Korea and marched through the town to the acclaim of its inhabitants the day before Hillary and Tenzing climbed to the summit of Mount Everest. It might have been the dawn of a new Elizabethan age in Great Britain but inside 6 Pennsylvania Avenue the atmosphere was inevitably affected by George's condition. Frequently, he would take the dog for a walk but then his legs would seize up and he would be unable to continue. Dulcie would have to go out looking for him and bring him home. Mike remembers watching his father coming home from work one day. He got to within 50 yards of the house, staggering, as Mike says, 'like Douglas Bader on two tin legs', when he accepted the fact that he could go no further and simply sat down on the pavement.

It was a summer's day, warm and beautiful, and when he eventually got inside he was freezing, and when I say freezing he was ice cold. Then when he sat down he couldn't get up again. His legs just wouldn't work. When my mother got home from work, she called the doctor and he said, 'It's just overwork,' and left. He probably gave him some aspirin or something but the trouble with his legs came back. In the middle of the night we were woken up by my mother asking us to rub my dad's legs because they were freezing cold and he couldn't use them.

One day in the spring of 1955, George could barely get out of bed. Dulcie called the doctor who examined the patient and gave it as his considered medical judgement that George was suffering from 'nerves'. This was the downside of the NHS – you got free treatment but sometimes it was of dubious value. The suggested cure was a fortnight by the sea. The logical location was Bournemouth, with Bunt and his family.

Bunt had resigned from the police force after the war but continued to play football, initially at Bournemouth and then

119

with non-league Weymouth and Dorchester, until he took up coaching and trained the A team at Bournemouth. When his brother-in-law bought the newsagent's shop in Sea Road, Boscombe, Bunt managed it. Across town, Joan managed a small general store in Holdenhurst Road above which was a flat. This was where George would stay while he recuperated.

On Tuesday, 19 April 1955, Bunt collected Vi from Winchester and together they made the journey to Cheltenham in an estate car (known in those days as a shooting brake) to pick up George and transport him down to the sunshine of the south coast. Apart from relieving Dulcie of the care and responsibility of looking after him for a few days, it gave her a chance to demonstrate to George's family how ill he was. She always thought that they believed that either Dulcie was exaggerating George's illness or that in some bizarre way she had managed to cause it. Relations between Dulcie and the other Summerbees remained awkward.

By the time they arrived at Holdenhurst Road soon after lunch on the Tuesday afternoon, Bunt realised that Dulcie was telling the truth. George was freezing cold so his brother and sister made a roaring fire and placed him on a mattress in front of it. By evening, George realised that the trip was a waste of time. His niece Heather, Joan's daughter, was 11 years old. She sat on the stairs and peeped through the open door of the dining room where the huge fire roared in the grate and her dying uncle whom she had barely seen lay motionless on a mattress by the hearth.

'I think he knew he was dying,' she says now. 'Somebody put his hands together and he said, "Don't do that!" – you know how it is when people die.'

George was dying and it didn't matter how many NHS doctors tried to convince him that a few days in the sun and a stroll along the promenade would cure him, he knew the end was fast approaching. He knew also that he didn't want to die in Bournemouth. George's final conscious thoughts were of

Dulcie and the boys. The last words anyone remembers George speaking were that he wanted to go home, back to Cheltenham and his family. Bunt and his sisters were too upset to argue. Heather and Bunt's son, nine-year-old Raymond, watched the mattress with George on it being loaded back into the rear of the shooting brake. He had been in Bournemouth for just a few hours.

Bunt began the drive back to Cheltenham in some panic. Dulcie knew George was ill, much more so than the doctors had told her, but nobody expected this sudden terrifying deterioration. At some point on the A350 between Blandford Forum and Chippenham, George groaned and lapsed into unconsciousness. They were still 35 miles from Cheltenham. Bunt and Vi decided they couldn't afford to drive for another hour or so. There wasn't much traffic about at this time of night but it was still slow going, conscious as they were that perhaps the end might be hastened by reckless driving. They decided to look for a hospital.

Approaching Cirencester, 15 miles from Cheltenham, they saw the signs to the Memorial Hospital and gratefully followed them. When they took George out of the car he was still alive. Bunt followed him into the hospital, hoping desperately they could do something. Any residual hostility because of the business with the ring had disappeared. This was his little brother, the one he'd tried to protect from getting sent off at Aldershot 20 years before, poor George who had tried so hard and who had been treated so shabbily by the game he loved.

There was no telephone at 6 Pennsylvania Avenue. It was late at night when Dulcie went to answer a knock on the front door. The boys were upstairs in bed. Michael had played a match that evening for Cheltenham Schoolboys on the Whaddon Road pitch. He would tell his father all about it as soon as he came home. It frustrated Michael that his father rated John so much more highly than him because, although he was only 12, he was already playing with much

121

bigger lads. He had captained his junior school side when he was nine and it was made up otherwise of 11-year-olds, but still his father believed that John was the one who was going to make it as a footballer. He looked forward to proving his dad wrong. He heard the knock at the door. Maybe the noise he could hear downstairs meant that his father had come back early.

Downstairs his mother was talking to a teacher who lived across the road, the only neighbour they knew with a telephone. He didn't mind the Summerbees giving his number for use in emergencies. This was one. He spoke in low, hushed tones. He had just put the phone down on a call from Bunt in Cirencester Memorial Hospital.

'What's he doing there?' asked Dulcie, frightened.

'His brother said he wanted to come home.'

'But he's only just gone to Bournemouth.'

'They want you to come to Cirencester, Dulcie. It's very serious.'

'I'd better get a taxi, then. Will a taxi go to Cirencester at this time of night?'

'I'll drive you. Get your coat and tell the boys you're going to be out for a while.'

Dulcie went upstairs and told the boys that their father was in hospital in Cirencester. She was going to see how he was but she'd be home in the morning when they woke up so they mustn't worry. The boys were worried, of course, but tried hard not to upset each other, or their mother who had enough troubles. John lay back on the pillow and thought of one of the last conversations he'd had with his father, the one he had never told anyone about.

'Mike doesn't believe me, but Dad took me out one day and told me he was dying. I said, "No, you're not," but I knew he was.'

By the time Dulcie arrived in Cirencester it was too late. She found Bunt in despair. George had passed away 45 minutes before she got there. 'A part'd ev'n just between twelve and one, ev'n at the turning o' th' tide.' Dulcie was devastated and stunned. Few words were exchanged with Bunt. This wasn't the time to prolong the family feud. Ironically, with George's death the feud effectively disappeared. It was George who was trying to keep the two halves of his family together. Once he had gone, they simply drifted apart.

A solemn doctor shepherded the distraught Dulcie into a side room and explained that George had died of Addison's disease.

> Just before he died, they took blood samples and all sorts. It's a very rare disease, you know. The doctors explained to me that near his kidneys there were two little round things like prunes, shrivelled up like dry leaves. They could have given him drugs but they didn't know about cortisone then.

Ironically, cortisone, which came into general use a couple of years later, was the staple ingredient of the many pain-killing injections Mike had to have in his legs during his playing career. It took two autopsies to confirm that George Summerbee had died of a disease that attacked fewer than one in a million.

In a daze, Bunt turned the car round and drove back to Boscombe. Dulcie was driven home by her neighbours to face the boys and the realisation that she had a family to look after and no husband to help her. It was seven in the morning when she got back to Pennsylvania Avenue. She climbed the stairs again and opened the boys' bedroom door. John remembers the moment he heard her key turn in the lock of the front door.

'I knew in my head he wasn't going to make it. He'd not been well for so long and it was getting worse. That morning when Mum came into our room, I knew what she was going to say.'

George Summerbee's short life, so full of early promise and bitter disappointments, was over. He was just 40 years old when he died. He was cremated in Cheltenham and a plaque was erected in his memory in the Garden of Remembrance. It's gone now. Plaques are removed after 25 years and so now there is nowhere for his wife and two sons to mourn him. In fact, there is nothing, except some yellowing newspaper cuttings, to tell posterity that George Summerbee ever existed. This final anonymity in death seems somehow appropriate for a man whom luck deserted at nearly every turn in his life.

CHAPTER EIGHT

Bristol and Swindon

The next few years were hard for all of them. George had never been a significant breadwinner but without his contribution they were entirely reliant on Dulcie. The boys were excused having to go to the funeral. They went off and played golf at a nine-hole course just outside the town as the friends and relatives assembled.

Dulcie appears to have been at her spikiest that day. Andy Beattie who was by then managing Huddersfield Town, with Bill Shankly as his assistant, came all the way from Yorkshire only to be berated for having betrayed George during his difficult time at Chester. Bunt drove his sisters Joan and Vi from Bournemouth and Winchester. Their father had died in 1948 and his mother couldn't face both Dulcie and the prospect of burying her younger son. Hostilities broke out almost immediately. It seems that George's family continued to draw a distinction between George's boys, who were part of George and therefore to be treated with consideration, and George's wife who, they felt, had somehow destroyed their ill-fated brother. It placed the boys in a very difficult position. Bunt died of a heart attack in 1983 at the age of 70 and it is therefore impossible to corroborate Dulcie's bitter memories of their final clash.

After George died he said to me, 'If I were you, I'd sell this house and get a council house. If you think for one minute that I am going to help you in any way you are mistaken, because I have no money.' I said, 'I've never asked you for anything. And I wouldn't take it.' He did offer to have the boys come down on holiday, though. 'Oh yes,' he said, 'they can come down any time they like.' But I paid for all that. I know he wanted money for the boys to stay there. He was always a very selfish man.

The boys remember being given money when they went down to Bournemouth and Winchester for their summer holidays but it seems reasonable to suppose that this was for their pocket money, as Bunt was always generous to them.

Mike, however, certainly remembers the fight over the clothes. George left behind him nothing but debts and a wardrobe of handmade Daks suits. After the funeral, Bunt and his sisters made a beeline for the clothes on the grounds, presumably, that they were too large for the boys. Dulcie refused to part with them, took them back to the shop in Cheltenham where George had ordered them and fitted the boys out with the proceeds.

The raid on the wardrobe wasn't the only such attack Dulcie had to repel. Someone from the Dowty factory who had worked with George knocked on the door one evening soon after the funeral and said George had promised to bequeath him his bicycle. The man went away without the bike but with a flea in his ear. Dulcie wheeled the bike back into town and, as she had with the suits, negotiated its sale in exchange for two smaller ones that could be used by John and Michael.

Dulcie's mother Lillian came down from Preston to take up almost full-time residence in Cheltenham. It was felt that the boys needed someone in the house when they came back from school. With £500 still owing to the builder of the Pennsylvania Avenue house, money was so tight that Dulcie had to take another job. After working during the day she would come home, make the tea and then go off to a cooking job in the evening.

The arrival of their grandmother did not please the boys. Although perhaps too old for the dreaded leather strap, they were still subject to what they regarded as a tyrannical regime. She would lean out of the window and embarrass them by yelling at them to change out of their school uniforms before playing football. John's show of defiance was countered by his grandmother breaking a bowl over his head.

Among the letters of condolence received after the news of George's death had travelled along the network of football professionals was one from Jack Hacking who was still the manager of Barrow. He wrote to inform Dulcie that she was due George's share of proceeds from the provident fund. As far as she can now recall, no such money ever arrived.

Perhaps it was because life was so tough that both Mike and John remember the occasional good times with such warmth. Chief among them was Wednesday afternoons, half-day closing. Dulcie would be there when they came back from school with a packet of Maynards wine gums and a large fire blazing away in the grate in the living room and there was the prospect of scrambled eggs and Marmite sandwiches for tea. Not exactly Enid Blyton with lashings of ginger beer but the ritual still evokes a pleasant nostalgia for them.

The summers were mostly spent with George's relatives, shuttling between households in Bournemouth and Winchester. John and Michael would leave Victoria coach station in Cheltenham, having said goodbye to their mother. Dulcie would never go with them. Grandmother Hattie still lived in the flat in City Road near Winchester railway station where George and his siblings had been raised. Vi and Bob and their three boys, Richard, Robin and Alan, lived a mile away in Stoney Lane. When they went to Bournemouth, the boys usually stayed part of the time with Bunt, Ruby and Raymond in the flat above the newsagent's shop in Sea Road and the rest with Auntie Joan and Heather in Holdenhurst Road.

Whatever the problems between the parents, the cousins

were mostly kept in a state of ignorance about them. Dulcie and Bunt might have been at loggerheads but Raymond, being three years younger than Mike, loved having his older cousins to stay and was happy to be part of their cricket and football matches from dawn to dusk. Raymond remembers John as the gifted cricketer, Mike was always the footballer. When they played on the beach, Mike's fear of the water kept him well away from the sea. Mike has never learned to swim and is resigned to the fact that nature has shaped him to remain forever on land. 'I've had women trying to teach me to swim. There was one who held me in the water and said, "Right, you'll float now," and she took her arms away and I sank like a stone.'

Winters were made tolerable by football. Now that privatisation has made us all nostalgic for British Railways, we should remember that in the 1950s Cheltenham was only just over an hour by train from Birmingham, which brought four major league grounds into the orbit of Mike Summerbee and his brother.

Kenny Skeen, me, John and David Shakespeare, we were train spotters as well. You could be on a Jubilee Class going in. Outside Birmingham we needed the Licky Banker – that's one train pulling and another one pushing the carriages up a slope outside the city. It came out of a siding and pushed us up the hill before we dropped into Birmingham.

There were four big sides then – Wolves, Albion, the Blues and Villa, all in the First Division – so there were two games to pick from every week. I'm talking about the time of Johnny Dixon and Pat Saward and Jackie Sewell, when Dave Hickson played centre-forward for Villa. When you came out of the station there was a fella selling rosettes and one selling roast potatoes and roast chestnuts. There was a sports shop on the way, owned by a man called Harry Parkes. He used to be a wing-half for Villa and we used to go in there to have a look round – it wasn't like today, there were only a few boots and things, but we had our *Charles Buchan's Football Monthly* in our satchels. We would get to the ground early. They used to open them about half past eleven, twelve o'clock. You could walk in when it was empty and there'd be a mad rush to get close to the players' tunnel.

We all went to Birmingham, regular as clockwork, to watch football and collect autographs. I used to like Villa because they played in a fantastic stadium but I used to like Albion as well because Ronnie Allen was our John's hero. It was brilliant to watch them play. We'd get the train back and be home at half past six, seven o'clock. We were so independent.

Football was always going to be Mike Summerbee's reason for living. It certainly wasn't school. He continued intermittently at Naunton Park Secondary Modern where he contributed to the school exclusively on the sports field. His name started to appear regularly in the local paper as he gave outstanding displays for Cheltenham Schoolboys in their matches against local teams from the Forest of Dean, Stroud and mid-Somerset in the English Schools Shield. Within a year of George's death, Mike had come to the conclusion that school wasn't going to help him in his determination to become a professional footballer so effectively, and apparently with the headmaster's connivance, he resigned from academic life. 'Just keep coming back for the games,' said Mr Wilson, the head. Mike was happy to oblige. By this time, Lillian had returned to Preston and Dulcie was unaware of the fact that her younger son had taken this unilateral decision to lower the school-leaving age to 14.

My mother used to go to work and I'd do all the housework so when she came home the fire was going, the potatoes peeled, and the house was nice and tidy. She thought I was doing it after school.

After a while, Dulcie twigged and told him if he wasn't going to school he would have to get a job and she sent him off to Dowty's where Mike suffered the same kind of mental anguish as his father had experienced there. Eventually, Dulcie relented and wrote to Pat Beasley at Bristol City.

My mother got me a trial there though she never wanted me to be a footballer. She wanted me to be a draughtsman at Dowty's and build bridges. I was to be an apprentice there and become an engineer. I said, 'No, I just want to be a footballer.'

Shortly after Mike's 15th birthday in December 1957, Dulcie received a letter inviting him to join the groundstaff at Bristol City. With some misgivings, she gave her approval. She was right to be worried about what Mike would discover when he got there.

I went to Bristol City, had a trial there and it didn't work out. I saw a fella break his leg in an A team game in a pit town just outside Bristol. I was in digs in Ashton and there was a fella staying there who worked on a sewerage farm. He used to come in at night and he never washed his hands. It was so cold I used to sleep with my duffel coat on. I used to wake up in the morning with the imprint of its buttons on my chest. I was terribly lonely.

In the summer of 2000, John surprised his brother when recalling the Bristol nightmare.

I remember taking Mike to the station and putting him on the train. 'Get on that fucking train,' I said. 'Don't let our Mum down.' I went round the corner and cried my eyes out. He never knew that. We'd lost him then, you see.

Actually they hadn't – at least, not for very long. By the time of the Munich air crash in February 1958, Mike was back in Cheltenham. He remembers the crash mostly for having left his new bike outside in the rain overnight. Dulcie fined him a week's pocket money, banned him from watching television and warned him severely about his future conduct.

With a heavy heart and his mother's ominous words, 'Right, no more football for you!' ringing in his ears, Mike returned to Dowty's to work in the stress section as a messenger boy, delivering the drawings of the draughtsmen to Dowty headquarters on the Gloucester Road on his kingfisher blue bike. It was a five-mile ride from Pennsylvania Avenue just to clock on in the morning. He loathed the job but there was no apparent alternative. O-levels and A-levels wouldn't help him to make the grade as a professional footballer but neither would working at Dowty's. Coincidentally, Dulcie's ambition for Mike to become a draughtsman and build bridges was the same as Francis Lee's father nurtured for his son. It wasn't one that either lad shared, fortunately for Manchester City supporters of a certain age.

Mike's refuge, as ever, was his football. He started to play for Baker Street YMCA, one of the best sides in Cheltenham. He was still slight of build and, playing with lads older than himself, was inevitably nicknamed 'Titch' Summerbee. By now he was starting to outstrip John as a player. Mike and Dulcie both think his father's death killed any ambition John may have harboured to become a professional player.

John could have been a wonderful player. He was bigger than Michael but much more aggressive. He had the wrong temperament. He'd have killed anybody who tried

131

to stop him. John loved his father. It broke his heart when he died.

Relaxing after a day's work with a large glass of red wine in his hand, John, now aged 59, claims that it was Mike who inherited George's volatile temperament. He didn't have the desire to follow his father into the game, although he concedes that he might have had the strength and possibly the skill. John is quick to denigrate his own abilities. Certainly it is true that John, gifted at both cricket and football as he undoubtedly was as a young boy, lacked the drive to transmute that innate talent into the necessary professional skills. He just stopped caring at the age of 15 or 16, precisely when Mike was at his most determined. John left school as soon as he could and became an extremely talented joiner and builder so he could see another career opening up for him. Mike stared myopically at professional football and, Dulcie's ambitions for him notwithstanding, could see no alternative. John also, quite understandably, found girls more attractive than the prospect of endless lapping, sprinting and sit-ups.

These, of course, are common reasons why talented kids don't make the grade as sporting professionals but in John's case the hormonal excuse was undoubtedly augmented by the devastating emotional upheaval caused by his father's tragic death. John didn't want that life of failure and despair, and his mother would have considered it her maternal duty to emphasise the negative aspects of football, if only because they were the aspects with which she was most familiar. Mike didn't want that life either. He wanted a better one and he was going to do anything and everything to make sure he got the chance.

One Saturday morning when Mike was playing for Baker Street YMCA, a well-dressed man stepped out of a Mark 10 Jaguar and joined the small band of spectators watching the match. His name was Cecil Green. Later that week, the Jaguar returned to Cheltenham and while Mrs Green waited in the car outside, Mr Green, as Mike always called him, knocked on the door of 6 Pennsylvania Avenue and changed his life. John was working full-time as an apprentice carpenter at Ford and Western and Dulcie was, as usual, out at work. Mike was alone in the house when he opened the front door. The appearance of the Jaguar Mark 10 outside his house impressed Mike more than anything.

Cecil Green was a director of Swindon Town football club and he wanted Mike to come to Swindon for a trial in the B team. Mike didn't need much persuading and, when she met him, even Dulcie was mollified by the appearance of this distinguished man and his expensive car, although it was agreed that Mike would continue to work at Dowty's. Even Mr Green could not deny that football was an insecure line of work for any young lad. Mike had hoped that Mr Green's offer might lead to the termination of his contract with Dowty's but Dulcie was firm about that, and after his Bristol City experience Mike didn't have the grounds on which to appeal against the Dulcie disciplinary committee decision.

During the week I was working at Dowty's as a messenger boy and then I was supposed to go to night school to learn to be an engineer but my heart was crying out to play football. I was doing something I didn't want to do. It's a rarity to earn a living doing something that you do want to do but I was doing something I hated doing because I wanted to be a footballer. It wouldn't have happened if Mr Green hadn't given me the opportunity.

The day Mike signed amateur forms for Swindon Town, John signed, too; but John played one match and didn't bother turning up any more. 'I only ever wanted Mike to do well,' he says. 'I think to myself now, I wish I'd tried, but I didn't think that then.'

Mike continued to play for Baker Street YMCA even when he had a B-team game in Swindon in the afternoon. He adjusted quickly to the level of skill and fitness needed for the B-team games but a judgement on his professional future was by no means straightforward. Mike was still skinny and underweight and some people at Swindon thought that he was physically unprepared for professional football. On the other hand, Swindon had a thriving youth team and the club's financial viability rested on maintaining a constant flow of youngsters. As decision time approached, the jury was still out.

> The club had a secretary called Bert Davies who had played for England and he always wore his England badge. They had a meeting to decide what to do with me and Bert Head [the manager] thought I didn't look strong enough, though he hadn't seen me play, but Bert Davies said if he let me go he was going to miss out. There was a game coming up, the reserves against Devizes in the Wiltshire Cup. They put me in the team for that one and I had an outstanding match. So Bert Head put me on the groundstaff with Ernie [Hunt]. If it hadn't been for Bert Davies and Cecil Green, I'd have gone into oblivion.

Dulcie was ambivalent about the news, but being on the ground-staff meant Michael would be happy, at least temporarily. On the other hand who would build the future bridges of Great Britain? Without Michael Summerbee to design them they might start swaying in the wind when people walked on them and then they would have to be closed down. There was also the question of where the boy was going to live. The only other boy on the groundstaff was Ernie Hunt and he was a local lad so he could continue to live at home. Mike had just been through one miserable experience in Bristol and Dulcie was desperately anxious for it not to be repeated. Once again Cecil Green came to the rescue. He owned a number of properties in the Swindon

area, one of which was a confectionery shop with an upstairs
flat, and he was happy for Mike to move in. Mr Green was
building a large detached house, The Divot, in the most affluent
part of Swindon and by the time it was ready, Mike had been
allowed to move into digs at 2 Tennyson Road. His landlady,
whom he liked, was Mrs Boreman and he shared rooms with
two old pros.

I lived with Johnny Stevens and Willie Marshall – one
came from Bradford and one was a Welsh international.
Willie was coming to the end of his career and Johnny
Stevens went to Newport. We had a bedroom and the
front room downstairs – it was very sparse. It cost me one
pound ten bob a week. Bed, breakfast, evening meal and
washing. You had to be in at a certain time for your
evening meal – Mrs Boreman was like a Blackpool
landlady but she was very nice. She died recently – she
was a hundred and two. In the morning I had a piece of
toast, I put on my duffel coat and caught the bus to the
ground. We never went out in the evenings. There wasn't
a lot to do so we used to play dominoes.

It all seems very basic – acceptable certainly for a young boy
who just wants to play football but depressing for those at
the end of their careers. It conjures up visions of a divorced
and broke actor, living in digs in a provincial town with a
decaying repertory theatre, surviving merely to be able to
play the Duke of Exeter in a tatty production of *Henry V*. In
fact, the accommodation had its drawbacks: 'We had a
gas fire in there and everyone started feeling tired. It was
about two weeks before they discovered there was a gas
leak. Fortunately nobody smoked otherwise we'd all have
died.'

Outside of the dominoes, the main attractions were the
swimming baths down the road, dating back to Victorian

times, and the dancehall, which attracted the local youth on Saturday nights. The Civic Playhouse was in full swing, its repertory season stretching from Rattigan's *Flare Path* to Shaw's *Candida* with tickets at all prices from one and sixpence to five shillings, but since Graeme Le Saux had not yet been born few footballers patronised it.

In 1958 Swindon was a company town and the company was British Railways.

There was no night life, no nightclubs. The dancehall was open on Saturday nights only, so there wasn't a lot to do. You only had to go a hundred yards and you were out of Swindon. There were fifty thousand people at the railway works and that's all there was. The hooter went at seven thirty in the morning and they all went in to work, and the hooter went at five and they all came out. We got good football crowds because there was nothing else to do. There were the working men's clubs and when they opened the bowling alley, you couldn't get in. We got free tickets for the pictures in the afternoons and sometimes we'd have a steak at one of those little grill places, but we weren't earning a lot of money anyway.

In other words, it was pretty much the life that George had led in Preston in 1935.

Mike, though, could get back to Cheltenham more easily than George could return to Winchester. After the game on Saturday, he usually caught the bus home to Cheltenham to see his mother. The journey took about an hour and a half, stopping everywhere *en route*. Mike got off the bus at the terminus in the centre of Cheltenham by which time the local buses had stopped so he walked the two miles home to Pennsylvania Avenue.

Mike's progress through the B and A teams was rapid.

136

They gave me the opportunity and within three months I was in the reserves playing at Fulham, Chelsea and Arsenal. On a Wednesday afternoon you'd run out at Highbury and there'd be maybe fifty people watching the Football Combination, but you'd be playing on the grounds you'd read and dreamed about. In your head there'd be fifty thousand there. If you shot and it went just past the post, you'd see the crowd swaying in your mind. I played against Johnny Haynes at Fulham when he was coming back from injury, Peter Brabrook and Jimmy Greaves and Bobby Keetch who used to kick lumps out of me.

In December 1959, Mike Summerbee made his Football League debut for Swindon Town in a 2–0 victory over Uncle Bunt's Bournemouth. The impact of his professional advancement on his social life was both immediate and spectacular.

There were always girls going to school on the top deck of the bus. I was like Adrian Mole in that first year, getting on that bus with my duffel coat. I did my best but I didn't have much decent gear. There was one girl called Cathy Phillips. She was going to the grammar school and she had eye make-up on at that age and was smoking a fag. She was very good-looking, a real rebel. She would never give me the time of day but when I got into the first team she suddenly started taking notice of me.

These days if a kid plays in the first team at 17 years old it's headline news. In 1959, Mike was just another precocious teenager, certainly nothing special. He also knew enough about the business of football to know when to keep his mouth shut. It might have been hard work on the groundstaff but it was paradise compared with the misery that was waiting for him if he failed and was forced to return to Dowty's. He was always one of the first into the ground, arriving between 8.30 and 9 in the morning to sweep out the dressing rooms and prepare the boots for the first team. Senior players like the centre-forward Maurice Owen, the goalkeeper Sam Burton and Pete Chamberlain would make Mike and Ernie the butt of their jokes but that was part of the learning process, a compulsory initiation rite. The reward came on the pitch when these players looked after the lads. Mike's room-mate Willie Marshall was a big help in these early years, retaliating instantly against any opponent who might bully his young colleague.

Mike needed looking after. Yellow cards weren't sprinkled like confetti. It was a man's game and when you were 17 years old and weighed eight stone soaking wet there was always the danger that the physical demands of the game would prove too much.

> They could be animals in those days. I remember going for a through ball against Derby once and someone caught me with everything. I thought I was going to die. I wanted the ground to open up. I couldn't suck air in anywhere. But you learned – you had to. These fellas were not like Sunday league players who just kick you; they could do serious damage. They could put you out of the game for ever.

There had always been an anxiety at Swindon that Mike wouldn't make the grade because he was too slight. This sentence will be read with a wry smile and a hollow laugh by Frank Clark and Terry Cooper and many another left-back who used to lie awake the night before he was due to mark Mike Summerbee. Mike turned into a very hard, aggressive player who could, in footballer-speak, 'look after himself'. It was Bert Head who taught him a lesson he never forgot after a match against Notts County. Mike was playing centre-forward and had pulled out of two tackles against a centre-half who was trying to boot him up in the air any time the ball came within five yards of him. After the match, Bert Head tore into Mike in the dressing room, deliberately humiliating him in front of his fellow professionals. 'Just shut your eyes and go in,' he stormed. Mike had never been subject to such a barrage of insults. It was a lesson he never forgot. I never saw him shirk a tackle in ten years at City and I'd be surprised if I get many letters from fans of his other clubs complaining of Mike's timidity. He quickly discovered how to compensate for his build.

I learned how to use the top half of my body. I was the strong and wiry type and I realised that the edges on my body were dangerous. People who are thin can be more dangerous to tackle because we're bony and I used that. Denis Law and George [Best] did that. You can ride things. It was survival.

I still had some bad injuries. I was out for a long time when I smashed my thigh when I was seventeen or eighteen. It was against West Ham. [Goalkeeper] Lawrie Leslie came out to the near post and he caught me with his knee in my thigh. I was in agony. It just blew up and there was no medical treatment then. Harry Cousins, the trainer, knew little compared to today's lot. He was just an old pro. The only way I could get the swelling down was to put a towel round my leg, sit in the bath and pour a kettle of boiling water on it to let the heat soak through.

Eventually the swelling subsided but it was a week before he could bend his leg again. The moment he could do so, of course, Bert Head put him straight back into the first team for an important match against Barnsley.

I thought I was OK but I took a corner near the end and

I completely tore the muscle from the knee cap right the way to the top of my thigh and I'm telling you now I have never known so much pain in my life. I was out for ages after that. There's still a lump on my thigh. There was talk of an operation but I just built the leg up again.

Mike harboured no resentment about this unsentimental managerial treatment. Indeed, it seems he positively welcomed it.

I felt I was missing out because I was young and I just wanted to play. In those days, unless your leg was broken, you could have been pulling the wool over their eyes. Who knew? I frequently played with stitches in the backs of my legs.

So how does he feel about players today with their BUPA treatments and their leisurely roads back to match fitness? Precisely as you would imagine he feels: 'What you've got in the game today is a load of hypochondriacs.'

One thing is for sure – he wasn't playing for the money. The game that Mike entered in 1958 was not so different from the one his father entered 24 years previously. The big differences with Mike were that he knew the downside of the game in advance, and he was 17 when he made his Football League debut, not 23 and a long-time reserve-team player as George had been.

Until he reached that 17th birthday in December 1959, Mike couldn't sign professional forms and his wages were, effectively, for his work on the groundstaff, cleaning the boots and sweeping the terraces. Then he got £7 a week in the first team and £4 a week in the summer. According to the Prime Minister we'd never had it so good but this sort of wage was never going to feed and clothe Mike Summerbee, professional footballer and bon vivant, wannabe man about town and Don

Juan. For some players, any spare time was spent on their second jobs – old pros Arnold Darcy and Pete Chamberlain were painters and decorators. After training and during the summer they donned the white overalls, strapped the ladders on to the roof of the little van and off they went – just like Beckham and Keane still do. Keith Morgan worked on building sites; Jack Smith and Cliff Jackson worked in the Wills cigarette factory, within sight of the County Ground. A summer job was imperative for both Mike and his new best friend, Ernie Hunt.

When I was on the groundstaff, I had to stay at the ground working through the summer, painting the stands, cutting the grass and so on, but when I became a pro, I took a fortnight's holiday [then did a summer job]. We used to line up a job before the end of the season.

Down the years, Mike and Ernie's jobs got more exotic. One summer it was cutting the grass verges for the council, the next year it was digging graves. 'We got paid extra for an eighteen footer,' Mike recalls somewhat ghoulishly. Another summer it was taking the money and giving out tickets for the deckchairs on the beach in Torquay. Mike enjoyed this job so much that he was willingly doing it in the summer of 1966, after he had won promotion to the First Division with Manchester City and was already featuring in Alf Ramsey's thoughts. Working the deckchairs wearing a pair of tight swimming trunks and a bus conductor's cap might have made him look like a premature refugee from the Village People, but it was a surefire way to meet girls – and unspecified others.

Ernie Hunt was replacing John as Mike's other half. When they were growing up together in Cheltenham, the two brothers were inseparable. If people saw Mike without John or John without Mike they would comment on it. Now, in Ernie Hunt, Mike had discovered a player whose skill he respected on the field and a mate whose sense of mischief was complementary to his own. I'm not entirely sure what they got up to in those graveyards but I have a strong feeling that the relatives of the dear departeds who were buried on the Hunt/Summerbee watch might be surprised by the results of an exhumation. One summer they worked as painters on an army base. 'Were you any good?' I asked, wondering if their artistry on the field might have produced a corresponding skill with the paintbrush. 'We were crap,' came the honest reply.

Coming out of the ground together after training one day, the lads were accosted by a man in a large black Humber car. He rolled down the window and asked them the way back to the A4. He had unaccountably missed the main road to London and driven instead into the car park of the County Ground, Swindon. It transpired that the lost driver was Sir Anthony Eden, who lived between Bath and Bristol and who, until recently, had been the Prime Minister. Perhaps it was no wonder that he lost Suez and his job if he was relying on Hunt and Summerbee to get him out of a jam.

Ernie's mother took a shine to Mike (as most women did) and at her invitation he left the digs at Mrs Boreman's and moved gratefully into the Hunt household at 40 Redcliffe Street. Ernie and Mike thought it was a hoot to travel to the ground on a tandem (as I believe the Neville brothers are also wont to do). Ernie usually took the front saddle because it made him look less like the rear end of a pantomime horse, but he was extremely fussy about his hair and on windy days he insisted that Mike peddle up front in order to provide him with a human windshield.

It was as well that Mike was settling into life in Swindon because affairs in Cheltenham had reached crisis point. Dulcie had met another man. In fact, she had met him while George was still alive because he was a neighbour. His name was Cecil Smith and he lived a few minutes' walk away from the Summerbee house in Pennsylvania Avenue. He was originally from the Channel Islands and had been in the merchant marine during the war. He had also been divorced which was enough to give him a slightly exotic, raffish air in the stultifying England of the 1950s. It certainly increased his attraction for Dulcie. Within a month of George's funeral, this new man was knocking on the front door of 6 Pennsylvania Avenue. It was just an innocent invitation to go to the pictures but to John it was tantamount to dancing on his father's grave.

> Frailty thy name is woman.
> A little month or ere those shoes were old
> With which she followed my poor father's body,
> Like Niobe, all tears . . .
> O, most wicked speed, to post
> With such dexterity to incestuous sheets . . .

I'm afraid this part of the story is inevitably going to turn into *Hamlet*. John plays the Prince of Denmark, Mike plays the part of Horatio.

Mike tried to rationalise that his mother had had an extremely difficult life and deserved some happiness. If it was Cecil who gave it to her, who was he to deny her? It was difficult for John to maintain that detachment.

> It was only months after my dad was dead that she was going out with Cecil. It was as quick as that. When they went off together, I used to wait in Mum's bedroom, looking through the window, waiting for them to come back. I was worried because if something had happened to her we'd really have been in the shit.

What worried both the boys was that Cecil appeared to have no visible means of support. They always appreciated how hard their mother worked and never more so than after their father died. Whether it was behind the perfume counter in the

Cavendish House department store or in the chemist's shop on the High Street, Dulcie always gave of her best. After George died, she changed jobs again, this time to work at a factory called Goddard's where she started on the production line and finished as an inspector. The boys had loved their father but they were well aware that it was their mother who kept the household together. This unwelcome intruder into their lives threatened their precarious existence. They didn't like him and they didn't know what their mother saw in him.

After Mike left Cheltenham to live in Swindon, Cecil moved into the Pennsylvania Avenue house. Once he was in, it was going to be difficult to get him out. John was incensed. One night he and his prospective stepfather came to blows in the living room. It wasn't a skirmish, it was a major land war and it meant the end of the prospect of any kind of relationship. John went to live with his friend Kenny Skeen and hoped never to speak to Cecil again.

The boys loved Dulcie as deeply as ever but they both had careers to occupy them during the day and a place to sleep at night. They didn't need their mother in the way they had needed her in the past. Dulcie knew that. She had guided her boys through the storms at sea and into their respective ports safely. Shortly after Mike Summerbee had established himself in the Swindon Town first team, Dulcie Summerbee née Ryan married Cecil Smith at the Registry Office in Cheltenham. Neither of her sons attended the ceremony. Within weeks, the newly married couple had sold the Summerbee home in Pennsylvania Avenue and moved to the small Devon village of Slapton. The precarious family existence Dulcie had struggled to maintain since the day she had married George Summerbee was finally over.

CHAPTER NINE

Swindon to Manchester

Just as decisively as the game's fortunes had turned their back on George, they smiled on his younger son. Mike joined Swindon Town in the season after they had finished second from bottom two years in a row during Bert Head's first two seasons in charge. Although results improved only gradually, the whole emphasis of the team was turned on to the youngsters. In one public pre-season trial match, the Probables, made up of the older professionals, were trounced by the Possibles 7–2. Bert Head decided to replay the match, this time behind closed doors, having warned the Probables that they were now playing for their places. The Possibles won again.

Mike and Ernie had joined Swindon Town just in time to be part of the flowering of Bert Head's youth policy. John Trollope and Terry Wollen formed the youngest ever Football League pairing of full-backs, and along with schoolboy international inside-left Cliff Jackson and wing-halves Keith Morgan and Bobby Woodruff, later to be joined by the left-winger Don Rogers, they formed the nucleus of one of Swindon Town's best sides. Playing so many youngsters kept the older professionals on their toes and it stimulated the crowd who liked to see good local youngsters coming through.

It also made sound financial sense. As evidenced by George's move to Chester and then to Barrow, it was always difficult for an impoverished club to sign a player at the end of his career.

An older player needed a house for his family or else he might waste time and effort in commuting; and his wages would have to reflect his seniority whereas teenagers tended to be grateful to be picked to play. Kids like Summerbee made few demands on the wage bill.

The boys needed time to mature, however, and Head still needed the right kind of older player to guide them. It is something of a surprise, therefore, to discover that at the start of the 1959–60 season, Swindon paid a record transfer fee of £6,000 to Plymouth Argyle to acquire the services of the inside-left Jimmy Gauld. His influence on the youngsters couldn't possibly have been the one that Bert Head was anticipating. At the end of the season, Swindon lost 6–1 at Port Vale in a display that aroused considerable speculation. At a board meeting held immediately afterwards, Gauld was placed on the transfer list. That was the least of his worries. In 1963 it was revealed that he had been the ringleader in a match-fixing scandal that horrified the football world. Gauld went to prison for four years. Mike remembers being puzzled by the 6–1 defeat.

Bert was due a bonus if we finished in a certain position. We had a right-back called John Higgins and he was marking Harry Oscroft who was Port Vale's outside-left. We were four down at half-time and Oscroft had scored all four. After the game, John Higgins said to Bert Head, 'There's something wrong here.'

Money has always been at the heart of any corruption in the game, from its earliest days. The public school gentlemen who administered the game and codified its laws remained aloof from, or deliberately ignorant of, the resentment that financial exploitation caused among the players. In the days of the maximum wage it is more easily understood than in recent times when overpaid managers are still unable to resist the lure

146

of illicit payments whether by bank transfer to an offshore account or in brown paper bags handed over in hotel lounges just off the motorway.

Swindon Town's Bronco Layne clearly regarded a bit of match-fixing as unremarkable because he took the practice with him to his next club. Layne was a free-scoring centre-forward for each of his clubs, averaging a goal every two games. In that 1959–60 season he was Swindon's top scorer with 20 goals. The following year he scored four times in a famous FA Cup victory. When he was transferred to Sheffield Wednesday, he maintained his scoring record and he was being talked about as a potential international when it was revealed that he, along with his Wednesday colleagues Tony Kaye and Peter Swann, had been involved in attempts to fix a home match against Ipswich Town. Layne went to prison for six months and like the other two was banned from playing football for life. To add to his misery, Layne lost his wife in a car crash.

Layne and Gauld, however, were responsible for Mike's league debut. In the 1959 Boxing Day fixture away to Bournemouth, Gauld injured his ankle. For the return match, neither he nor Layne, who was suspended for being sent off, could be considered. Bert Head breathed deep and gave debuts to young Mick Woolford at inside-left and the even younger Mike Summerbee at centre-forward. The irony that he should be making his debut against Bournemouth, where his father had given up the ghost and for whom Bunt was now a coach, was not lost on Mike.

Ernie Hunt had beaten him into the first team by a few weeks. Bobby Woodruff was already there at left-half and David Corbett at outside-right. Playing up front alongside Mike at Bournemouth was Willie Marshall, the flat-mate who looked after him on the field. He stepped on to the County Ground to make his debut in the Football League in the same division and at a younger age than his father had managed.

It was a typical December day, the wind swirling and the ground already well churned up, but Summerbee won praise for his 'industry and determination', words that were to be used about him constantly in the years to come. By contrast, Woolford showed 'neat use of the ball and alertness'. The game was won 2–0 with goals by Marshall and Darcy in the last 20 minutes.

Head was sufficiently pleased to keep the two young lads in the team for the next match, at home to Bradford City, and despite a 0–1 defeat, the boys received generous praise in the press. Swindon had previously been criticised for lack of fight. The introduction of Summerbee and his youthful colleagues appears to have put a stop to that grumble. The club kept out of trouble by finishing both the 1959–60 and the 1960–61 seasons in 16th place, but the success of his youth policy brought the same problems for Bert Head that George had experienced with Cheltenham Town when the scouts came crawling after Rushworth and Shiner. Suddenly the name Summerbee appeared in the newspapers outside Swindon and Cheltenham. Everyone had time for a bright, lively 17-year-old who might be a big star one day, particularly Bill Nicholson, manager of Tottenham Hotspur.

Nicholson was in the process of putting together his wonderful double-winning team. He had bought Cliff Jones but felt he needed another winger because Terry Medwin was coming to the end of his career, and Terry Dyson had yet to make a significant impact at White Hart Lane. Nicholson had been interested in Mike almost since his first-team debut and, having been rebuffed by Southampton when he tried to prise away Terry Paine and by Luton when he went looking for the Irish winger Billy Bingham who chose Everton in preference, Nicholson returned time and again to look at Summerbee. Soon there was a disorderly queue of managers and scouts looking at Mike.

I was reading constantly for two or three years that clubs were interested in me – big clubs including Tottenham and Newcastle, and there was Matt Gillies at Leicester. I played in a testimonial game at Reading with most of the Tottenham double side and I thought I was in with a shout. I'd have loved to have gone to Spurs. I thought I was as good a winger as anybody at that time, in the style I played – an aggressive player who could cross a ball, not the smooth, jinking type.

Nicholson got no joy from Bert Head. 'I refused two offers last season,' Bert informed him. 'I rate him at least in the Terry Paine class.'

Of course, Bert never spoke to the player about these conversations. As far as Mike was concerned, it was just paper talk. It would have taken a very mature man not to have been affected in some measure by the thought of being transferred to a top First Division club in London for a large fee, but it wouldn't have been surprising if, at the back of Mike's mind, lurked the ghost of his father and the fear of anonymity and failure at a big club. Going to Spurs sounded overwhelmingly glamorous but what if he didn't make it? What if Nicholson or the fates conspired against him and he was condemned to play out the rest of his career in the reserves? Typically, Mike refused to think that way. 'I wouldn't have gone there to be in the reserves. I would have gone to be in the first team. I don't care how much they'd won at Spurs. I might have started in the reserves but then I'd have forced my way in.' He'd made the Swindon reserves and been promoted within a year. He was a first-team player, learning his trade in the first team, surrounded by a bunch of mates he liked and a manager who rated him highly. Unless and until he was called into Head's office and shown a contract for his signature, he would try to ignore the paper talk and just concentrate on playing football for Swindon Town.

Although he was hardly a visionary manager, Bert Head certainly inspired loyalty and affection from the youngsters whose promotion into the first team he had overseen so carefully. He believed in them and was an engaging eccentric.

> The training was old-fashioned because Bert Head was an old-fashioned manager. We'd do a lot of lapping. Pre-season we'd go under canvas to an army camp at Weymouth, in a big tent. We were the advance patrol. He used to say to us, 'Woodruff, Hunt, Summerbee – advance patrol. Get down there and get the cooking tent up.' It was great fun; the *craic* was brilliant. Bert Head thought he was in the SAS – in reality, he was in the Home Guard.

When Summerbee damaged his instep before a big game, Head devised a fibre-glass protection to insert inside his boot. If Mike had kicked anyone that day he'd have broken his leg. When Ernie Hunt strained his groin before an important match, Bert Head asked Harry Cousins, the trainer, to 'strap it up'. Harry Cousins was a former player whose acquaintance with the latest medical practices was restricted to a bucket of cold water and a sponge, rather like Laurie Barnett, the Manchester City trainer who tried to fix Bert Trautmann's broken neck during the 1956 Cup final with the same ingredients. Nevertheless, Harry and Bert devised an original strapping for Ernie which involved the inside-forward being encased in plaster round his middle. It would have been like running around inside a bag of cement. Ernie stood up and couldn't move. He didn't play that day.

During their pre-season runs to regain fitness, Bert would drive his Zephyr 6 alongside the perspiring players and when they got to the finishing line he would hand out ice lollies from the boot of his car.

Perhaps his greatest escapade concerned the 'secret training' Swindon Town underwent in the week before a fifth-round

Cup-tie at home to the eventual winners of the competition, West Ham United. This was 1964, just as *From Russia With Love* was released and the country was swept by James Bond mania.

> He wouldn't tell us where we were going in case the news leaked out. We couldn't tell anyone or answer the phone if anyone rang and wanted to know. We had to get into our cars and follow him. He went through Cheddar Gorge, taking detours in case anyone was following us. We ended up in Weston Super Mare. In those days there was a sports programme on [the local TV station] TWW, so that night we gathered in the hotel to watch it. When it started it played the James Bond theme and a caption said 'Somewhere in England . . .' Then there was an interview with Bert Head and he was standing by the pier at Weston Super Mare.

The game and the lifestyle Mike was enjoying were still not so dissimilar to the ones George had known. The fact that Swindon were in the Third or Second Division and played in what was little more than a country town with a huge contingent of British Railways workers helped to keep Mike's feet firmly on the ground, despite his rapid rise to first-team status and local celebrity.

> We came back from Hull once because the game was abandoned after twenty minutes because of snow. The buses in those days were the old Corporation single deckers. We had a tea urn in the front with pea soup in it. We got as far as Silverstone. We were cutting across country to get to Swindon when we got caught in the blizzard and the road was blocked. Bert Head said to us, 'I'm not having this, get your gear on.' We put our football socks and boots on and overcoats and we got shovels and we cleared the road.

With Dulcie now living in Devon and John working in Yeovil, Mike was getting fed up with taking the bus everywhere. He wanted to learn to drive but decided not to use the traditional method of taking lessons. Instead, Mrs Green bought an old banger and allowed Mike to drive her around in it. 'I got to the stage where I thought I was good enough so I took my test. At the end of it the examiner said, "I'm passing you but I don't want you to go out on your own for six months." '

After this muted success, Mike saw a second-hand Hillman Minx side valve with the gears on the steering wheel and one long seat in the front. It cost £75. Mr Green lent him the deposit and he agreed to pay the rest on hire purchase.

At the end of the 1961–62 season, I decided to drive down to Devon to see my mother. I was going to pick up John in Yeovil and we were to go from there together. It was a chugger that Hillman Minx. You couldn't put your foot down. If you did it made no difference. You'd get overtaken by a man on a bike going up hills. Still, for seventy-five pounds it looked nice but as I drove into Yeovil there was an enormous bang and the big ends went. I looked underneath and there was oil leaking out of it everywhere. I managed to get someone from a garage to come out and look at it and he said I needed a new engine. I said, 'How much?' and he said, 'About a hundred and ten pounds.' That was about ten grand in those days. I phoned up Mr Green and he said, 'Tell them to fit a new engine and I'll pay the bill.' With labour it came to about a hundred and seventy-five. Plus there was the HP company to sort out. That made it about three hundred. Mr Green said, 'I'll do that. Don't worry about it.'

The holiday was a great success as far as the two brothers were concerned, passed as it was in a haze of alcohol and female company. The problem, of course, was that John still hadn't spoken to his stepfather Cecil. One night they went round to see Dulcie knowing that they would be bound to see Cecil as well. Whether it was because he was nervous or merely because he'd been drinking, John arrived at the house the worse for wear. In fact, he was suffering so much he eventually threw up the day's alcohol intake all over the lounge. Needless to say, the 'reconciliation' with Cecil never really got under way. Mike returned to Swindon in the Hillman without further mishap and rescheduled his debts with Mr Green.

> We arranged that I would pay him what I could every week. He had a little red Post Office notebook and I just took a pound or two pounds a week or whatever I could afford to Mr Green and he entered it in that little red book until I'd paid off every penny. Obviously as I got into the first team and the wages went up, I paid more each week. There was never any pressure from him. There was no interest or anything like that. He was just like a father to me.

At the start of the 1962–63 season, Mike was 19 years old and a regular member of the Swindon Town first team. The young lads had all come through by now, which was reflected in the club's rise to the dizzy heights of ninth in the Third Division at the end of the 1961–62 season. Swindon had been a founder member of the Third Division in 1920 and had never played at a higher level. Everyone knew that they wouldn't be able to hang on to their talented kids forever. If they were going to be promoted to Division Two, it had to be soon.

This was a time of change in the country; 1962–63 was the year of the big freeze with almost no matches played at all in January and February. In the middle of March, gales and driving rain turned the banked snow into thick grey slush. The

153

country seemed psychologically and physically paralysed and the government appeared powerless to do anything about it. The Conservative government of Harold Macmillan was in its dying days, stumbling from crisis to crisis. At the beginning of the season, a clerk in the Admiralty named William Vassall was sentenced to 18 years in prison for spying for Russia. The newspapers implied (wrongly as it turned out) that since Vassall was a known homosexual, the relationship between him and the Minister concerned, Thomas Galbraith, was compromised. Macmillan accepted his resignation. During the season, John Profumo lied to the House of Commons and at the end of the season he was given a free transfer out of politics because of his involvement with Christine Keeler. I always thought that the House was more irritated with Profumo because he was having sex with 'an undeniably attractive young woman', as Bernard Levin called her, in addition to being married to a former film star (Valerie Hobson) than with the fact that he had lied to them about it. Even in the early 60s the House of Commons was not exactly a hotbed of marital fidelity. Lord Hailsham nearly exploded in fury as he shouted, 'If you can tell me there are no adulterers on the front bench of the Labour party you must be stark staring bonkers.' He was probably right.

Britain seemed to be in the grip of a collective desire to reject the deferential society in which we had all lived for so long and to embrace something new, anything new – new was all that mattered. We wanted the 'white heat of the technological revolution' although few of us ever had much of an idea what that meant. Everyone still complained about the Post Office, and the public telephones, which were still under their control, were attached to huge black boxes requiring the user to insert four coppers and press button A, though not for much longer.

The world in which Mike had grown up was changing fast. Trams, steam trains and outside lavatories were vanishing. City centres unchanged since Victorian times were being rebuilt. Dr

Beeching was destroying the rail network that had been built up over a hundred years in the name of progress. Advertising and commercial television were creating a materialist consumer society that was in marked contrast to the self-denying era of our parents. The world of Anthony Eden who couldn't find the A4 without asking Swindon Town's right-wing pairing, and of the Old Etonian Harold Macmillan who admitted that he did not 'move greatly in the company of young people' was being replaced by the world of Harold Wilson who supported Huddersfield Town and who liked HP sauce and Gannex raincoats like the one worn by Kenneth Wolstenholme when introducing the new BBC 2 football programme *Match of the Day*. There were to be no more patrician Prime Ministers. When the Conservatives regained power in 1970, they did so with the grammar-school educated Ted Heath in charge.

What John Osborne started in 1956 with *Look Back in Anger*, Peter Cook, Dudley Moore, Jonathan Miller and Alan Bennett carried on in 1961 with *Beyond the Fringe* which mocked the Church, the monarchy, the Prime Minister and the reverence for what had been endured during the war. Television reacted to changing attitudes with Robin Day's searching interviews; and, in 1962, instead of closing down at 10.30 on a Saturday night, the BBC experimented with a live topical show called *That Was The Week That Was*. It had an impact greater than the quality of its somewhat rough and ready production, making a virtue out of the necessity of its live transmission. When the 1964 General Election was called, the BBC lost its nerve and cancelled *TW3*.

Television had outstripped radio and the movies as the greatest medium of popular entertainment ever devised and its power was steadily rising. By 1962, it was in 80 per cent of all British homes and it was to become a key component of the shift in status for professional football and its players. When George was at Barrow, over 40 million people passed through the turnstiles each season. By 1955 when he died, that figure had fallen to 33.3 million and when Mike was playing for Swindon Town it was down below 30 million and still falling.

The football authorities could not ignore these warning signs. In the post-war boom they could continue to reject footballers' demands on the grounds that the crowds would come to see them whatever happened and the political situation was not exactly conducive to granting a redress of grievances from the workers. But by the early 1960s, footballers were sufficiently motivated to call for a strike in pursuit of their claims for economic and social justice. When Jimmy Hill became chairman of the Professional Footballers Association he was fighting the same battles that Jimmy Guthrie had fought but the atmosphere in the country was significantly, if subtly, different. Guthrie used a broadsword; Hill favoured the rapier. Guthrie was an old-fashioned left-wing Scottish working-class firebrand; Hill was a smartly dressed, articulate, classless negotiator.

In 1958, the maximum wage had risen to £20 a week but the iniquitous retain and transfer system still kept the players firmly in their place. In the middle of the 1960–61 season, the PFA called a strike in support of their demands for the abolition of the maximum wage. Three days before the strike was due to take place, the FA capitulated. The maximum wage was abolished. For Johnny Haynes at Fulham this meant a weekly wage of £100. For players at Liverpool and Manchester United it meant an unofficial maximum of £35 a week. It seems that Busby and Shankly, having suffered themselves, were not keen to see the modern generation of players become rich; they decided that none of their stars would be tempted to drive down the East Lancs Road if they could earn no more at their rival's ground than they could at their own.

For Mike Summerbee, the abolition of the maximum wage was almost an irrelevance. Swindon Town had no money anyway.

When we got in the first team it was seven pounds basic and three quid appearance money – a tenner a week plus win or draw bonus. After the maximum wage was abolished, Ernie and I went to Bert Head to see if he would increase the basic wage to ten quid a week at the end of a season in which Ernie had scored sixteen goals and I got ten. Bert said, 'I can't go to the board and ask them for an extra three quid for two teenagers. We just can't afford it.' So he took us into town and bought us a couple of suits that didn't fit us from the fifty shilling tailors. He thought that'd keep us quiet.

It didn't keep Jimmy Hill quiet, though. In the person of George Eastham, who wanted to move from Newcastle to Arsenal, Hill found the perfect person to help destroy the retain and transfer system. Arsenal wanted him but Newcastle refused to sell. Legally, Newcastle could pay Eastham the minimum wage of £8 a week and retain his registration for as long as they wanted. In support of the justice of his claim, Eastham went a year without kicking a ball in anger. Eventually, Newcastle caved in and the transfer to Arsenal was completed but the court case still went ahead. In July 1963, on American Independence Day, the appropriately named Judge Wilberforce found in favour of Eastham in the High Court and the retain and transfer system was finally outlawed. As the player's counsel had pointed out, the system was like the bartering of cattle, a relic of the Middle Ages. Mike Summerbee (and obviously even more so his son, Nicholas) was to benefit from this judgement, liberating him and all players from the *ancien regime* under which his father had laboured.

At this stage, though, what made a difference to Mike Summerbee's life was not the politics of football or the country, but the quality of the team in which he was playing. Bert Head had done an excellent job of scaring away the First Division wasps from the honeypot and the newspapers in

1963 were full of his young team's achievements rather than rumours of their transfers. He had equipped his team to play successfully in the few matches the weather allowed by giving them basketball boots with thick rubber soles (at a cost of 12s 11d a pair) and yellow gloves to wear. Swindon's rise up the table was inexorable.

Over 25,000 people jammed into the County Ground to see the boys lose in the fourth round of the FA Cup to the Division One leaders Everton but the Robins' progress continued apace until Easter when the wheels appeared to come off. Going into the holiday, Swindon were tucked neatly into the slipstream of promotion rivals Peterborough United whom they were due to meet twice. Unfortunately, despite Ernie Hunt giving them a first-minute lead, Swindon contrived to lose the home match 2–3 and then compounded the error with a 3–1 defeat in the return at London Road. Despite trouncing Colchester 6–1, Swindon went down again on their travels, this time to Notts County, and their supporters were resigning themselves to the traditional mantra, 'maybe next year . . .'

They were given a boost by a run of victories in parallel with a stumble by Peterborough. Seven points out of a possible eight meant that if they won their last match of the season at home to Shrewsbury Town, Swindon would achieve promotion for the first time in their history. Eighty-nine nerve-jangling minutes passed scoreless before Swindon's Roger Smart joyfully crashed home the winner. As Groucho Marx commented, joy was unconfined and so were a lot of other girls that night. Mike Summerbee bought himself an MG sports car and Bert Head was awarded a five-year contract. It lasted for two.

Speaking at the Supporters Club annual dinner, the most successful manager in Swindon Town's history told his audience that he thought the club would reach the First Division 'in a couple of seasons'. He knew they would be expected to go on to greater things, 'even as far as the European Cup', but he warned his audience who sat there soaking all this up that 'we need to take it gently and gradually'.

Swindon began their first season in Division Two with these words ringing in their ears. Far from pricking the bubble of Head's hyperbole, the team's performance seemed to enhance it. They sat proudly on top of the table after winning their first four matches when the fallen giant Manchester City came to play at the County Ground. Although City had dropped calamitously through the floor of the First Division the previous May, causing 13-year-old boys all over Prestwich acute metal anguish (see previous volume), as far as Swindon Town were concerned, a team that included Barrie Betts, Vic Gommersall and Roy Cheetham was the big time.

The Swindon press made much of the fact that these giants in sky-blue shirts had spent the extraordinary sum of £200,000 in an attempt to win back their First Division status at the first time of asking. It is not possible to ascertain how this sum was arrived at. The City team included, in addition to Betts, Gommersall and Cheetham, Neil Young, David Wagstaffe, Alan Oakes, Paul Aimson, Harry Dowd and Graham Chadwick who were all signed as schoolboys. George Hannah came from Lincoln City and Derek Kevan cost £30,000 from Chelsea after Alex Harley went to Birmingham City and Peter Dobing to Stoke for a combined fee of £85,000. I conclude therefore that the Swindon papers were deliberately conveying misinformation in order to stoke the fires that would consume my helpless heroes. They succeeded perfectly. A record 28,291 people watched the Robins crush City 3–0 on that mild September night. Bert Head's musings on playing in the European Cup seemed relatively cautious.

Swindon's season, not surprisingly, fell away somewhat after this tremendous start. City adjusted to life in the Second Division with Derek Kevan and the newly arrived Jimmy Murray from Wolves forming an instantly successful striking partnership. They won their last three matches of 1963 by huge margins, scoring 18 goals. Then they went back to Swindon in the third round of the FA Cup just as I was busily examining my voucher sheet to see how many tokens I needed from that season's programmes to get my ticket for Wembley. I was spared the traditional aggravation induced by any dealings one might have with the City ticket office by the team's spineless capitulation. Swindon won 2–1. At 14 years of age, trying to understand Boyle's Law was easier than trying to understand Manchester City. At 50 years of age, I still find both concepts impenetrable.

Swindon beat Aldershot in round four before succumbing to a combination of Bobby Moore's West Ham, Bert Head's 'secret' training and Ernie Hunt's absence through tonsilitis in round five in front of yet another record crowd of over 28,000. More worrying was the transfer of Bobby Woodruff. It wasn't so much that the club had to sell him, indeed its finances had seldom been in such a healthy state, but Woodruff realised that if his career was to prosper it wouldn't be at the County Ground. After a bitterly contested board meeting at which the player was allowed to put his own case, a majority verdict granted his request. In March 1964, Woodruff went to Wolves for £35,000, the first of the talented local lads to leave.

Swindon finished in a respectable 14th position with the youth team reaching their Cup final but the following season was an unmitigated disaster. It began as badly as their first year had been triumphant. To lose 6–1 at Gigg Lane may be regarded as unfortunate but to replace the injured goalkeeper Norman Oakley, recently bought from Hartlepool, with the hapless Frank Haffey who had kept goal for Scotland in their 9–3 defeat at Wembley in 1961, looked like carelessness. The season was one long painful slog with draws and defeats interspersed with the occasional victory. The one that comes instantly to mind, of course, was achieved at Maine Road in January 1965. Swindon's 2–1 victory, achieved in front of Maine Road's lowest ever attendance of 8,015 (or 108,015 as it appears to us who were there when confronted by the fantasists who have since willed themselves on to the empty terracing in the Kippax stand), was a rare bright spot. Mike Summerbee certainly enjoyed himself that afternoon. Playing centre-forward, he skipped past City's newly acquired statuesque centre-half Roy Gratrix to score the winning goal with an ease that left the former Blackpool defender and the City spectators totally transfixed. Mike's Maine Road career had begun although none of us realised it at the time. Indeed the Swindon *Evening Advertiser* revealed that 'there were reports in the Manchester area before the game that City intended to make a transfer enquiry about Summerbee but their manager, George Poyser, was away on a scouting trip. It was thought he might have gone to watch Alan Skirton, the transfer-listed Arsenal forward.' Good old George Poyser, finger, as ever, firmly on the pulse of an egg and bacon sandwich.

The win at Maine Road was not enough to halt Swindon's slide which, hard as it is for me to appreciate it, was even worse than City's. Across town Manchester United were winning the League Championship so our position in the middle of the Second Division felt dire even if, by comparison with Swindon, it wasn't. A disconsolate Keith Morgan applied for a transfer and was immediately left out of the team. Everything Bert Head had been building for five years was starting to slip away from him.

Ernie Hunt had followed his tonsilitis with appendicitis and had then broken a bone in his foot. He tried to play on with another of Harry Cousins's strappings but it was hopeless. The team missed him greatly and were sucked into a frantic relegation scrap with Portsmouth and Middlesbrough. On the final day of the season they were level on points with Portsmouth but with a better goal average. If they did as well as Pompey they would stay up. They didn't. Away at Southampton they lost 2–1, the winning goal coming from Terry Paine. Portsmouth were away at Northampton who had come up from Division Three with Swindon the previous year and were now heading for promotion to Division One. A draw would suit both sides. A draw was duly achieved.

The Swindon team were on the coach coming back from the Dell when Portsmouth kicked off in their evening match. The coach stopped for dinner in Winchester, which brought back a few memories for Mike. It was a quiet party that climbed back on board. The coach stopped again in Andover. It was 9.20 and someone went to make the fateful telephone call. A minute later the whole team knew they were down. It was going to take a few more years for Swindon to make it into the European Cup.

At a stormy AGM, Swindon's chairman Wilf Castle, apparently a keen student of the world's philosophers, observed, 'No doubt mistakes have been made but unfortunately they never show up until after you have made them.' Then he announced that up to 12 full-time professionals would have to leave the payroll. Eventually, 11 players were sacked, providing an annual saving of between £9,000 and £10,000 in the wages bill. The loss of a derby match with Bristol City, who had taken Swindon's place in Division Two, was offered as another reason for cost-cutting.

By far the saddest case was that of Bert Head who was inevitably sacked. He had built his team so patiently, nurtured and protected his youngsters with such care, and guided them to the greatest days in the club's history to date. It seemed wrong that he should be expected to carry the can for a season of bad luck and a lengthy injury list. He announced his intention of leaving the game and opening a petrol station. Instead, when the new season kicked off in August 1965, Bert Head was the manager of Bury and still in the Second Division. At least he wasn't around to preside over the breaking up of his side.

It was obvious that the club would not be able to hang on to all its talented youngsters who were maturing into seasoned professionals. Mike was grateful to Swindon for giving him a chance and developing him as a player. He had given everything to the cause but he knew in his heart that it was over. The nature of his contribution to the team in this relegation season was recognised by the supporters, who voted him a £25 cash prize as their Player of the Year. He received 457 votes, over twice as many as John Trollope, his nearest rival. However, the big clubs who had been buzzing around Mike when he was playing in an ascending Swindon team were having second thoughts now that he was on his way back into the Third Division. He wasn't a promising teenager any longer. He was 22 years old and there were other promising teenagers around who might prove to be a better investment. This reasoning wasn't lost on Mike. In a public relations exercise, he was photographed in the kitchen of 40 Redcliffe Street, helping Ernie's mother, Doris Hunt, with the washing-up. He had vetoed the photographer's suggestion that he pose for the camera sitting in his MG sports car. He knew perfectly well that, just days after relegation, this was not what the supporters wanted to see. Unfortunately, this instinctive grasp of public relations does not appear to be genetic. During that anxious summer of 1965, at opposite ends of the country, Mike and I worried about the future. For all the fact that he was Player of the Year and had been playing first-team football for over five years, he felt wretchedly insecure. 'Ernie Hunt was always spoken of as a better player than me,' he says, 'so I did have a lack of confidence there. I'd never been to another club. I'd been at Swindon all my life.'

He was stuck in Swindon with no prospect of imminent release and I was stuck in Manchester as City failed to find a manager to fill the shabby, worn out shoes of George Poyser who had been sacked at Easter – a favourite time for culling managers in those patient long-ago days. The solution to both our problems came in July when Manchester City announced that they had appointed Joe Mercer to fill the vacant manager's chair.

Mike was working the deckchairs on the beach in Torquay when he heard the news and was immediately interested. He had first met Joe Mercer in 1960 when he brought a full-strength Aston Villa side to play at the County Ground in a joint testimonial match for Harry Cousins and the recently retired local hero George Hudson. Villa won 4–3 but Mike scored twice and after the game Joe, who had played in the match, introduced himself to the young winger with the information that he had known George and, of course, Bunt with whom he had played at Aldershot during the war years.

'He had an old Rover,' Mike recalls. 'I got into the car and it smelled of leather. Mrs Mercer was sitting in the back seat. He asked me, "Do you fancy coming to Aston Villa?" I said I fancied working with him and I'd go wherever he went. Then he had his breakdown.'

Mercer left Villa after a series of bad results and supporters' insults had contributed to a stroke. He was out of football for over a year. It seemed that Mercer would go the way of Bill Nicholson, Charlie Mitten, Matt Gillies and the other managers who had shown interest in Mike but made no commitment.

Joe's first signing at City was Malcolm Allison, the disruptive, charismatic coach who had recently left Plymouth Argyle because the directors wanted to pick the team. Whether he was pushed or he jumped is irrelevant. Mercer certainly thought he'd been sacked but Mike was now even more intrigued.

I heard the news that Joe Mercer had gone to Manchester City and that Malcolm had gone with him. I didn't know Malcolm but I knew his reputation as an innovative coach. I didn't need selling on City. I'd grown up on the Trautmanns and the Bobby Johnstones. I'd seen them at Villa and Birmingham in the days when John and I used to get the train every Saturday from Cheltenham to watch a match. John said they'd only just avoided relegation but for me there was never a problem in going there.

In fact, City had finished 11th in the Second Division. The fact that Mercer had fancied Mike in 1960 did not prompt an immediate enquiry in 1965. There was no approach from Mercer to Swindon. In fact, there was no approach from any club. As July turned into August Mike returned to Swindon to start pre-season training for life back in the Third Division. Danny Williams had arrived from Rotherham to take over from Bert Head. Mike had no problem with him but Williams knew Mike wanted to get away and raised no objections. Mike couldn't afford to wait any longer. He picked up the telephone, rang Mercer at Maine Road and outlined his position. Mercer said, 'Leave it with me,' and put the phone down.

Nine days before the first match of the season, Joe Mercer travelled to Swindon and met with the board. No deal was reached. On the Wednesday, the directors met again and though no deal was announced the clubs must have agreed terms because Mike was told he was to travel to Manchester for a medical the following day. The transfer fee was officially announced as £35,000 but the deal wouldn't be completed until Mike had passed his medical and agreed personal terms.

On the way up there I was thinking I'll get fifty quid a week here. By the time I got to Sale I was thinking maybe seventy-five, but they sent my contract up from Swindon where I was on thirty-five. Joe Mercer said to me, 'Right, son, we're in the Second Division and we're skint. You're on thirty-five quid a week, I'll give you forty.' I said, 'That'll do for me.'

Mike's initial impression of the Maine Road set up was positive.

I parked the car and went up the stairs into reception. There was a girl on a white telephone. I was shown into the players' room. It had a snooker table and there on the walls were photographs of the great players of the past and I thought this is a really big club. The changing room was bigger than both changing rooms at Swindon knocked together. It had the smell of a big club.

Joe Mercer wasn't in his office but in a greasy spoon café across the road. Mike walked over to join him, bought himself a cup of tea and looked for a spoon to stir it with. Next to the urn was a piece of string to which at some point in history a teaspoon had once been tied. Mike took his cup of tea to the table and sat down opposite his new boss, commenting on the fact that the only teaspoon in the place had been stolen. Having spent most of his footballing life in such establishments, Mercer reached into his pocket and produced a teaspoon before launching into his speech about City being skint. Mike couldn't help noticing that there was still a small residue of string around the handle of the spoon. Life at Manchester City had begun.

CHAPTER TEN

Manchester –
the Glory Years

The French have a phrase for it. They call it *le coup de foudre*. Somehow it sounds grander than its prosaic English translation, 'love at first sight'. Mike fell in love with Manchester immediately and I fell in love with him at much the same time. Admittedly, I had to share him with 20 to 30,000 others but I wasn't the possessive type.

In the summer of 1965, Mike was largely unknown outside Swindon. Even those of us who had seen him score the winning goal in January had never heard the name before. As soon as he'd signed the forms, he was summoned by his new coach.

'I put some gear on and went on to the pitch to meet Malcolm. I'd never met him before and he had no idea what I was like. It was the Friday before the first match at Middlesbrough next day and he worked my bollocks off.'

They were all glad the first match was away from home. The players and the new management team found Maine Road an intimidating place. Mercer was worried that nobody would come, that they would play their games in that rotting iron hulk of a stadium in front of ten people. It was a losing side with ten years of disappointment behind it. Across town . . . well, that was the point. Much as everyone connected with City would have liked to ignore the other lot completely, if you lived in the same town it was impossible.

The team that travelled to Ayresome Park included nine players who had been part of the previous disastrous campaign. The newcomers were Summerbee and Ralph Brand, a £25,000 buy from Rangers who scored two goals in two seasons and was eventually transferred to Sunderland. Mercer and Allison had to work with the players they were given because there was almost no money for purchases. Fortunately, among the players they inherited were Mike Doyle, Glyn Pardoe, Neil Young, Alan Oakes and Johnny Crossan.

Listing the names does not convey the tension of the atmosphere surrounding those early games. These were not the players who Allison was to boast would terrify the cowards of Europe and who were duly knocked out of Europe in the first round by an unknown team from Turkey. They were nervous and insecure, by no means reassured by the appointments of the men who were to guide them. Allison was unknown as a coach and Mercer was a sick man who, as a manager, had not achieved anything like what he had achieved as a player. On the coach to Middlesbrough, Allison alleges that Mercer told him he would retire in two years and bequeath him the team. Neither of them could have imagined the nature of what that legacy might be but, to Mercer's eventual discomfort and the destruction of almost everything they were to achieve together, Allison was never to forget those fateful words.

The week in which Mike moved to Manchester and played his first game for his new club had a suitably dramatic conclusion.

After the Middlesbrough game we came back to Manchester and I knew I had to go back to Swindon to get all my clothes. I'd left my MGB outside Maine Road, which apparently you shouldn't do, but I came back and went out for the evening with Peter Gardner [sports writer for the *Manchester Evening News*], Harry Dowd and Matt Gray. We went to the Corn Exchange and it was wall-to-wall girls in mini skirts at ten o'clock at night – Swindon was closed at ten o'clock at night. I had on a tweed sportscoat and I drank Mackeson. They were all drinking Bacardi.

Next day, Paul Doherty [sports agent] picked me up to take me to Maine Road to get the car. Someone had loosened the nuts on the front wheel. I got as far as Penkridge when the wheel came off. I hit a car head on and rolled over. I had stitches above the eye and the elbow but the car was a write-off.

Walter Griffith, the secretary of the club, broke off from his task of blotting the ink on the Summerbee contract, drove down to Penkridge to pick up the new signing and took him back to Manchester, hoping that his new manager hadn't signed a player who was going to cause him many more sleepless nights.

Initially, his worries were soon calmed as the team lost just once in the first 15 league matches. A crowd of 25,000 attended the first home match, against Wolves, and for a midweek 0–0 draw against Norwich at the end of October, over 34,000 came to watch.

Mike was in his element as the popular adulation took hold. Relieved that his gamble in joining what seemed to be a failing Second Division side fallen on hard times and going nowhere had paid off, he never ceased to marvel at the difference between life in Swindon and life in Manchester.

I'd always been a country boy, a small-town boy. Cheltenham and Swindon were small country towns. Don't forget there were gas meters in those days – and you had to go down the hall for the toilet. It was so different when I came to Manchester with people wanting to know you. If you were any good, you soon became an icon to these people.

If Allison ever had cause to doubt the wisdom of Joe Mercer's decision to sign the right-winger, it was dispelled when he saw the way Mike responded to injury. He pretended to be unhurt by the car crash but in reality he played the next two games feeling very stiff and sore from the impact and the subsequent stitches. The first match was won, the second drawn.

In the fourth match of the season, the midweek return game with Wolverhampton Wanderers, a Wolves defender unceremoniously barged Mike off the pitch and into the stand where he collided head-first with a metal post. He was led off the field looking like a stuntman in a Sam Peckinpah film with blood spurting in a fountain from a deep cut in the top of his head. Ten rows back, a woman who was three months pregnant was so traumatised by the sight that she suffered a miscarriage. Informed about it later Mike took the trouble to send her flowers. Also watching the match from the stands were two particularly interested observers. The Wolverhampton manager, who had recently taken over from the legendary Stan Cullis, was none other than Andy Beattie, whose last sight of Mike had been on the day of George's funeral. Sitting next to him was Ernie Hunt who was about to become the club's record signing. Hunt's departure from Swindon had been more acrimonious than Mike's and it was not until mid-September that Swindon, desperate for the money to rebuild, finally agreed to let their popular inside-forward have the move he wanted. As Mike was led into the changing room, with City 2–0 up, Ernie was waiting for him. His old friend held Mike's arm tight as the doctor inserted 17 stitches into Mike's head, pulling them through with a pair of metal pliers. Roy Cheetham trotted out to take Mike's place in a slightly rearranged City side and thereby made history by becoming the first substitute ever to be used by Manchester City. Of more relevance to everyone else was the fact that City left Molineux with a 4–2 victory.

Cecil Green had come to Wolverhampton to collect Mike and take him back to Swindon to complete the journey that had been aborted so abruptly in Penkridge. It had been ten eventful days since Mike left Swindon for his medical at Maine Road and all his clothes were still in Ernie Hunt's house. Mr Green might have been anticipating a warm convivial chat with his protégé as his maroon Bentley Continental purred its way back to Wiltshire. In fact, his still dazed travelling companion sat in the passenger seat with a towel round his head, trying but failing to stop the blood from seeping out of the wound and on to Mr Green's nice leather interior.

Allison would not have been surprised if Mike had pulled out of Saturday's match at Highfield Road against Coventry, but with stitches and a plaster on his head and stitches in his arm, the prototype of the Bionic Man lined up at outside-right and performed well, without much thought of self-preservation, in a 3–3 draw. 'Malcolm said to the team, "Whatever you do, don't knock the ball to him in the air because he can't head it." First one came over and I headed it.'

The battered and bruised hero returned to stay in a Manchester hotel where he remained until well into 1966, somewhat to Mr Griffith's dismay. 'I stayed in the Grand Hotel in Aytoun Street for six months. The club paid. They kept sending me to digs but I wasn't having any of it. They were all crap.' Eventually, to the club's financial relief, he did manage to find suitable accommodation.

I was sitting in reception at the Grand Hotel when Sandra, one of the receptionists said, 'It's my twenty-first tonight, Mike. Do you want to come to my party? It's in Sale Moor and we're all going in my car, a Morris 1000.' I got in the car with about five birds, all receptionists, and we got to her house which was nothing fancy but nice. It was Sandra's mother, who used to be a dancer, who said, 'Why don't you come and stay in the back bedroom instead of the hotel?'

It was just bed but she'd make me a meal if I wanted one. I used to get up in the morning and go and have some breakfast at a Cypriot café in Rusholme. I was paying eight quid a week for the room. You could go out with a fiver on a Saturday night and have a meal and get drunk and get a taxi home and still have change. I enjoyed it there because they looked after me and the club was happy because they wanted me out of the hotel so they didn't have to pay the bill.

An added incentive for Mike was that George Best lived just down the road in Chorlton. Within weeks of arriving in Manchester, the two of them had met and struck up a friendship that has survived the vicissitudes of 35 years – which is more than can be said for most of George's women friends. This friendship, however, was to cause havoc in the suburban street of his new digs.

Bestie would come and visit me there and suddenly it wasn't a quiet little cul-de-sac any more. We'd come in at three in the morning – I was driving a Volvo 1800 then – or I'd roll up sometime on Sunday and they'd all be out there mowing the grass. Me and Bestie'd been in Phyllis's all night.

Phyllis's was an after-hours drinking club in Moss Side where the windows were draped with heavy velvet curtains that kept out the light until midday on Sundays. Best and Summerbee would wander from there to a steak house on Bridge Street where they held court with the likes of the rising young actor Ian McShane. Afterwards they would drive to the ever-welcoming house of the bookmaker Selwyn Demmy who introduced Mike to his future wife. Then it would be back into town to a club like Mr Smith's or The Phonograph, but not too late this time. Monday morning meant Wythenshawe Park and two and a half hours of physical hell as Malcolm Allison worked off the excesses of the weekend's dedicated socialising.

It was shortly after Summerbee and Best became friendly that the latter completed his transformation, turning from George Best, talented Irish footballer, into Georgie Best, superstar ('Walks like a woman and he wears a bra,' as City fans later sang to the strains of 'Jesus Christ Superstar'). In early March 1966, Best scored twice as United destroyed Benfica in the original Stadium of Light. On his return from Portugal the following day, he was photographed by the tabloids wearing a large sombrero, provoking the caption 'El Beatle'. Best had officially joined the swelling ranks of the working-class heroes of the 1960s. Michael Caine and Terence Stamp, David Bailey and Terence Donovan, Twiggy and the Beatles had all become the darlings of the media. Ten years before, as Sir Anthony Eden drove round and round the County Ground looking for the A4, these young men and women would have been proletarian factory fodder. The 1960s, for all its self-delusion, was the decade that broke down social barriers and created the conditions for the rise of a genuine meritocracy.

Young people now had significant purchasing power. Their horizons had expanded and they didn't want to be junior versions of their parents. Tom Courtenay in *Billy Liar* (1963) captured the mood of a 19-year-old, desperate to break away from the stifling conformity of his petit bourgeois existence with his job in an undertaker's and his bedroom in his parents' semi-detached house. What he wanted was Julie Christie and her free-spirited liberated woman, life in London as a script writer for the comedian Danny Boone, a new kind of a career and a new kind of lifestyle for a lower-middle-class lad from a Yorkshire town. He just didn't have the bottle to go out and get it.

As you can see, this film made quite an impact on me, partly for its promise of what lay 'out there' for someone from that sort of background and partly because I was captivated by the sight of Julie Christie swinging her shoulder bag and tossing her blonde hair in St Peter's Square in Manchester. I spent many hours looking for any trace of Julie Christie in that square, or indeed of any other girl who looked remotely like her, but without success. My sole triumph was that while doing so I once saw Willie Donachie in Percival's bookshop. I can't remember what he was reading, although I know I was very impressed, so it probably wasn't *The Manchester City Football Book no. 3* – I was the one who had gone in there to buy that Pulitzer prize-winning effort.

As London transformed itself into a swinging city in the mid 1960s, so Manchester made an effort to be a provincial version. At the start of the decade, the *Manchester Guardian* moved its centre of printing operations to London or the 'branch office' as the paper's distinguished northern sports writer Eric Todd always called it. In 1959, when we were on holiday in Cornwall, my family had to wait two days before the paper reached our hotel by post from Manchester. When we returned the following year we could buy it in any newsagent's shop in St Ives the same day but we could no longer be certain there would be a report on the Lancashire cricket match. At the end of the decade, the paper, with its sister publication the *Manchester Evening News*, moved out of the Cross Street building where C.P. Scott had written his leaders denouncing the jingoism of the Boer War and Neville Cardus had complained of Paderewski's piano technique and Harry Makepeace's slow batting, into new purpose-built offices on Deansgate. It was symbolic of Manchester's desire to be seen to be moving with the times, though some Mancunians regretted what they saw as the abandonment of the city's distinctive radical tradition.

The success of this repositioning of Manchester was cultural rather than architectural because although the slums were slowly being cleared, what was erected in their place was a new and equally disastrous mixture of tower blocks and sink estates, patterned after the brutalist, realist architecture beloved of East German town planners. Even as *Coronation Street* anachronistically celebrated the folksy community of back-to-back terraced houses, inner-city areas such as Hulme were being rebuilt as instant slums, harbouring the germs of the disease that 20 years later would produce gangs and drug-related crime on a scale previously unimagined in Manchester.

Granada Television, on the other hand, transmitting from its production base in Quay Street, was an almost instant success, drawing creative inspiration from its Manchester location. *Coronation Street* gave the world not just a host of unforgettable characters in a soap opera still going strong after 40 years, but a sense of the heightened reality of life in Manchester. By contrast, *Crossroads*, made by ATV in Birmingham, gave absolutely no sense of the place where it was made, which many people thought was perhaps as well.

As Granada TV's drama department started to gather and nurture the creative talents of Jack Rosenthal, Arthur Hopcraft, Michael Apted and Colin Welland among others, across town Michael Elliott and Braham Murray were beginning to build a national reputation for their newly founded University Theatre, the forerunner of what became the Royal Exchange. Manchester was 'in', Manchester was sexy, but wherever you went in the world from 1966 onwards, to the vast majority of the population the city meant only Manchester United and Georgie Best, with a dash of Bobby Charlton and Denis Law on the side. Football continued to be the city's greatest ambassador. Footballers, freed from the shackles of the maximum wage and the old retain and transfer prison cell, were ready and anxious to join the party and celebrate this shift in cultural values. In the summer of 1966, England won the World Cup and footballers received official recognition of their new social status. When Eddie Hapgood captained England in the 1930s it was inconceivable that Stanley Baldwin would think it politically beneficial to be photographed standing on the steps of 10 Downing Street with the Arsenal left-back. When Bobby Moore held aloft the Jules Rimet trophy, Harold Wilson knew very well that to be associated with Bobby Moore or to recommend the MBE for the Beatles was a vital part of the politician's ongoing campaign for public approval.

Sixties celebrity was a potent mixture of pop music, television, fashion, advertising and a physical beauty which the camera lens could convey to an eager public. The old style of Hollywood beauty – the cut-glass voices and immaculate grooming of David Niven and Audrey Hepburn – was giving way to an appreciation of other ethnic styles – the black Sidney Poitier and the Jewish Barbra Streisand. George Best slipped easily into the new élite and Mike Summerbee was right behind him, probably threatening to bring him down if Best tried to get away; both of them had an appreciation of and an attraction to this new lifestyle.

Summerbee and Best made a perfect partnership – out-of-towners but immediately accepted by Manchester. It needed the red–blue combination to capture the public imagination. After all, who else at Maine Road could have credibly been seen in nightclubs with El Beatle? Georgie Best and Roy Cheetham? The two Georges – Best and Heslop? Colin Bell had the footballing talent and the floppy-haired looks but not the personality to complement Best. Francis Lee had the talent and the personality but not the interest. Lee preferred to spend his spare time building up his waste-paper and launderette businesses. He is now an extremely wealthy man so, in retrospect, his decision seems to have been a wise one.

Best and Summerbee both had one vital extra ingredient –

FATHERS, SONS AND FOOTBALL

they were key members of successful sides. We all saw what happened to Best when United plunged into their eagerly anticipated fall from grace. Not surprisingly he got fed up with playing teams entirely on his own and found he didn't need to win a championship to open a bottle of champagne. In the second half of the 1960s, however, United were an excellent side and Manchester City sought to match them trophy for trophy.

The night Best became El Beatle, Summerbee travelled with City to Leicester where they knocked the First Division side out of the FA Cup in a fifth-round replay. The following month at Rotherham, the recently signed Colin Bell scored the goal that secured promotion back to the First Division, giving Mike his second promotion in three years. City were the champions of the Second Division and unlucky losers in the sixth round of the FA Cup to eventual winners Everton. Mike Summerbee's first season at Maine Road could scarcely have started better and he was soon happily ensconced in what passed for football society in Manchester.

If you went out on a Saturday night in Manchester, everybody knew you. Malcolm Allison had a house-warming party and I was one of the few City players there – along with Denis Law, Paddy Crerand, Noel Cantwell and Maurice Setters. Of all the people in Manchester at that time, I couldn't name one I didn't get on with, and a lot of them were United players. There were never any problems between the players. It was the fans who had the problems.

The problems got worse quite quickly. Initially, however, City had to justify their First Division status. Like many another recently promoted team, they started as they had finished the previous year. They drew the first game, away at Southampton, with Mike scoring City's first goal back in the First Division.

177

Then came two home victories in three days at Maine Road against Liverpool and Sunderland so that, by the end of the first week of the new season, Manchester City were top of the First Division. It didn't last of course. By late October, they had won just one more game and were second from the bottom.

'The pace of the game wasn't that much different in the First Division,' says Mike, 'but looking at the fixture list was a frightening thing. There were no easy games. Every game was tough and you had to fight just to survive.'

Mercer and Allison responded to the slump by switching Glyn Pardoe to left-back. Summerbee responded by fighting.

In one game I got sent off for head-butting a wing-half. It was in the eighty-ninth minute and it was right in front of the ref. He just tapped me on the shoulder and said, 'You know where you're going, don't you?' I said, 'I certainly do,' and trotted off. I used to get booed on to the field at away grounds, and booed off at half-time and at the end. I think I might have been regarded as overaggressive by opposing fans.

Mike's combative nature meant that he was forever treading the narrow line between legal aggression and what referees took to be illegal violent conduct. Francis Lee is eloquent in defence of Mike's physical bravery.

Mike used to retaliate first. He'd come up in a hard school. If you let them do you, you'd soon find your leg in plaster. He was a very powerful player, strong and aggressive and full-backs didn't like him for the simple reason that their old adage was to go tight on a winger, clatter him and sooner or later he'd go deeper and jack it in. With Mike that was the worst thing you could have done because it was like a red rag to a bull. If you kicked him, he'd be doubly annoyed and he would definitely do you. There were some full-backs who had sleepless nights before facing Mike.

One of them was the future City manager, Frank Clark, who was a left-back at Newcastle United for 13 years.

He was the hardest, toughest winger I have ever played against. Bestie was close behind him but Mike was nastier than Bestie. We had some great tussles and great respect for each other. I remember kicking him once and I spent the rest of the game apologising. He was terrific to play against because you knew you'd never get any moaning from him.

Mike's combative nature lurked just below the surface at all times. Notoriously, he was to become one of the few players ever to be sent off in a testimonial game. It was played at Loftus Road on 12 December 1972 and it followed in the wake of Rodney Marsh's transfer to City from Queens Park Rangers.

It was close to Christmas and we were going to Great Ormond Street Hospital next day to see the kids. I came in at half-time and complained that Hazell had been kicking me. I said to him, 'I've travelled two hundred miles to play in this testimonial match and it's Christmas and you're kicking lumps out of me! Now just stop it.' Anyway, the second half starts and I'd only been on the field two minutes when he starts again so I smacked him one – I gave him a good 'un and all – and Belly hadn't even come out from half-time yet so I passed him going off. He said, 'Where are you going?' I said, 'I've been sent off.' It went to a tribunal and Terry Venables represented me and got me off.

It wasn't only referees and the Football Association who found Mike's short fuse less than amusing. One night after a black-tie dinner, a marital row ended somewhere on the Lancashire moors as Mrs Summerbee turfed her husband out of the car and drove the next 20 miles home by herself in peace and quiet. The international winger had plenty of time to mull over the consequences of his actions as he set off on the long walk home. An hour later and seemingly no nearer civilisation he came upon a red telephone box. He found sixpence in the pocket of the trousers of his dinner suit and rang home. The attempt at cajoling his wife out of her nightie and back into the car was abruptly terminated when the injustice of what he had suffered swept over him and he started the row again.

'Mike, where am I?'

'I suppose you're in bed.'

'I am. And where are you?'

'I'm in the middle of the moors, it's snowing and I've got no coat.'

'Exactly. So what was it you wanted to say?'

'And another thing . . .' he began to shout before the line mysteriously went dead. He searched in his pocket for more money. He didn't have any. With a sigh he continued his midnight hike over the moors, haunted by the baleful stares of the sheep that were as surprised by his presence as his wife was puzzled by the temperament that never ceased to land him in trouble.

Despite the ever-present threat of the FA's suspensions, Mike never stopped scrapping and fighting. Throughout the winter of 1966–67 the team were battling just to stay in the First Division. They lost both their Easter matches against Leicester City and it wasn't until April that they settled sufficiently to finish, in the end, a comfortable 15th in the table. Mike was incapable of changing his temperament so for him there was no such concept as a 'dead' match.

I remember a 0–0 draw at Chelsea. The game was dead so I decided to give that Bonetti one. They all gathered round me, all the assassins – Harris, McCreadie, Hinton, Boyle, Webb, Osgood – animals they were. They were all threatening me and I said, 'Listen, if I'm going, I'm taking two of you bastards with me.'

The upturn in City's league fortunes came immediately after they had lost narrowly and unluckily at Leeds in the sixth round of the FA Cup. Up until then they had been playing the right-back, Tony Book, as a sweeper behind a four-man defence and barely registered as an attacking force at all, so concerned had Mercer and Allison become to stop leaking goals. Contrary to all expectations, City came out at Elland Road and ran Leeds off their feet. It was the precursor of what was to be a spectacular league campaign the following season. Just for the moment though, with his First Division status secure, Mike could turn his attention to an extremely good-looking young blonde woman.

Her name was Tina Schofield and she was 19 years old when she and Mike met, quite appropriately, in The Phonograph, introduced by their mutual friend Selwyn Demme. Tina's father was a wealthy businessman who ran a business that involved manufacturing travel goods at his factory and selling them in his shops in Oldham and Ashton. Besides Tina, there was a younger sister, Anita, and three older brothers. The family were all Christian Scientists and Tina had been expensively educated away from her northern roots at the Christian Science boarding school near Esher in Surrey.

The point of the school was to turn out young ladies, but religion came into it quite a bit. In a way, it distanced me from my parents and Mummy says now that she wishes they hadn't done it. She would have liked her daughter at home with her and when I came back I was terribly refined. My parents were still "'Ello, love' and all that. It made me into a bit of a snob, I suppose, because I became different from them.

After acquiring five O-levels, Tina left school and started work in the family business as a receptionist. The 1960s may have been a decade of great social change, but when Tina left school in 1963 the careers open to a woman, even of her social background, were strictly limited. Much as she enjoyed working, it was still a curtain-raiser to the main play – marriage.

Daddy wanted me to learn from the bottom up, to work in reception, in the factory and in the shops to learn how the business worked. I wasn't planning a career as such so this was a logical place for me to start but I soon realised that I had absolutely no interest in it. I wanted to become a beautician so I went on a course and then I worked in Manchester for Steiners at the Midland Hotel.

It was while she was working at the Midland that she got to know Mike. The attraction was instant and mutual but Tina's training-ground routines were just as rigorous as Mike's.

He asked me out a few times before I said yes. It didn't mean anything to me that he was a footballer. I asked my brothers about him and they said, 'Oh yes, he's a good player, he's just signed for City,' so they knew about him. I thought he was going to take me out for dinner so I was all dolled up but he took me to a pub.

There was a perfectly sound reason why Mike sought the traditional security of a pub rather than the intimidating uncertainty of a restaurant – he had never taken a girl to a restaurant before.

He didn't know which fork to use or what the food was if we went to a French restaurant. I didn't know much about wines but he knew even less. That's why we went to a pub, but I found his lack of social graces endearing. There was something about his very chiselled look that made him different.

If Mike was intimidated by Tina's social circle, the feelings of awe were immediately dispelled when at his first formal dinner he was hit on the head after five minutes by a flying bread roll. It was hurled across the room by one of the many Young Conservatives in the room, no doubt anxious to demonstrate to the famous footballer the sport at which he was most adept.

The romance was helped by the fact that Mike had rather more time on his hands than Tina's traditional suitors.

He was just so different from anyone I'd met before. Sometimes he'd come round and see me in the afternoons in a lovely car and he always wore sweaters and smelled of wintergreen. He only wore a suit for match days. Other boys I knew wore suits and went to the office till six o'clock. He talked to me and he was really nice. He was quiet then. He was the country boy, a bit of an 'oo aah'. He told me about his mum and the cottage in Devon where she lived. I soon knew where he'd come from and that was it really.

Only, of course, it wasn't. The course of true love didn't run as smoothly as one of Mike's dashes to the corner flag. Much to his surprise, Tina tackled him from behind. More than thirty years after the event, this is still sensitive territory. During the course of the first stage of the relationship, Tina took a two-week holiday in Majorca with a girlfriend and, as she puts it, this being three decades before *Ibiza Uncovered*, she went out with another man.

As if being sent off at Newcastle, having lumps kicked out of him and struggling to stay in the First Division were not sufficient to occupy his mind, Mike received intelligence from Majorca of Tina's dalliance. In her defence, she would like to state that she wasn't wearing an engagement or wedding ring and no hint of anything permanent had passed between them at this point. Nevertheless, Mike decided to act with the full majesty of the FA Disciplinary Committee. He met her at the airport, went out with her twice and then dropped her with the words, 'I know what you've been doing and you're not the girl for me.' Tina was stunned. She was, and remains, an extremely attractive woman which, by and large, always gave her the whiphand in her relationships with besotted young men. She had no PFA to defend her and she was made perfectly aware of the finality of Mike's decision.

It was at this time that her former boyfriend's star status became a problem. Before she started going out with him she had never heard of him. Now, every time she picked up the *Manchester Evening News* there was a picture of him. She had to get out of Manchester. Steiners transferred her to the cruise liners for a short while. Then she moved to London to become an air stewardess with British Caledonian.

The family was surprised. None of the other Schofields had wandered too far from their home in Mottram Road, Stalybridge, but much as Tina enjoyed the life of an air stewardess it soon became apparent to her that her father was not a happy man. In fact, he was terrified that his beloved daughter would be involved in a plane crash. Still, the prospect of returning to Manchester after having been dumped by Mike was too difficult to contemplate.

'It shook me up. I could be quite superficial. I had no ring on, we weren't engaged, so I went on holiday and had some fun, but that was how he felt.'

Tina lived in a flat near Heathrow with a number of other girls, all of whom knew that if a certain Mike Summerbee were to call, his message should be relayed to her instantly. Eventually he did call, usually on a Friday when City were playing in London.

> They stayed at the Waldorf and he would ring up and tell me where he was and I would go to see him. I'd be shaking. I had my hair done and my nails done. Can you imagine walking into a hotel where there's a whole bunch of players sitting around looking at you, talking about you? You know what lads are like, but I'd do that just to see him. We'd just have tea or coffee for an hour then I'd come home.

Mike obviously needed all his strength to boot Cyril Knowles round White Hart Lane.

The story of Manchester City's championship season 1967–68 has been told many a time and oft. The key to their triumph was the signing of Francis Lee in October 1967 and the move of Mike Summerbee from outside-right to centre-forward. Lee, unhappy at Bolton, had been looking for a transfer; Mercer and Allison knew they were a proven goalscorer short of turning City into a very good side. After £60,000 changed hands, Lee made his debut in a 2–0 victory against Wolves at Maine Road and the team embarked on an unbeaten run. Lee and Summerbee became friends the moment Francis signed for City and have remained close ever since. Neither has ever been frightened of expressing their opinions. But Lee was excited with the way his City career started.

> We went ten games up to Christmas without losing, and we were hammering teams. I thought, 'We can win this.' I'd never played in a side that had gone ten games unbeaten and we were enjoying ourselves and playing some brilliant football. We lost at West Brom twice and

everyone said we'd gone, blown a gasket, because we'd come from bottom of the league to second so fast.

In fact, even the defeat at West Brom on Boxing Day was a little unlucky. Colin Bell was out injured and City had gone two goals down before Summerbee and Lee scored to pull them level. The momentum was now with City but it disappeared when one of the goalposts collapsed with only a few minutes left and 15 minutes elapsed before the game could be restarted. In the last minute, a mistake by the City goalkeeper Mulhearn presented Jeff Astle with the winner.

Mike drove home after the game so angry with the result that he was stopped by the police for speeding. However, his mind wasn't entirely consumed by irritation at the way the team had thrown away two points. As the traffic cops approached his car, he rolled down the window and came up with the story, 'Malcolm Allison's just passed me doing over ninety and he's pissed out of his mind.' The police leapt back into their car and drove off in pursuit of bigger fish. They were probably United supporters.

Four days later, City lost the return match at Maine Road and a week after that, on 3 January 1968, Tina Schofield watched her first game of football as Manchester City took on Reading in the third round of the FA Cup.

Tina's brothers were rugby supporters and would have been much more impressed had their glamorous sister pulled the Sale flanker or an Orrell prop forward than a mere footballer. Tina had never been interested in football and wasn't particularly keen to sit out in the cold on a freezing day in early January, even if her boyfriend was in the form of his life and being talked of in England terms.

Tina's scepticism was well founded as City played out a witless, sterile 0–0 draw with the Third Division side. The ghastly 90 minutes was enlivened by one moment of pure farce. After 75 minutes, City were awarded a penalty. Everyone expected the result would now be a witless, sterile 1–0 home win. Francis Lee was City's penalty king.

> I put the ball on the spot and I'm thinking to myself, 'Right, I'm going to knock this to the keeper's left, and it's going in, boom.' I'm focused and all psyched up for it and I turn round and walk back to the edge of the box. As I'm walking away from the ball, Tony Coleman runs in and smashes it straight into the crowd. I looked at him and I said, 'What are you doing, you stupid ****?!' He said, 'I just fancied it.' I said, 'You won't fancy it so much when you get in the dressing room.' Joe Mercer went berserk because the replay at Reading was now a tricky Cup-tie.

In fact the replay at Reading was the match Tina should have gone to. City awoke from their collective dream and won 7–0 at Elm Park, the ground on which George Summerbee had started his last match as a player–manager in a sad defeat. Mike scored a hat-trick. As the players trooped off to the generous applause of the home supporters, the disembodied voice on the public address system announced in spontaneous admiration, 'Ladies and gentlemen, you have just seen one of the greatest teams England has produced in a long time.' City were duly knocked out in the next round.

Mike was on song. When City beat Spurs 4–1 in front of the *Match of the Day* cameras on an ice-bound Maine Road pitch, the whole country appreciated how magnificently he was playing. Joe Mercer's old Everton colleague, the legendary centre-forward Dixie Dean, was fulsome in his praise and predicted a certain international future for Mike.

Summerbee couldn't have done it all by himself of course, and he always paid due acknowledgement to the efforts of his team-mates, but his outstanding performances during the season were vital to the winning of the league title. Francis Lee was always aware of Mike's qualities.

> When I joined City, they played the ball to feet and it was controlled. Mike was the guy who was making it happen. Of that championship side, Mike was the fulcrum. The ball was always played up to him, he would control it, shield it and everything would happen from that. My first impression was, 'This guy can play because his control is so good. When he goes down the line he's got enough pace and strength to take him there.'

In February, Mike missed his first game of the season for City when, after the traditional press speculation, he was finally chosen to represent England in the European Nations Cup match against Scotland. He had featured in Alf Ramsey's plans since he had been chosen at the end of the previous season to travel to Canada as part of an FA XI who were taking part in a tournament to celebrate the centenary of the Canadian FA. Now he was brought into the full England team in preference to Jimmy Greaves, which did not go down well with the southern press.

> I was rooming with Bobby Moore and he told me, 'You're playing tomorrow. When he tells you, look surprised.' We were training at Kilmarnock. It was icy, difficult to keep your feet. Alf came over to me and said, 'You're playing tomorrow, Michael, good luck, son.' We came down to the ground by bus with a police escort and there were hundreds and thousands of Scotsmen. Alf said, 'Take no notice of these Scottish barrrstards.'

Ramsey's antipathy to the Scots was famous, born of the long years of abuse he had suffered from them when he was an international full-back. As the players stepped off the coach a

voice called out, 'Welcome to Scotland, Sir Alf!' That very
gentil, parfait knight riposted swiftly with, 'You must be
fucking joking!'

Mike couldn't help but be caught up in the powerful emotions
swirling around the game. In the dressing room he opened his
telegrams of congratulation (including one from 'the Boss and
Malcome', courtesy of the illiterate GPO) and then walked out
to face 134,000 Scotsmen, all of whom held him personally
responsible for the slaughter at Culloden in 1745 if not for the
massacre at Glencoe 50 years earlier. Mike's thoughts were
nearer to home. The banks of Scottish fanatics, which seemed to
reach all the way to the sky, brought back those long-buried
memories of the England v. Scotland games played on the rec at
Penwortham, when the sons of George Summerbee played
against the sons of George Mutch and the O'Donnells in their
own version of the Auld Enemy confrontation. It was when Bill
Shankly played for Scotland against England that George made
his debut for Preston. The thought of his father overwhelmed
Mike. George had never rated his younger son. How Mike
wished that George could have been spared, just for this one
sublime moment, to see his son kicking off at Hampden Park
wearing the famous white shirt of his country.

There wasn't much time for these thoughts. After presentation
to Princess Alexandra, the match started and the Scottish defence
soon let him know he was being kicked by internationals. The
defence also included Bremner and McCreadie, old enemies from
the First Division. It was hard for Mike playing up front on his
own with Geoff Hurst running free off him, but he struggled
through and England gained a creditable 1–1 draw. As he came
off the field Bobby Moore reminded him, 'You've played for
your country, Mike. They can never take that away from you.'

Two men above all *kvelled* for Mike, that untranslatable
Yiddish word which in crude English terms means bursting with
pride at the achievements of one's children or grandchildren –
Joe Mercer and Cecil Green. Joe Mercer was just delighted. The

Boss, as he would always be to Mike, had recognised that talent years and years ago and was thrilled to see it nationally acclaimed. Mercer was to be a father figure for many years although even he could never replace the one man whom Mike has always acknowledged was more instrumental in his career than any other – the deeply unselfish and constantly supportive Cecil Green, now chairman of Swindon Town.

'The rest of the team went back to London,' Mike says, 'but I stayed with Bobby Charlton till the next day to fly back to Manchester. When I got back, I met Mr Green who'd been to the game and I gave him my shirt and my cap.'

Without Mr Green there might never have been a Mike Summerbee of Manchester City and England, Manchester United might have won the league championship in 1968 and my world, and that of many of my contemporaries, would have been infinitely the poorer. It is typical of Mike to give Mr Green such significant items. He knew how much Mr Green would value them. More than words, they indicated the depth of feeling Mike retained for the man who had saved him from obscurity.

A few weeks later, as Mike and City girded their loins for the climax of the championship battle, Mike thought he'd better get the domestic side of his life sorted. He couldn't be sure that City would beat United at Old Trafford or that they would win their last four games to take the title, but he felt he had Tina Schofield where he wanted her so he asked her to marry him. He had already persuaded her to move back to Manchester in terms no girlish heart could long refuse.

I was getting ready to fly to Canada via Prestwick when he told me to pack it in. He said, 'If you pack it in, I'll take you out.' So I dropped it like that. You were supposed to work out your notice but I told Daddy I wanted to come home. I was also supposed to be going to Australia to represent British Caledonian and Daddy had to get me out of it. He did and I came home – no engagement ring or anything and I'd loved flying as well, but I packed it in.

Well, it was the summer of love – what was a girl to do? The significance of what Tina was giving up made a limited impact on Mike. Fed up with waiting for him to proceed to the next stage, Tina found a job appearing in safety films for the National Coal Board. When they threatened to send her up to Scotland, Mike was in no mood to watch her trip across the border – he had just survived being sliced open there – so he proposed marriage. A glittering diamond cluster engagement ring was displayed for the edification of the popular press. Tina was relieved to discover that the NCB had commuted her sentence to work at Bank Hall Colliery in Burnley.

Her parents had always worried about the insecurity of her life if she married a professional footballer. They did not enjoy the prospect of their expensively educated daughter being reduced to running a newsagents and confectionery shop like Bunt or, more typically, standing behind the bar of a public house pulling pints.

'Mike told my parents that he would always look after me, that I was his responsibility now – and he has, which is why they have the highest respect for him.' Mike was soon to discover the reality of what that entailed.

Meanwhile this season of seasons continued from one high to another. A week after an earth-shattering 3–1 win at Old Trafford which changed the balance of football power in Manchester for a decade, Mike played his second game for England and his first at Wembley. A goal by Bobby Charlton five minutes from time was enough to secure a narrow win over Spain but Mike's selection was still not popular with the London-based press. He returned with relief to Manchester and embarked upon the final series of matches which would determine the destiny of the league championship.

Manchester United had long been favourites to retain their crown and add to it the European Cup. The night of City glory at Old Trafford had caused a stutter at the end of March and United's catastrophic 6–3 defeat at the Hawthorns suddenly gave City the edge. If they won their last three matches, they would be champions whatever United did. They duly beat Everton 2–0.

On the penultimate Saturday of the season, United walloped Newcastle 6–0 but City went to White Hart Lane and ran rings round Spurs in a scintillating 3–1 victory. Bell scored twice and Summerbee once as City outran and outpassed a Tottenham side that looked pedestrian in comparison. Dave Mackay decided that day that he was almost finished as a First Division player and ended ten glorious years in north London by moving to Derby County.

City's final match was at Newcastle while United entertained Sunderland. A win for the Reds was assumed to be a formality so City had to win to be sure of securing the title on goal average. Mike and Colin Bell were both injured and the team left for Newcastle without them as the two City stars underwent last-minute treatment from the physiotherapist, Peter Blakey. It obviously worked – 20,000 Blues travelled up the A1 to watch Summerbee put City ahead after 12 minutes. Three goals from Newcastle were not enough to dampen City's ardour that day – they scored four and had two disallowed. As Mike says, 'There was no way we were going to lose that game. No way. If they'd scored six, we'd have scored eight.'

This was no idle boast. The way the City defence was playing, Newcastle could quite easily have scored six that day. Fortunately, even if they had, it wouldn't have mattered. Manchester United tripped over their own feet losing to Sunderland and little Michael Summerbee, Titch Summerbee, George's little boy who couldn't ride his bike or tie his own shoelaces or tell the time was now not just an England international but also the league champions' centre-forward.

> Thou hast it now – King, Cawdor, Glamis, all
> As the weird women promis'd; and I fear
> Thou play'dst most brilliantly for't.

Macbeth, Hamlet, Lear, Othello – they all discovered sooner or later how the fates treated their hubris. As Birnam Wood and 'man that is not of woman born' were to prove the undoing of Macbeth, so a little-known Turkish team called Fenerbahce was to prove to Mike Summerbee (and me).

CHAPTER ELEVEN

Manchester – Cups and Cock-ups

There was no point in delaying tactics now. A date for the wedding was set at the end of September 1968. The man of the moment and his beautiful bride needed a house befitting their status. Tina was deputed to find it. What Mike was expecting was something like Pennsylvania Avenue, which cost £700 with the extras, a nice semi, a house for a growing family. What Tina found was a large detached house with stables and land attached in Hatherlow near Romiley in rural Cheshire. The purchase price was £10,500. Mike had been awarded a bonus of £150 for winning the league championship. Fortunately, Herbert Schofield came through with the deposit and Mike, as he did with Mr Green, paid back his father-in-law in full. When they moved in, all Mike's furniture fitted into one corner of one room.

Hatherlow House wasn't so much stockbroker belt as *House & Gardens*. In fact, the Schofield family house in Stalybridge was the first house Mike had ever visited that he couldn't see from the road. He had missed it at his first attempt, confused by the fact that it was hidden away at the end of a long drive. Mike was doing more than moving up a class. Mercer and Busby still lived in their semis. The players who had reached the top of their profession were not yet slaves to conspicuous consumption. Bobby Moore was living in a pleasant detached house in

Chigwell. Apart from Mike, George Best was the other player who bucked this trend. He moved from sharing digs with David Sadler at Mrs Fullaway's boarding house in Chorlton-cum-Hardy straight into a much photographed new house near Bramhall, designed by an architect who had seen too many Antonioni movies. The City and United players were mostly to be found in smaller houses in Sale or Timperley, but Mike was determined to prove to Tina and her family that he could continue to keep her in the style in which she had been raised, although the spectre of the mortgage payments continued to haunt him for some years.

Tina's idea of her wedding, as you would expect of a well-brought-up, middle-class girl, was probably based on what she read in *Bride* magazine. What she was going to get, she soon discovered, was whatever could be fitted into Manchester City's hectic fixture list. As league champions, Manchester City had been invited to play in the European Cup, which in those long-ago days involved just the champion side of each country. In the first round they were drawn to meet Fenerbahce from Istanbul, the champions of Turkey. They strode into battle carrying the colours of Malcolm Allison. The day after the championship-winning victory at Newcastle, he had foolishly declared, 'We'll terrify the cowards of Europe.' Allison's belief was that most European sides were too defensive and could be beaten by teams who attacked them boldly. The logic was impeccable but, unfortunately, City started the season with only one win from their first nine matches. For their first game in Europe, Summerbee was in the worst form of his life. The home leg ended in a dreadful and disappointing 0–0 draw, with Mike missing a chance in front of goal that he could have blown in.

Two days before the return leg in Istanbul, Mike and Tina were married on a foul Monday morning in the church of St Michael and All Angels in the pretty village of Mottram-in-Longdendale, on the edge of the Peak District. George Best, with whom Mike was about to open a boutique called

Edwardia, was the best man. The church was full but somewhat lop-sidedly arranged. The Schofield family was well known in the area and their acquaintances were numerous. Mike's family situation was rather different. John came with their childhood friend Kenny Skeen, and Dulcie travelled up from Devon, but without her husband Cecil, who had not reacted well to Mike's growing fame. Mr and Mrs Green, his former landlady's family from Sale Moor, Joe and Norah Mercer, Malcolm Allison, Tony Book and Francis Lee together with half-a-dozen Manchester United players completed Mike's entire contribution to the guest list.

It wasn't the bad weather that nearly caused a postponement but the temperaments of the groom and his best man. George and Mike were driven to Stalybridge on the night before the wedding by George's temporary chauffeur – George had been banned for speeding – to be inspected by the Schofields and to be informed yet again of their responsibilities for the upcoming festivities. Having passed muster, Best and Summerbee were dropped back at the Piccadilly Hotel in the middle of Manchester where they were supposed to go to bed early and make sure they had clean socks and underpants for the next day. It took about seven minutes for one to suggest to the other that the next few hours could be spent more pleasurably at the Brown Bull in Salford. At 5.30 in the morning, three and a half hours before they were due to leave for the church, Best and Summerbee staggered out of the Brown Bull and back to their hotel room from which wild horses failed to drag them at 8 o'clock when the alarm went off.

Eventually, George's chauffeur, with the help of the hotel staff and the master key, discovered the groom and best man at the wedding of the year passed out on their beds and, when shaken awake, facing that most solemn and binding act with enormous hangovers. Roused in this unfeeling manner, they decided when they got to the church to avoid the waiting press and well-wishers, and they hurried round to the back where the vicar made them a cup of strong tea on his primus stove. They sat nursing their mugs and their hangovers while George faced up to his responsibilities for the day.

'Look down there,' he said. Mike followed the direction of his finger and, through the driving rain, he saw the green fields of the Peak District stretching out before him in the mist of the cold, wet September morning. 'Just run down there, across that field, over the fence and you're away, free as a bird. They'll never catch you.' Mike thought about the advice but rejected it. After all, they were in God's house and God was presumably listening. If he needed proof of that, as he and Tina left the church for the reception in Marple, he noticed with some amusement that the chauffeur and the best man had their heads under the bonnet of the car, wondering why it wouldn't start. Sometimes even the RAC and the AA have to bow to a Superior Power.

There was time for a reception but no time for a honeymoon. The chartered plane to Istanbul left Ringway Airport at 10 o'clock the following morning. Two days later they were back in Manchester with their tail firmly between their legs, knocked out of Europe by the unfancied Turkish side and traumatised by their first experience of the 'Welcome to Hell' reception thoughtfully provided by their hosts.

It was a crushing disappointment for the team and their supporters. Already by this time, the first week in October, they were so far behind Leeds United that they had virtually given up any realistic prospect of retaining their title. Tony Book had suffered an Achilles tendon injury in pre-season training which caused him to miss the entire first half of the season. After the débâcle in Istanbul, Ken Mulhearn the goalkeeper was replaced and played just six more games for the club before being transferred. George Heslop similarly fell out of favour and was replaced by the teenager, Tommy Booth. League results failed to improve and of all the championship team players whose form disappeared, Mike Summerbee disappointed the fans the most.

> I found my metabolism had changed. My whole lifestyle changed when I got married. I felt great in training but when it came to the games I couldn't lift my legs up. I was living in a centrally heated house for the first time and getting breakfast in the morning and a meal at night. I'd never had that. All my adult life I'd had my breakfast in a café – bacon and beans on toast – lunchtime, too. Suddenly, I get married, I have regular food and clean clothes and it completely threw me. It wasn't because I was shagging too much.

I don't think I asked that question. Mike simply volunteered the information.

The season turned round after Christmas. Tony Book returned to skipper the side to a 4–1 home win over Chelsea and in the next match, at Hillsborough, Mike and Francis Lee swapped positions. Mike went back to being the fast aggressive right-winger he had been during his first two seasons at Maine Road. It was an unqualified success. The FA Cup run suddenly began to assume significant momentum. Having fortunately scraped past Luton in the third round, City travelled to St James' Park where they fought out a scoreless draw. At Maine Road in front of 60,000 fans they completed a 2–0 victory and, after the winter postponements, finally defeated Blackburn Rovers 4–1 at Ewood Park. Spurs came north, desperate to avoid their usual pasting in Manchester. Francis Lee's second-half goal separated the two sides at the end of a desperately hard-fought encounter. The following week, City returned to Old Trafford, anxious to prove that their magnificent 3–1 win there the previous year was not a fluke. United were on their way to a place in that season's European Cup semi–final, but that meant nothing to Mike.

There was more of a build-up to the derbies in Manchester in those days. Now it's all done on television. Frank Clough and Frank McGhee were proper sportswriters. You weren't afraid to be included in their articles because you knew it was going to be about the game. Then, of course, you got the lunatic Doyle on the Friday night saying, 'We're coming to destroy you.' Just to wind them up.

Mike Doyle was hardly the only culprit. City were testing their strength and everyone enjoyed it, though it meant slightly more to Doyle, Oakes, Pardoe and Young who were City youth-team graduates and had, like the rest of us, suffered years of humiliation from arrogant Reds.

Malcolm used to love to walk out on to the pitch early, holding up five fingers to the Stretford End, meaning we'd beat them 5–0. 'Bring it down to four, Malcolm,' I used to say. 'Five puts too much pressure on us.' He'd strut around with his coat draped across his shoulders. They used to hate him. He'd brush away a speck of dust like he was doing that to United. He thought we'd never get beaten there.

We rarely were in those days. United were the champions of Europe but City were champions of Manchester. A single goal confirmed it. The scorer was Mike Summerbee whose rehabilitation was now complete.

Much as he enjoyed the victories and hard as he fought to achieve them, Mike was always friendly with the United players and respected them enormously, particularly Tony Dunne the Irish full-back who was his regular marker. He jokes now about asking for his studs back, having left them embedded in his marker's shin but he will also readily admit that when he got past Dunne, City needed to score because the number of times he would succeed in doing that during a game was limited.

There was a subsidiary anxiety in most of the derby matches. George Best was always threatening to come over to Mike's side of the field and nutmeg him – push the ball between his legs, run round, collect it and be on his way – which he was always eager to do against lesser opponents. Mike warned him in no uncertain terms to stay on his own side of the field and not to try any of that 'impish Irish genius' malarkey on him. He explains his reasoning with commendable honesty: 'I didn't want to be going out with him afterwards and see him limping badly and know that I was the one who'd been kicking him.'

Not even George Best could slow the City bandwagon in the spring of 1969. A dramatic injury-time winner by Tommy Booth brought City victory over Everton in the semi-final at Villa Park and a place at Wembley. Tina, by now six months pregnant with their first child, agreed to watch her husband playing football for the second time, having been assured that the eccentric Tony Coleman would not be taking the penalties. The left-winger confined himself to fatuous remarks made to Princess Anne during the presentation ceremony before kick-off which were later reported as 'give my regards to your mam and dad'. I have no doubt that the Princess became an instant fan of the opposition, Leicester City. If so, she was in for a rotten afternoon as we ran out winners by the single goal of the game scored by Neil Young after Mike Summerbee had battled his way to the dead-ball line and crossed into the path of that sweetest of left feet.

Mike had experienced his second epiphany that day. Walking out to face the traditional 100,000, he again felt the presence of his father looking down on him. George had been so near yet so far with his three 'appearances as 12th man' for Preston and Portsmouth. Mike so badly wanted his father to be there at Wembley that he could feel him, almost see him. Dulcie was working in a hospital in Devon and John preferred to watch it on television, so the people who knew how hard George had struggled were not there to witness his son's triumph.

Thirty-one years later, Mike learned that there were two Summerbees in the crowd that day. His uncle Bunt was still connected to Bournemouth through whom he was able to acquire his precious tickets for himself and Mike's cousin Ray, now an officer with the Metropolitan police. The two of them had followed Mike's career with considerable interest. Bunt would have been as aware as Mike of the poignancy of the moment and the presence of the ghost of George Summerbee.

It never occurred to Ray or Bunt to ask Mike for tickets. They weren't the kind of people who asked for favours and, according to Ray, Bunt didn't want Mike to feel under any obligation. Sitting with the Bournemouth party meant they were in no danger of running into Dulcie. If she could launch into Andy Beattie on the day of George's funeral over something that happened eight years previously, it would be unlikely she would have forgotten about the affair of the loan and the engagement ring despite the years that had passed.

After receiving the Cup, the City heroes went on their traditional lap of honour, Harry Dowd, the goalkeeper, wearing the base on his head, also in the traditional manner. Eventually, they approached the section of the crowd where Bunt and Ray were sitting. As he saw Mike with his team-mates coming towards him, Ray wanted to rush on to the pitch to hug him. He and Bunt were bursting with pride, eyes filling with tears, but they couldn't do it. They wanted to shout out, 'It's Ray and your Uncle Bunt!' but to Mike they were just faces in the crowd and he went on his way. Ray and his father filed out of the ground and walked back down Wembley Way to the tube station, the pride they took in Mike's triumph mingling oddly with the feeling of being weighed down with an indefinable sorrow at the gap that had opened up between them.

Oblivious to all this, Mike was taken to the Waldorf Astoria

Hotel with the rest of the team to get changed, and then set off for the Café Royal for dinner, where the *Match of the Day* cameras were waiting for them. The night, however, was still young.

> Afterwards we all went on to the Sportsmen's Club in Tottenham Court Road. The atmosphere was great, the champagne was flowing, we were having a great time. Then I went downstairs to find a cab. Tina came down after me but before she arrived I got into an argument with four Leicester supporters. They started on me so I gave them one. Tina saw me brawling with four men and ran back upstairs to find Francis.

'Francis!' she cried, 'Your best mate is scrapping on the pavement outside. Can you sort it out?' Which he did but not in the way Tina expected.

> Francis waded into them and knocked them all out. So both of us had bruises, torn shirts, blood all over our nice new suits. I think I slept on the couch or on the floor. I remember waking up in the morning and looking at Tina lying in bed with this large stomach and she started on at me. She said something like, 'You! Dragging me down to the depths. You're no better than a common hoodlum.' I said, 'I don't bloody well care what you think. We've just won the Cup.'

Very soon it became a question of which cup was being referred to. The following season looked set to become a duplicate even down to the disastrous Summerbee start. Just as marriage had affected Mike in 1968, so the birth of his first child, Rachel, appeared to wreak similar havoc during pre-season matches. This time Allison was not prepared to wait until Christmas for Mike to rediscover his form. During

202

the Charity Shield defeat against Leeds United, Allison took Summerbee off at half-time. It had never happened to Mike before.

Mal said, 'We're carrying you. You're finished, you.' He never spoke to me at all that week. It really woke me up. I like being free. I didn't know much about responsibility and Tina had just given birth to Rachel. When he said, 'You're finished,' I said, 'You fucking what?' but it helped me because I just wasn't functioning. I was fit enough. I never missed training. Tina might have been there supporting me but she didn't know about the life of a professional footballer. My mother did.

Dulcie was seemingly more upset by Allison's behaviour than Mike, who at least realised that he had been playing poorly. Dulcie, however, was incensed, no doubt worrying that George's fate might overtake Michael. She had to do something before Malcolm Allison turned into Jim Taylor. The day after the humiliation at the Leeds match, Dulcie came roaring up from Devon, fire billowing from her nostrils, demanding that her son drive her over to Allison's house right now!

Michael wanted to know what I was going to say. I said, 'I'm going to tell him off.' I went to see Malcolm Allison and he said, 'Hello, Dulcie, it's nice to see you,' and I said, 'It isn't nice. You're a bugger, you are. Don't say things about Michael that aren't true. Everybody has a bit of a lapse some time or other and now he's got a lot of responsibility but he's still a very good player. And you want to remember something. He's got a very good name. His name is Summerbee and that's very important. Anyone connected with the name Summerbee will not let the side down.' I told him, 'Don't you dare say anything about him again that's not good.' He said, 'Hang on a minute, don't you realise what I'm doing?' I said, 'Yes, you're goading him into playing better but you could do it a bit better instead of humiliating him in the papers.' He's paid plenty of bills for Malcolm Allison.

You crossed Dulcie Summerbee née Ryan at your peril. Mike Summerbee was miraculously restored to the side for the opening match against Sheffield Wednesday. Goals by Young (2), Bell and Lee gave City a comprehensive 4–1 victory.

It was still a patchy season in the league, redeemed by success in the Cup competitions. After the fiasco of Fenerbahce, there were no wild predictions from Allison this time, just a careful and methodical disposal of each opponent in turn. In March 1970, just before the ritual slaughter of Manchester United at Old Trafford, City travelled to play Academica Coimbra in the warmth of a Portuguese spring. Returning to a snow-bound Britain for their next Wembley final, their flight to London was diverted to Birmingham. They eventually arrived at their London hotel at 2 a.m. on the Friday morning. They were due to kick off against West Bromwich Albion in the League Cup final 37 hours later.

The Wembley pitch looked, in Joe Mercer's words, 'like a cabbage patch'. It was not the surface to play on with tired legs, and the prospect of extra time after a gruelling 90 minutes was not one City anticipated with relish. In the event, their worst fears were realised and with the score level at 1–1 at full-time, they had to play the extra 30 minutes, eventually running out 2–1 winners. By that time, Mike was no longer on the pitch. A long ball down field seemed to be bouncing in his favour when it scurried away from him to the Albion defender. Still haunted by Bert Head's words all those years ago, Mike refused to pull out of the tackle, went through with it and broke his leg. The seriousness of the injury was not immediately apparent and he stayed on the field for a few minutes. It was as well he did for he was instrumental in creating City's equaliser, heading on Pardoe's corner for Bell to set up Mike Doyle for the goal. If you look at the video of that moment not only does Mike not celebrate with his team-mates, he can barely move. He soon made way for Ian Bowyer, was taken to hospital for an X-ray and missed seeing Glyn Pardoe's winner as surely as the hospital missed seeing the hairline fracture of his leg.

Mike was in agony during the evening celebrations so on his return to Manchester he went for another X-ray and this time they found the break. He was back for the two legs of the European Cup-Winners' Cup semi-final against FC Schalke, which City won on aggregate 5–2, and then he played in a meaningless last league game of the season at Hillsborough where he damaged the broken leg again. The club was desperate for him to play against Gornik in the final in Vienna but, despite half a dozen pain-killing injections from the club doctor, Sidney Rose, a fitness test on the morning of the match left nobody in any doubt that he would have been a liability on the field. Mike was and always has been a wonderful team man. No matter how much he wanted to play, he knew in his heart that he couldn't risk letting down his team-mates. They had travelled so far together but they would have to complete the journey without him. With goals from Neil Young and Francis Lee, and only one in reply, they did just that.

It was Tina, the practical one, who encouraged her husband to look ahead to the prospect of life without football. She was still not used to the idea of the man of the family going off to work in the morning and coming back in time to hear the lunchtime edition of *The Archers*; she was determined that her husband wasn't going to be opening a newsagent's shop on his retirement.

Mike and George Best had already invested in a boutique. The son of George Summerbee had inherited his father's love of clothes and since his wife-to-be had once been a part-time model and his best friend was a fashion icon, it's not surprising that Mike's first business venture should be to do with fashion. The shop was called Edwardia and it opened, behind Kendall's department store, in a blaze of publicity. Edwardia had the exclusive rights to Ravel shoes but its key assets were Mike Summerbee and George Best. They each invested around £1,000 in the shop, which was to be run by Malcolm Mooney, their mutual friend.

Neither player approached the business as Francis Lee approached his off-field activities. Lee was building up his company, which recycled waste. There were no photo-shoots with skimpily dressed models but then Mike rarely kidded himself that he was a businessman. He had good ideas but they tended to benefit others and he lacked the zeal for business that his friend Francis displayed so dramatically. Edwardia was not to be the start of Mike Summerbee's career as a businessman but a place for him and George to hang out after training. I confess that as a teenager I made the occasional sortie into the shop hoping to see my hero checking the inventory, but I was never fortunate enough to do so. Still, that was presumably the ethos of the business. Both players are happy to admit that they approached the business as a means of enjoying themselves rather than as a means of making money. In this they succeeded admirably. Mike eventually got back his original investment but neither of them made anything out of the venture. Later, Mooney opened another shop of a similar nature in Sale but Mike didn't invest. By this time, Tina was urging him to exploit his local fame by going into a respectable business that would build a platform for a future career after football, and he had found a more congenial business partner.

Frank Rostron worked for John Michael in the Arcade and met Mike at Edwardia. Frank was looking for a way to open his own business and in partnership with Mike and a cutter who had made some individually tailored shirts for Mike (having measured him up, you should forgive the expression, in the toilets of a pub in Cheetham Hill Road), they began a small shirt-making business in an office off Corporation Street in the centre of Manchester. Mike's job was to build up the customer base with his vast range of contacts and Frank ran the business. It worked significantly better than Edwardia and eventually, as Tina hoped, it provided the basis for his life after retirement as a footballer. It certainly helped that by the summer of 1970 and after five unbelievably successful years in the city, there were very few people in Manchester who did not know the great Mike Summerbee.

City had now won five trophies in those five years (unlike Signor Vialli we don't count the Charity Shield), in the process becoming the first English club ever to win a European and a domestic trophy in the same season. The team Mercer and Allison had built was maturing nicely. Mike was now 28, Colin Bell was 24; youngsters Joe Corrigan, Ian Bowyer and Tommy Booth were established first-team players; Willie Donachie, Tony Towers and Derek Jeffries, products of the fertile youth-team system, had made their debuts. Matt Busby had retired and Manchester United were a spent force, the butt of jokes from City supporters in the days when the two sets of rival fans actually lived in the same town. The future could not have been brighter for Manchester City.

They blew it. There were still great games to come, great players, a growing, passionate crowd and even a trophy but the team in which Mike had been a central figure, and which should have gone on to even greater success, started to unravel. At the heart of it was the relationship between Joe Mercer and Malcolm Allison. The day after Mike signed for City, the two men sat on the coach taking the team to their first match at Middlesbrough. Joe Mercer was popping pills to steady his nerves. He couldn't possibly have imagined how much success he was shortly to enjoy when he made the fateful comment to his lieutenant that he could have the club to himself in two years' time. As it turned out, that was when City were embarking on their championship season. The greater City's achievements, the happier Joe became and the less willing he was to surrender any part of it.

Malcolm Allison couldn't walk out at the head of his team at Wembley in 1969 or 1970. He sat on the bench. He thought he had the vision but Joe was hidebound by traditional thinking. It was Joe Mercer's penny-pinching that cost City the services of Gordon Banks; he tried to beat Leicester City down to £40,000 when a further £10,000 would have sealed the move. With the best goalkeeper in the world in their team, who knows what City might have achieved?

The growing gap between the two men was exploited by others, greedy for the prestige of being seen at the helm of one of the country's top clubs. An unedifying spectacle was played out in the newspapers as Malcolm Allison's supporters on the board tried to wrest control of the club away from Albert Alexander, the incumbent chairman, and his allies who were Joe Mercer's biggest supporters. Mike and the players were understandably appalled at this internecine warfare.

It was the arseholes who came along who broke it up. They made me sick and all we could do was watch Malcolm getting sucked up into it. Joe Mercer saved his career and I felt those people had jumped on the bandwagon because of the success we'd had and were planting ideas in Malcolm's brain. I said to him the other week, 'You could never be a manager as long as you've got a hole in your arse.'

The day before an important match at Leeds, Mike, Francis Lee and Colin Bell took their coach to one side and demanded to know what was going on. Much as they respected Malcolm's work as a coach, they realised how important Joe Mercer's stabilising influence was as a corrective to Allison's style. Yet, without Allison's ability as a coach, Mercer knew that he would be severely handicapped in his ambition to keep the success going. According to press stories at the time the board had apparently fought off the takeover and, as a result, Allison's job was said to be in jeopardy. After the Leeds game (lost 1–0), Mercer told the board that if Allison was fired he would resign. The board rescinded its dismissal notice but the Mercer–Allison ship was holed beneath the waterline. It was only a question of how long it would take to sink.

It was during the following summer that I joined the club to participate in close-season training. I was horrified to see the way Joe Mercer was treated. There was no trace of the genial figure of popular mythology who had guided the club so successfully with the lightest of touches. I could see why the players revered Allison. He was a big, broad-shouldered, handsome man with great charisma. Mike still speaks of him with enormous respect.

> He's still the top man in this country as a coach. Venables is close but Malcolm's the top man. People are still afraid of him because everyone's always been vulnerable in football. We all are.

Allison was close in age and attitude to the players, enjoying the traditional activities of the professional footballer of that era – drinking and tossing money away in nightclubs and at the bookies. It was as if, having been forced to retire prematurely by the onset of tuberculosis, he had refused to acknowledge that he was no longer a player.

Within weeks of the start of the 1971–72 season, Joe Mercer was officially kicked upstairs to the post of general manager. Malcolm was the new team manager. The fans hoped that this was just a nominal rearrangement and that the partnership would continue undisturbed. From the inside, it was obvious that the partnership was in reality already just a memory.

The players were not happy at the way Mercer was being treated but they were torn in their loyalties. Mike has never lost his respect for Joe Mercer, the man who tracked him when he was at Villa, who made him feel wanted and successful. Indeed, they were so close that Joe sometimes lacked the necessary disciplinary qualities. It is doubtful if Joe would ever have humiliated Mike in the Charity Shield game the way Malcolm did.

> Joe rarely said anything to me. He thought of me as his son and I think he was too embarrassed to give me a bollocking. I was very close to him. And even when he did do it, the next day he'd come up to me and ask how I was, as if to say he was sorry. He didn't say sorry but I could have a bit of fun with him without him thinking I was being disrespectful.

That 1971–72 season was the Mercer–Allison team's last hurrah. For all the problems off the field, the players were determined to do well. Malcolm Allison was doubly motivated. If City won the championship this year, everyone would have to recognise that his was the guiding hand. Wyn Davies was bought from Newcastle and, although it cost Neil Young his place, even through the sentimental mist that descended on me I could see what Allison was planning. Davies's role was the same as Mike's had been during his time at centre-forward – holding up the ball for the forwards and midfield to join in, laying it off for Lee to run through defences. Although Davies scored just eight goals that year, Lee notched an incredible 33, still a post-war City record.

At Maine Road, the team lost just once all season after an opening-day defeat by Leeds. Spurs received their traditional four-goal thrashing. By this time, Bill Nicholson had seemingly become paranoid about his team's inability to perform there and devised a cunning plan that would have surely won Baldrick's approval. The idea was that straight from the kick-off Martin Chivers would belt the ball into touch just before the corner flag, like a rugby fly-half kicking for a line-out on the opponent's try line. The Spurs midfield would move up and Spurs would keep the pressure on City in their penalty area for as long as they could.

Unfortunately, Chivers's standing leg gave way just as he made contact and instead of soaring in a neat arc towards the corner flag, the ball shot off at right angles like an exocet. It nearly decapitated a surprised Mike Summerbee standing on the edge of the centre circle, and smashed into the face of an inoffensive old man sitting harmlessly in his seat in Row W in the Main Stand and broke his glasses. This plan was devised by a man who had long been respected as one of the tactical masters of British football.

Mike was still only 29 years old during this season. He was a seasoned professional with a top club (even if it had just committed suicide by electing Peter Swales on to the board), the owner of a large and impressive house in the country, the husband of a beautiful young wife and the father now of two children. Two days before the Spurs match Tina gave birth to a baby boy, Nicholas John. Like his father, Mike had chosen the difficult career path of the professional footballer, married a girl six years younger than himself and was now a proud paterfamilias.

To add to his feelings of accomplishment, Mike regained his place in the international side for a match against Switzerland in 1971 and went on to feature in home internationals against Wales and Northern Ireland and in the infamous Gunther Netzer-inspired win by West Germany at Wembley in the European Nations Cup in 1972. There he was joined by Francis Lee, whose last international match it turned out to be, and a new club colleague, Rodney Marsh, a pure Allison signing if ever there was one.

City were four points clear at the top of the table when Allison signed Marsh from Queens Park Rangers for £200,000. He was glamorous, skilful, an entertainer who brought in the crowds and attracted media attention. He was to be City's answer to Georgie Best. In fact, he was a disaster. The key to City's success had always been their direct style of play. Now they needed to accommodate a player who preferred to dribble towards the corner flag and stick the ball between defenders' legs rather than link the play with Summerbee, Lee and Bell.

On Easter Saturday, Stoke came to Maine Road and won 2–1. Gordon Banks had an outstanding game and made the extra £10,000 that Mercer had refused to cough up look like small change to Allison. Although the crowd sang 'Oooo Rodnee, Rodnee' the dressing room did not join in. City lost the championship to Derby County by a single point. Joe Mercer left the club and went to Coventry City. It was the beginning of the end.

When we came in one day and found that Joe Mercer was going to Coventry it was a body blow. As soon as he went we knew it was going to break up. Joe was the stabilising influence and after he went the team split up almost immediately.

Now Allison found himself with a club split in two, its greatest manager gone and boardroom problems that would take 25 years to resolve. In September 1972, City were knocked out of Europe by Valencia in the first round of the UEFA Cup and out of the League Cup by Fourth Division Bury. By the end of the month, they were lying bottom of the First Division. In March 1973, the board of directors, his board of directors, forced Allison to sell Ian Mellor to Norwich City. Three days later, Coventry City won 2–1 at Maine Road and a beaming Joe Mercer acknowledged the full-throated heartfelt cheers of a City crowd who bitterly resented the manner in which he had been treated by the club. Allison was photographed sitting in front of genial Joe, glowering at the result.

212

It was no wonder. Since Christmas, City had won precisely two games. After nearly eight years at City, Allison now found he could no longer motivate the players, some of whom had lost confidence in him. The month of March produced a 1–1 home draw and four defeats. Allison threw in the towel. He resigned as manager of Manchester City and took up a similar position at Crystal Palace. Despite the glory of a Cup run to the semi-final with Palace, Allison never achieved anything of comparable significance as a manager with any of his numerous clubs.

The players were happy enough to see Johnny Hart, their old trainer, take over as manager but they knew he was neither Joe Mercer nor Malcolm Allison, and his principal virtue was that he had been an insider during the glory years and therefore provided a degree of continuity in unsettling times. They also knew that he was not a physically robust man and it came as no surprise to them when Hart was taken to hospital seven months later. To ask him to replace both Mercer and Allison was demanding too much.

Sometimes Mike would kiss the family goodbye, drive into work and think it was just as it used to be. The ground was still impressive; the playing staff now included Denis Law as well as Lee, Bell and Marsh; the fans were as vocal and demonstrative as ever. He couldn't walk through Manchester without attracting attention from strangers (he still can't) yet something had gone out of the club.

Johnny Hart couldn't sort out the troubles that beset the club on and off the field and contacted his chairman to inform him he would have to resign. The days of the Manchester City managerial board game had arrived because the new chairman was the ill-fated, ill-starred Peter Swales, whose first public pronouncements told of his intention to rid City of its showbiz elements. He brought in a sergeant-major figure to set about this job. The man he chose was the

Norwich City manager, Ron Saunders. This combination of inept, incompetent chairman and his new manager effectively brought Mike Summerbee's playing career to an anti-climactic close.

CHAPTER TWELVE

Around Lancashire

The end of Mike's career at Maine Road infuriated me then and saddens me still. I didn't know exactly what happened until recently but I could see the malaise reflected in the style of play I was watching. Put simply, Summerbee and Lee no longer felt welcome. Saunders and Swales wanted a different type of player, and they thought their faces didn't fit any more. Excuse me? *Their* faces didn't fit?! And who was it telling them? A nudnick and a chocham – the Yiddish words are scarcely worth translating; just saying them out loud gives you their meaning. City's established stars thought Saunders set out to break their spirits like a sergeant major dealing with conscripts on national service. They saw themselves as professional players, who didn't need such handling.

The team made progress in the League Cup, but they had received a remarkably kind draw, playing Walsall, Carlisle, York City and Plymouth, all lower division clubs. Coventry provided their only First Division opposition before the final.

The FA Cup run ended in the fourth round when Brian Clough's resurgent Nottingham Forest (still a Second Division club) hammered City 4–1 early one Sunday morning during the three-day week. Howard Davies and I had left Oxford at some unearthly time on a Sunday morning to watch the then unknown Duncan McKenzie slice our defence apart with humiliating ease. As City kicked off for the fourth time inside 20 minutes, Lee remarked to Summerbee, 'I told you we weren't much of a Sunday League side.'

It was somehow fitting that this was taking place during the three-day week. Joe Gormley pulled the National Union of Mineworkers out on strike, causing widespread power cuts. In Cambridge, my new wife lit candles as the lights went out and wondered why she had ever left her native California where local phone calls were free and you paid for gas and electricity with the rent so it didn't matter how much you used. I lit candles and prayed to my dead mother's soul to keep my marriage going.

Edward Heath called a general election, challenging the country with the question 'who governs Britain?' The answer, from 636 constituencies was, 'it's the miners, stupid!' Heath was ill-advised to ignore the conventional political wisdom advocated by his predecessor in office, Harold Macmillan, who warned that there are three bodies no sensible politician directly challenges – the Roman Catholic Church, the Brigade of Guards and the National Union of Mineworkers. Harold Wilson took office, gave the miners what they wanted and the engineers and the electricians and the car workers, and NUPE and ASLEF and COHSE and SOGAT and then we had inflation heading for a rate normally associated with the banana republics of Latin America.

In early 1974, Edward Heath and Ron Saunders vied with each other for the position of who could cause more despair in our household. Saunders was simply the wrong man for City at the time, though his ability to get results was shown by his success at Aston Villa, whom he took to their only league title since 1910. We City fans never warmed to him. In February, a week before the League Cup final at Wembley, the City team travelled by train to Southampton. As they settled into their seats the players were told they couldn't leave the car in which they were travelling. Summerbee and Law exchanged glances. Halfway there, the two internationals went down to the buffet car for a cup of tea and a piece of toast. No sooner had they arrived than Ron Saunders came down the corridor, furious that his order had been ignored. Summerbee and Law continued to drink their tea.

'Go back and sit down,' said Mike, the team captain.

'We're professionals,' added Denis. 'We know what we're doing.'

Saunders, a limited player to put it kindly, went back and fumed. Denis scored the first goal and Rodney Marsh the other in a comfortable 2–0 win at the Dell, but Saunders was still not happy.

The following week, Law, Lee and Summerbee were told to stand behind the goal while the reserves and the youth team played a practice match. The much-vaunted famous five forward line of Summerbee, Bell, Lee, Law and Marsh were all told to train separately from the rest of the first-team squad. It was certainly not because they were such good players that they were too good to train with everyone else. They felt as though he was telling them that the rest of the world might consider them great players but to him they were just superannuated ballboys. It was perhaps no surprise that City went out at Wembley and lost the League Cup final to Wolves 2–1.

Mike knew he had to get away to continue his career, despite all the great memories. That was all they were now – memories. The new chairman showed what a master of psychology he was by taking down all the photographs of the Mercer–Allison side which had been on display at Maine Road and hiding them at the back of a cupboard. That really made Corrigan, Pardoe, Doyle, Booth, Oakes, Lee, Bell and Summerbee feel wanted and valued.

The week after the defeat at Wembley, on 9 March, City travelled to Elland Road for their annual 1–0 defeat by Leeds United. Mike remembers how the conversation in the players' lounge after the game took a very interesting turn.

Billy Bremner asked me if I fancied coming to Leeds, so then I knew Don Revie was going to come in for me before the transfer deadline, which was about ten days away. He wanted me as cover for Peter Lorimer. I had to be in London on the day before the deadline for the shirt business, so I left a number where I could be reached. Sure enough, I got a call from Ron Saunders. He said, 'We've agreed a fee of thirty thousand pounds for you with Leeds. Will you come back and sign before the deadline?'

I rushed back, drove to the ground and there was nobody there. Eventually I found Saunders and said to him, 'Where's Revie?' He said, 'Revie's pulled out of the deal.' I asked him why but he said he didn't know. I phoned up Don Revie. He said, 'Mike, I agreed a fee on the phone of thirty thousand pounds, which is as good as shaking hands for me. Then Swales tried to up it to fifty thousand pounds.' I found out later that the club was trying to sign Stuart Pearson from Hull and he needed the extra money for him. Revie said, 'I still want you, Mike, but I don't deal with people I don't respect. He went back on his word.' That was it for me. My life at City was over.

By this time, the players of Manchester City seemed to me to be in open revolt. On 9 April my friend Howard Davies and I stood on the terraces at Loftus Road watching City lose 3–0. They didn't just lose to a better side or give one of those inept displays you become resigned to over a lifetime of supporting a team – they looked to roll over and kick their legs in the air. I had never seen a City side play like that. It seemed to me as if they were holding a large banner draped across the width of the pitch proclaiming to the world 'We hate our manager'. QPR appeared almost embarrassed to be present at this family row and took their three goals as delicately as they could.

Howard and I noted that only Summerbee looked as though he could be bothered. Even now, in extremis as it were, Mike's innate professionalism never allowed him to turn in anything other than his best possible performance.

Swales took decisive action. Seeking now to dissociate himself from the manager – who had been doing exactly what he had been asked to do – Swales called a notorious meeting of the entire playing staff from the famous five to the apprentices. Each was encouraged to slag off the manager in front of the chairman. Francis Lee thought this was outrageous. He was no admirer of Saunders but he believed that the guy should at least be present to hear what his players were saying about him. It was not an honourable way to behave but it made no difference. Swales couldn't afford a repetition of the QPR performance. Saunders went and Tony Book, the captain of the great side, the heir apparent who had half expected the job when Johnny Hart resigned, was made the manager.

Great was the jubilation among the faithful when the news was released. Booky, the quiet man, who always nodded a smiling welcome to me in the morning when I trained with them, seemed the logical choice. He also smoked which came as a huge surprise to me but he was reputedly over 80 years old when he retired and still as fit as a fiddle. Howard and I had long assumed that the players' campaign had been specifically designed to replace Saunders with their former skipper.

Book's side which had flirted with relegation during that abysmal 1973–74 season concluded with two victories. The second one was the infamous 1–0 win at Old Trafford when Denis Law's instinctive backheel sent United down into the Second Division. For the old City hands it was a memorable day and the coach taking the players home celebrated by driving through the centre of town so they could see the faces of the relegated Reds' fans. I remember it as a day of incipient violence. You knew it was going to happen but you didn't necessarily know when. Appropriately it came eight minutes from time as Stepney stooped to retrieve the ball from the net. The move had involved Summerbee, Bell and Lee before Law finished it off. Neither Denis nor Francis Lee kicked a ball for City again.

Denis retired but Francis was transferred against his will to Derby County by Tony Book, who disappointingly to many seemed too close to Peter Swales. Book's appointment should have brought success in the wake of peace and harmony. It certainly brought limited success over the next three years but at a cost. For Mike, Tony Book's succession to the title produced a Solomon–Rehoboam situation. For the few of you not entirely familiar with the First Book of Kings – confusingly, also called the Third Book of Kings – Rehoboam, the newly enthroned son of the late King Solomon, begins his reign with the sort of political gaffe now associated with Ann Widdecombe: 'And the king answered the people roughly and forsook the old men's counsel that they gave him; and spake to them saying, "My father chastised you with whips but I shall chastise you with scorpions." ' If Mike Summerbee thought that life was going to get better for him under Tony Book, he was in for a rude shock. Swales might have lost one manager to player power but appointing Tony Book and then forcing him to proceed with the same policy meant that he now had a PR card in reserve to play if things got too hot for him. Besides, it was unlikely that the players could be united against Book as they were against Saunders.

I felt that Tony as manager was completely different from the guy I'd roomed with and eaten with and worked with for years. I helped him to become Footballer of the Year in 1969 because he only had to pass the ball ten or fifteen yards to me. He was a good reader of the game and a good skipper. He knew what kind of people Francis and I were but he didn't know how to handle us properly. I know it's different when you become the manager but if you work with someone for a long time and you've been with someone through thick and thin, even if you do become their manager you should know how to handle them. But he didn't. Simple as that. He changed and my relationship with him has never been the same since. I just say hello to him now.

It's a damning indictment and for my generation of Manchester City supporters an extremely sad one, rivalling the future breakdown in relations between Colin Bell and Mike during Francis Lee's Second Coming.

In his last season, Mike played just 26 games for the first team. At various times his No. 7 shirt was worn by Phil Henson, Barney Daniels, Mickey Horswill and Ged Keegan. I know, I know. It defies belief. Mike played in a comprehensive 4–1 defeat at Anfield on Boxing Day 1974 and was dropped for the next match, against Derby County, two days later. While Mike was playing for the reserves against Bury Reserves at Gigg Lane, Francis Lee made a spectacular return to Maine Road scoring a famous winning goal for Derby at the Platt Lane end and celebrating in front of the home supporters. The *Match of the Day* cameras and Barry Davies's hysterical commentary recorded the moment for posterity. To me it felt like an own goal and I would have preferred it if Francis had behaved as Denis Law did after his backheeled goal against United. I did not know, of course, what Lee had had to suffer at the club. Now I assume that those celebrations were for the benefit of Peter Swales rather than directed at us who had revered him for so long.

When Mike returned from Gigg Lane to discover what his friend had done, he was delighted. This was not a healthy atmosphere. On 22 March 1975, he played his last game for the Manchester City first team, a 1–0 victory at home over Coventry City. Dennis Tueart scored the only goal and he and Peter Barnes were to ensure with their exciting wing play that the fans didn't dwell too much on Mike's departure.

In the summer of 1975, Mike Summerbee left Manchester City where he had spent the key ten years of his career and joined Burnley. The headlines that day were made not by his departure but by the arrival at Maine Road of the England centre-half Dave Watson from Sunderland for £275,000. As a footnote it was announced that with the signing of Watson, City would drop their interest in Alan Ball for whom they had bid £100,000. Arsenal had wanted £150,000. If only that studied lack of interest in Alan Ball had been made legally permanent, many thousands of people would have had their lives greatly enriched.

I was sad to see Mike go. He was always (and, as you can see, still is) the player I most enjoyed watching in a pale blue shirt. But I'm a fan, and though my memory is longer than most, my emotions are wrapped up in the club I support. I would see him occasionally on television in the next year or two wearing a different coloured shirt and experience a glow of nostalgia for the old hero but my heart remained at Maine Road no matter where Mike would now wander.

Burnley's Jimmy Adamson and Dusty Miller had said to Mike, 'Don't leave your house, just come over and play for us.' It was a relief to be out of what he clearly felt had become a poisonous atmosphere at Maine Road, and Burnley treated Mike particularly well, especially as the transfer was conducted with the unpleasantness that seemed to surround Peter Swales's transactions.

It was great at first because I was on a free transfer and then suddenly Peter Swales decided he wanted twenty-five thousand for me. I'd given them ten years and we'd won everything. I'd made a contribution to that and now when I had the chance of a decent contract at a superb club like Burnley they could have said, 'Goodbye and thanks for everything you've done.' Instead, they asked for twenty-five grand. Bob Lord said to Swales, 'Right, we'll pay it, but we won't be dealing with you any more.'

Mike drove over to Turf Moor and signed for Burnley on the same day that Willie Morgan made his return trip to Burnley from Manchester for a further £32,000. Jimmy Adamson introduced Mike to the chairman Bob Lord.

I was a bit concerned because Lord had the reputation of being a tough guy. There was a large shiny desk in the room and there was nothing on it except the contract. I sat down and looked at it for the first time. It was a fantastic contract – inflation-proof. At that time inflation was going berserk, up by twenty-five per cent a year or something. I said as much to Bob Lord. He said, 'You deserve that.' I asked him why, what he meant. 'You've met Jimmy Adamson and Dusty Miller four times now and you've never mentioned money,' he said. 'That's your reward.' I signed immediately. He was a superb man and Jimmy Adamson was brilliant.

Mike found it a relief to join a club where he made immediate friends with players and supporters.

I had a great time with those lads – Colin Waldron, Dougie Collins, Jim Thompson, Peter Noble, Taffy [Leighton] James, Ray Hankin, Brian Flynn, Paul Fletcher, really a great bunch of lads. I had a fabulous time there. I played outside-right, sometimes inside-right, and when they were struggling I played full-back. The crowd understood and liked me and I had a bit of fun with them.

The Burnley crowd appreciated Summerbee's attitude – you gave everything you could for the cause but if you lost there was no law of football that decreed you couldn't also demonstrate your enjoyment of the game. As an injured player lay on the ground near the touchline being treated, Mike would stand over him and indulge in banter with the crowd. Sometimes his relationship with the crowd became even more expansive. Youthful supporter Alastair Campbell, currently Chief Press Secretary at 10 Downing Street, vividly remembers a game just before Christmas 1976 away at Notts County. The match was called off after the Burnley supporters had arrived at the ground, leaving them irritated and frustrated. During the referee's inspection of the pitch, Campbell and his girlfriend edged nearer to the players' tunnel and were thrilled when Mike came out to talk to them.

'He was still there when the game was called off,' Campbell remembers, 'and he invited us to the players' bar for a drink. We left the worse for wear, hours later. I have a vague memory of him selling some shirts to the other players.'

One incident from Mike's time at Burnley gives an indication of how much he enjoyed his time there. It occurred during a very hot pre-season training session. For a change of scenery, coach Dave Merrington took the players up to a plateau on the moors.

We ended up training in the middle of nowhere; there were no trees or anything like that to guide us as a landmark. We did exercises and running and everything and when we'd finished, Dave said, 'Right, back on the bus.' We looked round and no one knew which way to go. We were all lost. We decided to split up into groups. I was with Ray Hankin and Fletch. We went the wrong way, up and down the moors, past reservoirs and on for miles until we ended up in Skipton. Only we had no money and we just had our training gear on.

Through the kindness of a Burnley-supporting bus driver, they eventually made their way back to the training ground at Gawthorpe Hall. By this time it was past three o'clock and they were comfortably the last group to arrive. The conclusion was that they had been on an extended pub crawl but it was regarded as a joke rather than a breach of discipline. We can only speculate on how Ron Saunders might have viewed such an incident.

Sadly, for all the fact that Mike enjoyed his time there, results started badly and deteriorated from there. It looked like a good side on paper – Summerbee and James on the wings, Morgan, Flynn and Collins in midfield with Peter Noble and Ray Hankin up front – but the combination mysteriously only ever worked fitfully. Burnley had won the Second Division championship in 1973 and reached the FA Cup semi-final in 1974, losing to Newcastle, but they failed to sustain their success.

We were a good side in the mid seventies with lots of good players, but in those years there were so many good sides. I think it was me who set Burnley on their decline. My pal Mike King, the comedian said, 'Burnley signed him for a record fee and regretted every single penny.'

Burnley took six points from the first ten games and by the end of September they had managed only one win although even amid the wreckage of another home defeat, this time 0–1 by Leeds United, it was noted in the local paper that 'Summerbee followed up his outstanding display against Sheffield United with his best home performance so far.' Shortly afterwards they were hammered 4–0 at St Andrews by Birmingham City who had lost their manager, Freddie Goodwin, the day before when they were residing in 21st place. The victory allowed them to swap positions with Burnley who couldn't keep their heads above water thereafter.

Unlike Francis Lee's epic return to Maine Road, Mike's matches against Manchester City both finished in dull, scoreless draws. City went on to win the League Cup that year, their last trophy to date, the 1999 Second Division play-off final trophy notwithstanding. Mike experienced again that unpleasant sinking sensation he remembered so well from his last days at Swindon Town 11 years previously. It wasn't quite as desperate this time round of course. At Swindon he was worried that his entire career might go down the pan if no decent club came in for him. At the age of nearly 34, he knew he'd achieved enough in football not to worry about failing to leave his mark on the game – and on a few defenders.

Despite being in his twilight years and on the best contract of his life (£350 a week), Mike continued to fight for the Burnley cause. The fighting was noticeable in his very first pre-season warm-up game, which took place at Plymouth.

I got involved with the Plymouth full-back just in front of the dugout. Their trainer, Alan Brown, the ex-Sunderland player, started ranting and raving at me so I just wound him up further. Anyway, after the game he came into the players' lounge like a bull, looking for me. Johnny Crossan had warned me about him. I'd never seen anything like it.

Alastair Campbell kept a cutting from the *Daily Express* of Mike Summerbee pictured with fists raised and a smile on his face above a caption reading 'Anyone fancy a bash at the Burnley Battler?' He also recalls an incident in a midweek match at Bramall Lane in which Leighton James was fouled on the edge of the penalty area on the left-hand side of the field. Summerbee was 70 yards away on the opposite wing and watched the inevitable skirmish with growing interest. The referee eventually calmed things down and Leighton

James prepared to take the kick. As he did so, Summerbee arrived at the end of his 70-yard sprint and tried to reignite the flames by squaring up to the defender who had begun the incident by fouling James.There was absolutely no reason for Summerbee to adopt this attitude of wilful aggression but it was exactly the kind of incident that left Campbell with such a vivid and positive memory of the man. There may be some justified scepticism among fans at the manner in which certain politicians scrounge for votes by pretending a passion for football they do not feel, but of Alastair Campbell's own fanatical devotion to the cause of Burnley Football Club nobody should entertain the slightest doubt.

It wasn't just these acts of unprovoked aggression which so endeared him to Burnley supporters. There were still moments of sublime Summerbee skill left to savour. One afternoon he so tormented his opposing left-back that a fan was recently moved to write to Campbell in order to relate

the most unexpected thing ... which I have never witnessed before, or after, by any player in my 50 years' support of Burnley FC. Summerbee got down on one knee immediately in front of the startled defender as if to tie his left shoe lace, or as if to be knighted, for what seemed like eons with the ball directly in front of him. Not only was the left-back transfixed but the fans were also partly amused and partly perplexed, not knowing what was going on. Then he calmly raised himself, continued his dribble round the hapless defender and the game continued. For sheer audacity and confidence in his own ability that incident will live with me for ever.

Despite these burnished memories results continued to disappoint. The one bright spot in an otherwise depressing year was Burnley's run in the League Cup. Summerbee was outstanding at Anfield where Burnley drew before disposing of Liverpool in the replay at Turf Moor. As Campbell notes, 'He always looked the part on the bigger stages.' The stages, however, continued to get smaller. In the first week of 1976, Jimmy Adamson was sacked and moved to Sparta Rotterdam. He was replaced by Joe Brown but the slide continued unabated.

Burnley were relegated on Easter Monday after a depressing 0–1 home defeat by Manchester United who arguably had their impending (and ultimately losing) appearance against Southampton in the FA Cup final on their minds. The local paper, while writing the obituary notice, nevertheless observed, 'Summerbee continued where he left off in the previous match [a 1–0 win at Newcastle], showing the younger members of the team a thoroughly professional example by his enterprising approach and use of the ball.'

There followed the usual clear-out of unwanted players. Colin Waldron and Doug Collins were among six players shipped out on free transfers; Mick Docherty, son of Tommy, ended up at Manchester City. Mike stayed but his body was starting to betray him. A groin strain that he should have been able to shrug off in a week or two gave him persistent discomfort. The new season didn't look as though it was going to lead to an immediate triumphant return to the First Division so when Blackpool came in for him just before Christmas 1976, Burnley offered him the chance to move on a free transfer. In one way he was extremely sorry to go.

> I enjoyed Burnley. They were a fantastic club and I found
> the people round Burnley very similar to Manchester City
> supporters. There's lots of them and they're very loyal –
> they support the club through thick and thin.

If Mike had hoped for an Indian summer at Blackpool he was to be confronted instead by grey skies, a vicious wind along the prom, white horses on the Irish Sea and a shuttered Pleasure Beach. It was all brought on by that persistent groin strain. The problem with pelvic injuries is that you can't see them. Mike tried his best but it appears that the Blackpool management thought he was shamming. After all those years of going through brick walls for his team, it is sad and ironic that he should be faced with such an accusation right at the end of his career.

It didn't help that, as he discovered after he got there, his transfer had been the idea of the club's chairman rather than the manager, Allan Brown (no relation to the man still tearing through the players' lounge at Plymouth looking for him). Brown had been a Blackpool player during the great days of the Matthews–Mortensen era. He and Mike did not get on, although Mike admits that he really shouldn't have gone there in the first place.

> I couldn't get the injury right. I just wasn't fit and when I got there I said, 'Cancel the contract,' because I just couldn't perform. Allan Brown had no idea. He thought I might be pulling the wool over their eyes. I went to see a specialist called Markham and he looked at the X-ray and said, 'Well, at your age, you might as well retire.' He said it just like that, as if it meant nothing. My whole life as a footballer would have ended just like that.

As the Chancellor of the Exchequer, Denis Healey, cut public spending and begged the International Monetary Fund for loans to bail out the country which was suffering the consequences of rampant inflation, Mike Summerbee made a grand total of three first-team appearances for Blackpool during the rest of that unsatisfactory 1976–77 season. He had a growing family to think about and a thriving handmade shirt business to worry about. More to the point, he had lost that blistering burst of speed that used to leave full-backs trailing in his wake. Full-backs were catching him now or, as he himself puts it, 'Managers were catching me now, never mind full-backs.' Maybe retirement was for the best. Tina was certainly of that opinion but Mike still couldn't let it go. Football was in his blood.

Mike met Freddie Pye who expressed an interest in taking him to Stockport County if he could regain his fitness. The physiotherapist Freddie Griffiths eventually effected a repair job and at the start of the 1977–78 season, Blackpool sent him off to Fourth Division Stockport on loan. At the beginning of October the move was made permanent.

As at Burnley, Mike soon showed he wasn't there just for the weekly wage packet and thoroughly committed himself to the cause. Over Christmas on an ice-bound pitch at Oakwell, he produced a display reminiscent of the ballet on ice against Tottenham ten years before. He retained the ability to keep his feet on a treacherous surface while all around him were going down like ninepins. He even survived being attacked by frustrated home fans – shaping to take a corner kick, he was bombarded by snowballs thrown by frozen Barnsley fans. Greatly amused, Mike gestured grandly for police protection. He didn't care. They won 1–0 to take County to the fringes of the promotion race. It is a measure of social change that, in similar circumstances, Beckham is now pelted with pound coins. Nobody at Barnsley was going to throw away hard-earned brass in 1977, even before Thatcher and Heseltine destroyed their local industry.

The player–manager at Edgeley Park was the 26-year-old Alan Thompson but after he found the combination too arduous with a bad run of seven defeats in eight games during February and March 1978, Mike was invited to succeed him. Twenty-eight years after George Summerbee became the player–manager of Cheltenham Town in a last desperate bid to maintain a toe-hold in the game, his younger son took on the same responsibility.

Mike was as full of plans as George had been and he quickly made use of his wide variety of contacts in the interests of his new club. He attracted some good players to Stockport, including George Armstrong from the Arsenal double-winning side on a free transfer, Phil Henson, who had been an apprentice at Manchester City, from Sparta Rotterdam for £11,000 and Les Bradd from Notts County for a bargain £15,000. Armstrong was not a success but Bradd was an inspired signing, giving the sort of total commitment that Mike immediately recognised. Stuart Lee came from Wrexham on a free transfer, scored a few goals and was quickly sold on to Manchester City for £112,000 on the same day that Steve Daley was signed by Swales and the newly returned Malcolm Allison for over £1,400,000.

Despite the pantomime that would shortly engulf Maine Road as Allison seemed to the fans to be selling good players and buying bad ones at inflated sums and yet still hope to win the European Cup and turn a profit (he couldn't), Mike was quick to pay tribute to his old coach as the inspiration behind his training ideas. Allison would no doubt have approved of Mike's total overhaul of Stockport's poor facilities at the Silver Wings training ground in Timperley.

We were struggling for gear – it was rubbish to be honest. The Lacrosse World Cup was shortly to take place at County, teams from all over the world were coming, but the showers were hanging off the wall and the tiles were cracked. I talked to the Quiliogotti family who are old friends and got the whole training area redone – a hundred thousand pound job for five hundred and a couple of seats in the directors' box. I got the Argentinian World Cup strip with the County badge sewn on it from a great friend at Adidas, and boots and fifty balls, all for nothing, but soon after I left the Falklands War broke out and they couldn't use the strips any more.

The highlight of Mike's managerial career was his last

performance at Old Trafford, the scene of so many of his previous triumphs. In the second round of the League Cup, Stockport had been drawn at home to United but Freddie Pye's financial reality clouded any romantic thoughts Mike may have harboured of beating United at home. The tie was switched to Old Trafford and Mike was thus determined to beat United in front of 42,000 on their own ground.

Stockport went a goal down to a Joe Jordan header after ten minutes but nevertheless took the game to United. In the second half, Summerbee and Bradd gave the shaky United defence a torrid time. Lou Macari spent the game chasing Mike, so worried were United by what the old campaigner could still do to them. Paddy Roche, the panic-stricken United goalkeeper, brought down Stuart Lee and Alan Thompson scored from the resultant penalty. With 12 minutes to go, Terry Park burst through a feeble tackle from Brian Greenhoff, sprung United's fragile offside trap and drove home what everyone thought would be the winning goal.

Two minutes from time, just after he had sent off Gordon McQueen, the referee awarded United a contested free kick on the edge of the area. Sammy McIlroy's shot was unluckily deflected past Rogan in the County goal. Sixty seconds later the referee was pointing to the penalty spot amidst a storm of protest. Jimmy Greenhoff stroked home the penalty and Stockport were out. Summerbee led his team on a well-deserved lap of honour round the ground. The weak, indecisive and petulant United players slunk away to be deservedly knocked out in the next round by Watford. This time not even the partisan home crowd could save their blushes.

The inevitable bad patch for Mike came along shortly after the start of the 1978–79 season. On 13 October, Stockport went to Valley Parade and were crushed 6–1. They were then 17th in the Fourth Division and appeared to have slipped back down the snake having painstakingly hauled themselves up the ladders. Mike spoke to the press after the defeat in

Yorkshire, attempting to put the traditional managerial brave face on things.

'We're not such a bad side really,' he said. 'We gave away two silly goals and they finished by giving us a football lesson.'

On the following Wednesday, Mike resigned as player–manager of Stockport County. Freddie Pye said, 'We've called it a draw. Mike found it very difficult, playing, managing and at the same time running his shirt business.'

Mike Doyle was allegedly keen to take over but Pye was now wary of someone with an outside business interest and Doyle had for years been running a motor dealership. During the great days, the City programme had always contained an advert reading 'Why not shoot over and see Mike Doyle?' which I had always reconfigured in my mind as 'Why not see Mike Doyle shoot over?' – which I had done, a lot.

It was more than just the results that caused Mike to withdraw from the job. He had disagreed with Pye about the sale of Derek Loadwick to Hartlepool for £6,000 and with another director about the purchase of Lawson, the former Everton goalkeeper, for £10,000. Having his judgement questioned by those who knew less about the game and whose opinions he did not respect was the final straw for Mike. Freddie Pye generously paid up the remainder of his contract and that was it. Two months short of 20 years since he had made his Football League debut for Swindon Town at home to Bournemouth, Mike Summerbee retired. He was nearly 37 years old.

> I said goodbye to the lads, slung my boots in the dustbin and next day I was out selling shirts – I sold thirty that first day. I didn't miss it, you know. I really didn't. I played one Sunday morning for one of Francis Lee's charities and he said, 'If you were a racehorse, they'd shoot you,' so I thought that was pretty much the end.

Only it wasn't quite. There was a final coda at Mossley of all unlikely places. Bob Murphy, who managed the local football club, was a friend and customer of Mike's and during the season after Mike retired he mentioned that he was short of players and asked Mike if he would mind turning out as a favour. Mike, being Mike, said yes, not really believing the situation would arise. So when Murphy rang him two days before the FA Cup first-round tie against Crewe Alexandra, it was with some trepidation that Mike agreed to play. Murphy tried to make it as easy as he could for Mike.

'Can you get here by two o'clock on the day?' he asked cautiously.

Mike thought of the pain involved and the very strong likelihood that he would be making a total pillock of himself.

'I'll be there at one. I'll need two hours to warm up.'

'I'll probably bring you on as sub in the last thirty minutes.'

'Listen, you'd better play me from the start. I told you, it'll take me two hours to warm up. The crowd'll have gone home before I'm ready. If I'm an embarrassment, you can bring me off any time.'

The manager of Crewe at the time was Tony Waddington. One look at Summerbee in the colours of the opposition and the former Stoke City manager's face dropped.

'Oh no! Not you again. I thought I'd finished with you,' he groaned, remembering previous encounters when Summerbee had destroyed his careful plans. His fears were well founded although the home crowd were none too impressed at the sight of this 38-year-old taking the field, looking a little heavier than his fighting weight.

'Oi, Summerbee!' yelled one diehard local supporter. 'What are you doing out there, you useless fat bastard?'

He didn't know Mike's propensity for bantering with the crowd.

'How does five hundred quid sound to you?' he yelled back.

It was a lie of course. Mike was playing for free as a favour to Murphy but the supporter wasn't to know that and he shut up. At half time it was 0–0 and the manager gratefully clapped Summerbee on the back and thrust a cup of tea into his hands.

'Well done, Mike. Sit down and drink this.'

'I can't sit down,' said the exhausted Summerbee. 'If I sit down now I'll never stand up again.' He spent half-time on the move round the dressing room.

The Mossley pitch had a slight slope which was unnoticeable for the first 45 minutes, but in the second half Mike felt as if he were running up Mount Kilimanjaro. Five minutes from the end, with the game still scoreless, Mossley were awarded a corner. Mike took it and the ball finished up in the back of the net. The following day, all the papers were digging out their old 'Hero Summerbee' headlines but by his own admission he had made minimal impact on the game.

'I tell you what, though. I was so sore afterwards that it took me about five months to recover. That was when I knew I really was finished.'

It was the end of his career and the end of the 1970s, a decade that had begun with a League Cup final victory at Wembley. Now it was 1979 and Mrs Thatcher was in Downing Street, shutting down Britain's manufacturing industry and nursing the unemployment figures towards the three million mark. Mike's career in football seemed to me to belong to the world of Harold Wilson, seminally influenced as it was by a childhood spent in the days of post-war austerity and a maturity in the days of 60s prosperity. The time when Hugh Scanlon could manoeuvre the tanks of his engineering union on to the lawns of 10 Downing Street was past. Union power belonged to history, like Mike Summerbee's football career.

Tina was looking forward to having him home more. The children were growing up; Rachel was ten and Nicholas was eight. A happy family life and a small business were the prospects for the next few years. It seemed inevitable that Mike Summerbee the professional footballer would be replaced by Mike Summerbee the shirt manufacturer. It was a big surprise to everyone when Mike Summerbee the footballer was replaced by Mike Summerbee the movie star.

CHAPTER THIRTEEN

Budapest to Swindon

It all began one spring day in 1980 when the telephone rang in Hatherlow House. It was Bobby Moore, who uttered the fateful words, 'Do you want to be a film star? They're making a film in Budapest. Do you fancy it?'

Mike went to London and met the casting director as a result of which he got the part of Syd Harmer, outside-right and currently right inside a German prisoner of war camp. No acting lessons, no drama school, no humiliating auditions to play a chicken in a KFC commercial, no curt negative responses from the National Theatre or the RSC – if this was acting, it looked like an easier living than professional football. Recruiting other players for *Escape to Victory* starring Sylvester Stallone was not difficult. Some of the Ipswich Town team had apparently also been captured by the Germans. It cut into pre-season training so they knew they were on to a good thing and didn't argue much about money and not at all about billing. No wonder the casting director liked them.

Tina and the children were going to be on holiday in Portugal for the six weeks that Mike was expected to be on location in Budapest. They weren't too fussed about his disappearance. He'd done plenty of filming before, giving his opinions on football in general or a particular match. As far as they were concerned, he was just doing a few days' filming for Granada.

Mike's experience of Hollywood film-making was almost entirely pleasurable.

When we were there, most of the filming was of us so there was very little hanging about. We were working nearly all the time. We had very few days off. It made me appreciate how difficult it is to be an actor. It's not easy hanging around after you've got up at a very early hour of the morning. It's not as easy as people think. Plus you've got a script. Mind you, most of the stuff we did was ad libbed. That was the way John Huston wanted it.

It's fairly clear from watching the film that what John Huston knew about the sport of Association Football could be written in marker pen on a linesman's flag. Huston is an interesting director, a man who moved easily from personal films to hack studio work with equal facility. The man who made *The African Queen*, *The Maltese Falcon* and *The Treasure of the Sierra Madre* was also capable of putting his name to such turkeys as *The Barbarian and the Geisha*, *The Bible* and *A Walk with Love and Death*. Although a big fan of American sports, the only footballer he had ever heard of was Pelé – which is why Pelé had also been incarcerated in this extraordinary POW camp along with Ossie Ardiles, Bobby Moore, Mike Summerbee and Russell Osman.

For Mike, the six weeks in Budapest, billeted in a luxury hotel with plenty of spending money, were like a well-paid holiday. Unfortunately, John Huston directed the film as if he, too, was lying on a sun lounger. The footballers didn't care. They thought they were film stars and were amused to find that the actors all wanted to be footballers. Maurice Roeves, Tim Piggott Smith and Clive Merrison used to come out for a kick around with the lads most mornings. Mike took to the discipline of filming like a duck to water.

In the final scene where Sly Stallone has to save the penalty, there's a close-up of me sweating, encouraging him, saying, 'Come on, Hatch, you can do it.' They sprayed me with water. Stallone said to me, 'Just act normal. Be yourself.' Huston said, 'OK, Mike, you know what to do,' and I did it on the first take. Huston said, 'Cut! Print that one!' and I said, 'Clark Gable was never like that, was he?'

Huston was forced to agree but then the last film Huston made with Gable was the Arthur Miller scripted *The Misfits* and Gable died during its making.

Predictably, Mike took to the hedonistic side of movie-making with equal facility.

Most of the players went as soon as the football scenes were completed and there were only four of us left – Russell Osman, John Wark, Mooreo and myself – so we threw a party for John Huston in a suite in the hotel. The weather was so hot that we put six cases of wine into the bath, which we filled up with ice. Huston came and had a ball. 'If you're ever in Puerto Vallarta,' he said to us afterwards, 'make sure you come down and see me.'

His younger daughter Allegra came and stayed with us at the house in Hatherlow. She was very attractive. One night we were at a do together and she said to me, 'Come on, Mike. Dance with me like you did that night in Budapest.' Tina overheard and wasn't impressed. Allegra left shortly afterwards. I think she was evicted. Tina always said it was the worst part of our marriage because I thought I was some sort of superstar when I came home.

The reason Bobby Moore suggested Mike for the part was that they were good friends and got on well together. They had first met when Mike was 16 and Moore was 18. They roomed together on England tours and the room was always spotlessly clean. They were very similar in many ways, especially the tidy way they looked after themselves and the way they dressed.

> It's terrible for someone who's tidy to be with someone who's untidy. At City, I roomed mostly with Booky and he had to be tidy otherwise we wouldn't have stayed room-mates. Francis fluctuated between Tommy Booth and one or two others. His room-mate had to be in the bed by the door so that if room service knocked it was him and not Francis who had to get out of bed and open it. I couldn't room with Francis now because of the snoring. The last time, I got up at 2 a.m. and went and slept in my car outside. I was laughing for half an hour.

If Bobby was in Manchester he would always stay with the Summerbee family at Hatherlow. Bobby Moore was a true hero in a game which doesn't always respect its heroes and Moore's treatment by the game's administrators after he retired was a national disgrace. Despite his unfailing tidiness and courtesy Moore had one major problem. He hated sleeping alone, as the young Nicholas Summerbee was to discover.

> I was in bed asleep and I felt someone pushing me over and getting into bed with me. He got up in the morning and left. I came down in the morning and I said to Dad, 'I think Bobby Moore slept in me bed last night,' and he said, 'Yeah, he would have. He gets lonely at nights.' When Dad played for England he said they'd wake up in the morning and there'd be three fellers in bed together. They couldn't get to sleep on their own.

In 1980, when his dad made *Escape to Victory* with Bobby Moore, Nick Summerbee was nine years old and coming to the end of his Jimmy Greenhoff phase. Greenhoff with his blond hair had been Nick's first soccer hero, as a consequence of which he became a Manchester United fan. He persuaded his embarrassed parents to buy the United kit and proudly wore Greenhoff's No. 8 on his back. So total was his identification with the former Stoke City player that he issued a demand that his name be changed to Nicky Jimmy Summerbee. They weren't buying that one.

When Nick was eight and Rachel was ten, the house next door to Hatherlow was bought by Peter and Mary Cobb with whom the Summerbees struck up an immediate friendship. The Cobb girls were a little older than Rachel but they shared an interest in horses, which later became Rachel's consuming passion. Peter Cobb was a City fan, the son of a City fan who had watched his team play at Hyde Road before the Maine Road stadium was built in 1923. Nicholas, inevitably, took enormous pleasure in sitting by the gate waiting for Peter to come home in order to taunt him mercilessly about City's defeat that day. This was 1979–80, the time of Malcolm Allison's Second Coming, of Steve Daley and humiliating Cup defeats at Shrewsbury and Halifax. Nick was a true Red – he rarely went to matches at Old Trafford but he made his parents buy him the kit. Unfortunately, when he signed for City some of this history was to leak out in quite the wrong way. Nick was always more interested in playing than in watching football.

The large garden at the rear of Hatherlow House made a perfect pitch for the football-obsessed boy, and the gardener, George Batey, soon became a major influence in Nick's life. George was not just a gardener but a general handyman around the house. He seemed to spend more time there than its titular owner.

We used to stop George from working in the garden and make him play five-a-side with us. He was an old man was George and he must have been knackered going

241

home on a Saturday. We used to put him through it – bringing him down with sliding tackles and all that. I mean, he was supposed to be there doing stuff for the house but I don't remember him doing anything. When I played in the Sunday leagues he used to drive us all there. He used to love it. Dad stayed distant from all that except when there was a big game on. Dad wasn't a part of it, but George was.

Tina wanted Nicholas to work with either food or photography because he displayed an early interest in both. His interest in football she attributed to his age rather than any genetic inheritance. To this end, she enrolled him at Hillcrest, a local private school where Rachel was already a pupil, but the appeal of academic life was as lost on Nick as it had been on his father. All he, too, ever wanted to do was to play football.

His general lack of interest in school inevitably brought him into conflict with the headmaster. Being an expensive private school, Hillcrest reserved the right to beat the children of the parents who paid them so handsomely. Unlike Mike's day when this was a routine matter, the headmaster had to request permission from the parents before ritually caning a pupil. Nick had no doubt that this was a legal loophole he could exploit.

They had to ring up Dad to ask permission. I thought, 'My old man'll get me out of this one,' but he just said, 'Go ahead, beat the hell out of him.' That night when I came home, Dad was in the bath laughing his head off.

Nick hated school. The only lesson he showed any interest in was cookery. There was a large room at the top of the building which had been turned into a kitchen and cookery lessons became the one period in the week he looked forward to. To this day his interest in cooking has remained intense and his fiancée, Leonie, is delighted to find herself in a relationship in which she is banned from the kitchen when Nick is making dinner.

Reluctantly, Tina accepted that there was no point in forcing the boy to go down an academic road he was so reluctant to travel. Mike recognised that if Nick wanted to be a footballer as badly as it appeared he did, that was at least a sound start. Without that dedication and determination, the game would simply swallow him whole and spit him out as it had so many other young hopefuls. Tina did not at first appreciate the difficulty Nick would encounter in being taken seriously by a professional club. She and Rachel both thought his name and his obvious talent would be sufficient. Mike knew the game and didn't share this sublime certainty. Nick, inevitably, went to Manchester City for a trial as soon as he was old enough. It was not a success.

> They had hundreds of kids there from all over the country. I made no impact at all. If I had, I'm sure they'd have rung back. So I started going to United at the Cliff on Tuesday and Thursday nights.

At United, Nicky soon found himself swamped by the vast numbers of kids who had felt similarly about Jimmy Greenhoff. He liked the coach Eric Harrison, who was responsible for bringing on the bright crop of youngsters in the early 1990s, but the sheer impossibility of making the grade at Manchester United overwhelmed him and after one summer holiday, he decided not to return.

His father never pushed him to achieve. Mike was no doubt subconsciously recalling his own experiences as a kid and the way in which George had so blatantly ignored him. Hard as it might have been at the time, it stoked his ambition; the fire to succeed burned brightly inside Mike. Maybe the same would be true for Nicholas. Meanwhile, there were still the Sunday league games with Poynton Boys to absorb Nick and George the gardener; Mike continued to keep his distance. Nick didn't mind too much. He could see only too well the way the other fathers behaved and he was not anxious to see his own father caught up in the traditional Sunday morning aggravation.

> You'd see some of the kids' dads really getting involved – it was quite an eye opener. He didn't want to be one of those and we accepted that. When he did turn up he always would get involved, nearly getting into a fight with some other bloke or arguing with people. I didn't want him to be like those other kids' dads so I was happy he stayed out of the way. It would have been really embarrassing.

In 1987, despite his background and pedigree, Nicholas John Summerbee was just another young hopeful with no guarantee of employment. Mike knew somebody on the board at Norwich City who arranged for Nick to have a trial and it was at Carrow Road that Nick thought he would be making his Football League debut.

> My first trial was at Norwich when I was fourteen or fifteen. The trials were to see if you could get a YTS apprenticeship after you finished school. I was born in August so I was young for my school year. I'd have been fifteen when I finished school in July 1987, but sixteen by the first of September when the school year started again.

It was the first time Nick had ever left home and he was understandably nervous when his father dropped him off at a bed and breakfast hostel where the other trialists were also staying. Fortunately for him, the name Summerbee meant nothing to the other boys of his own age; only the first team and the coaching staff were aware that Nick was Mike's son.

Even though he had been around football and footballers all his life, Nick was shocked by his first genuine experience of the world of professional football.

> I was there for about two weeks. The bloke who ran it was really strict. He went ballistic at us. Everything was fucking this and fucking that. I was gobsmacked. It really bothered me. I mean, we weren't apprentices, we weren't getting paid. I thought it would be along the lines of, 'Go on, get out there and enjoy it. If you're good enough we'll soon see' – but it wasn't.

Still, this was what he had dreamed about for as long as he could remember. He was not going to wimp out now and he applied himself diligently to the work, expecting to be told that he had passed the first exam he had ever cared about. Back at home, Tina was worrying about his welfare but she, too, never had a moment's doubt that Nick was good enough. They were both wrong. Towards the end of the second week he was pulled to one side and given the dreaded news.

> This bloke said to me, 'You're not what we want. It's just not right so I wish you all the very best in whatever you're going to do.' I held it in at first but I was crying by the time I phoned Dad. I thought, 'How can he tell? How can he tell now what I'll be like when I'm older and bigger and stronger?' It was a big shock. Maybe I didn't do that well but it was still a shock. I remember crying my eyes out when I was talking to Dad. You think it's never going to happen to you so you're very emotional. It'd been my dream for the whole of my life.

Nick travelled down to London to meet Mike who was with a group of friends on their way to Chester races. They had a helicopter and were happy to offer the Summerbees a lift.

Mike wanted them to land in the back garden but was dissuaded. Nevertheless, the spectacular homecoming, which had been observed by his friends, relieved some of the humiliation for Nick.

After Norwich, Nick went to Leicester as a result of an intercession on his behalf by Russell Osman who, since filming *Escape to Victory*, had become a friend of the family.

I stayed at his house, went to the club for a couple of days and finished off in a trial game. I was desperate by now. I think we played against Mansfield Reserves, proper blokes, not kids, and I did really well. Russell said I did really well and I deserved a contract. But I think they must have had their minds made up before the game started because they just said to me, 'We haven't got any room for you on the YTS.' I was gutted. If they'd already got their apprentices, why bother with me?'

The end of his schooldays was fast approaching and still Nick was unable to push open even the back door to the world he wanted so desperately to enter. Tina's pleas for him to reconsider the professional worlds of cookery or photography fell on deaf ears. It was to be football or nothing; or in his case, football or window cleaning and working on the street markets. It was September 1987. The boys of his age were either back in school or had already started as YTS apprentices. Eventually, through Cecil Green, Mike secured a trial for him at Swindon. Could lightning strike in the same place twice?

Both Mike and Tina were delighted. If it had to be anywhere, Swindon was the logical place. Lou Macari was the manager and he had taken the club from the Fourth to the Second Division in successive seasons. The club and the town were buzzing on the back of successive promotions. Mike couldn't help thinking that perhaps Nick would be lucky as he had been lucky, joining Swindon just as they were starting to rise. As they drove down to the west country, they encountered a swarm of police cars with their lights flashing and sirens sounding. The news on the car radio was of a massacre in Hungerford. It was a day they would never forget.

Nick played centre-forward in a trial match and scored three or four goals as his side ran out easy 9–0 winners. There were celebrations in the Summerbee household as Nick was invited down to join the apprentices. It seemed so fitting that Swindon should be the place for Nick to start his professional career. After his miserable experiences at Norwich and Leicester, Nick was in seventh heaven.

I'd done it. I'd got my dream job. I packed my bags because I thought I was leaving home for the two-year YTS scheme. Mum and Dad took me down to the hostel. The landlady was a fat woman who wore polyester and smelled. Mum was crying her eyes out when I went up to the rooms where all the lads were staying, three or four bunk beds to each room. I'd got what I wanted but I was already homesick. That's when I met one of my best mates – Fitzroy Simpson. I was on the top bunk, he was on the bottom. He's going to be the best man at my wedding.

Despite the homesickness, Nick was eagerly anticipating his first day as a fully fledged YTS apprentice. He went down to the County Ground with the other lads, expecting to be allocated a number to identify his boots and kit, but John Trollope took him to one side and told him there was no number for him.

He said, 'I think you've misunderstood what I was saying. I never said I was giving you an apprenticeship. We're just offering you another two-week trial.'

Trollope had played alongside Mike at right-back in the young Swindon side of the early 1960s, so carefully nurtured by Bert Head. He went on to make a record 770 appearances for the club between 1960 and 1980 when he took over as manager. His record as a manager was undistinguished and in 1983 he was relieved of the responsibility, but he stayed on as the youth-team coach. However, both Nick and Mike thought they had understood the conditions under which Nick returned to the club after his first successful trial. Just how the mix-up occurred is unclear. Perhaps there was a failure in communication, or perhaps Trollope was playing psychological games with Nick to see if he was made of the right stuff. Whatever the origin, Nick was so incensed that he played out of his skin for two weeks and was officially awarded his two-year apprenticeship.

A two-year YTS apprenticeship may be the dream of every young would-be footballer, but the lifestyle is not necessarily easy. Once a month Nick and the other 17 apprentices would be informed of their manifold weaknesses which were written down for future reference; and they still had to do the traditional mundane tasks of sweeping the terraces and picking up the dirty kit. This wouldn't have mattered much to Nick if he had been playing regularly but he was surprised and disappointed to find how infrequently he was involved in a match.

The first year passed with agonising slowness as the home-sickness took hold. What made it worse was the nature of the landlady and the club-approved hostel where the boys were living. The landlady was paid by the club to look after the boys but they weren't impressed.

> She rarely left any food in the fridge. Instead of putting a loaf of bread or two in the middle of the table, she handed round two slices each. I mean, we were growing lads. You weren't allowed to bring any food into the

house and if you went round the corner to the chip shop she used to report you to the club. She used to make the toast and tea then come upstairs and get you up. By the time you got down it was all cold.

Young Fitzroy Simpson decided he was going to report her to the club, especially as Lou Macari was particularly scrupulous about the boys' diet. He never drank alcohol and was determined that the apprentices should look after themselves similarly, an attitude which certainly appealed to Tina. Macari decided to see for himself what was happening at the hostel. Nick was faced with something of a dilemma because one of the first things he had learned in the cruel world of professional football was that if you want to get on you don't go looking for trouble.

I was just a kid playing for a professional contract. But we'd told Fitz, 'Don't worry, we're all on your side. We'll back you up.' So when Lou Macari came round to the digs and said, 'What do you think of the food?' I said, 'There's nothing wrong with it.' And the next lad said, 'Yeah, it's all right.' We stitched up Fitz good and proper. He's never forgiven us to this day. I think we didn't complain because we were frightened of causing trouble. I know I didn't want to be put out of the game.

At the end of that first difficult year, John Trollope called Nick into the office and said, 'If I was you, I'd go home. I'd go home and I wouldn't bother coming back because you're not going to make it.'

I was amazed. An apprentice had two years – you're growing up, anything could happen and I wasn't even playing in games. That did me in, did that. I mean, we'd had that start when he seemed totally out of order. I was homesick and I hated the hostel and now Trollope was saying I wasn't good enough and I'd better go home.

A sorrowing Nick told his father, 'I don't think I'm good enough for this game. I don't think I can do it.' Mike didn't say much beyond, 'You do what you feel is right.' He left it for a couple of weeks but during that time Nick thinks he must have contacted Lou Macari, who took a different view, because the manager was soon on the phone to him encouraging the young lad to give it another year.

Although he had to run the gauntlet of his coach's disapproval, the second year of the YTS scheme went particularly well for Nick. For a start, his wages increased from £21 to £32 a week. He scored more than 30 goals and, at the end of the season, when the decision was made about whether or not to offer him a professional contract, he took great pleasure in sitting in the room with John Trollope as Lou Macari gave him the good news. The boys traditionally gather in the dressing room and are summoned individually to hear the fateful decision. They return ten minutes later with the verdict clear from their demeanour. Nick returned smiling.

Nick Summerbee was now a professional footballer earning in the region of £80 a week – in 1989, ten years after Mike had retired, there still wasn't that much money in the game.

Swindon Town was a good experience for Nick. His parents were both pleased to see him taking the first steps into the adult world. He moved out of the dreaded hostel with the apprentices and into digs which he shared with Alan McLoughlin, who later moved to Southampton and then Portsmouth, and Nicky Hammond, now the goalkeeper at Reading. He had a professional contract, a small amount of money in his pocket and his freedom. There was one problem.

> There were no women, it was just football. Sometimes I'd
> go home with Fitz. His mum lived in Melksham between
> Bath and Bristol. She's Jamaican and whenever we stayed
> the weekend she looked after us. We had this great West
> Indian food. That was where I developed a taste for hot
> spicy food, I think.

Within weeks of awarding Nick his first professional contract,
Lou Macari, Swindon's most successful manager since Danny
Williams, left to manage West Ham United for a brief and
unhappy season. His replacement was the Argentinian World
Cup star and former Tottenham Hotspur favourite, Ossie
Ardiles. What Nick saw around the club after Ossie arrived
caused him some anxiety.

> Everyone loved Ossie but it was his first managerial job
> and everyone was walking all over him. He was too
> nice a bloke. He was giving people silly contracts. He
> had his mates there, including Mickey Hazard and Dave
> Kerslake, and the club was getting into a mess because
> it didn't have that much money.

Still, it was Ardiles who gave Nick his Football League debut
in that 1989–90 season when he brought him on at Boothferry
Park in the match against Hull City. It was a proud moment
for Mike who was remembering his own debut against Bournemouth in 1959, and for Tina who sat there thinking, 'My
baby! My baby is playing outside-right for Swindon Town in
the Second Division.'

Although Nick didn't play again for the first team that
year, Ardiles's first season was crowned with success despite a
2–0 defeat against Sunderland in the first match, in which six
players were booked and Fitzroy Simpson was sent off. At

the end of September, Swindon were in 21st place but Duncan Shearer and Steve White scored nearly 30 goals apiece, Alan McLoughlin had a magnificent season, and Swindon eventually defeated Blackburn 4–2 on aggregate in the play-off semi-finals. The showpiece Wembley final against Sunderland was won by a single goal from McLoughlin after 25 minutes.

Swindon celebrated promotion to the First Division for the first time in their 73-year history, but the party was cut short as the dark financial clouds which had hovered over the club for months deposited their contents indiscriminately. In February, the FA fined Lou Macari £1,000 for betting, and the chairman Brian Hillier had been banned from football for six months in connection with a bet of £6,500 at odds of 13 to 8 for Swindon to lose an FA Cup tie at Newcastle in January 1988. The club was also fined £7,500. Hillier appealed against his ban which was upheld and his banishment was increased to three years.

On 1 May, days before the play-offs began, the captain Colin Calderwood along with Hillier, Macari and the club's accountant had been arrested by the Regional Crime Squad. Three days after promotion had seemingly been secured, the Football League Commission announced that the club had pleaded guilty to 35 breaches of Football League rules connected with irregular payments to players. Cecil Green, now the President of Swindon Town, along with five directors, was severely censured by the League who announced that Swindon would not be promoted to the First Division but relegated to the Third. The town and the club were in shock. On appeal, the draconian sentence was reduced. Swindon were denied promotion but permitted to remain in the Second Division.

The following season was an anti-climax for everyone. Nick made just seven scattered appearances for the first team. Ossie Ardiles departed for Newcastle to add to the blows Swindon had received in the space of a few months. For Nick, it meant proving himself all over again to another new manager. Fortunately, Swindon found an inspired replacement – Glenn Hoddle became player–manager. Nick was an instant fan of the future Chelsea, England and Southampton manager.

> I liked him because he gave me loads of confidence. He loved all the continental stuff because he'd been at Monaco, and he turned me into a right wing-back. He liked all the tactics and he made training fun. We'd be doing volleys and overhead kicks in training. Most of the players respected him and when he started playing himself you saw what a fantastic passer he was.
> We were playing one day at the County Ground and he was spraying balls down the left, just knocking all of them left-hand side, so I thought I'd show him I had a bit of interest and I shouted to him, 'Hey! What are you fucking doing passing left side all the fucking time? Pass it fucking here!' He said, 'Don't just fucking stand there looking at me! Fucking make a run and I'll fucking find you.' [Author's note: this constitutes authentic footballers' dialogue.] I thought, 'He's a flash bastard.' So I set off on a run and the ball came about forty yards right into my path and I think I mis-controlled it.

Hoddle, reasonably enough, harboured some doubts about whether the 20-year-old Nick was ready for regular first-team football. With his assistant John Gorman, Hoddle explained that his formation would be played by all Swindon teams so that anyone called up to the first team would understand the tactics immediately. Nick's problem was that Hoddle favoured Dave Kerslake over him.

I had lots of arguments with him. 'I'm better than him,' I said. 'Give me a chance.' And he kept saying, 'You'll be a good player one day but you're not ready yet.' Eventually, I fell out with him. I didn't think things were going to work out for me but I went back there the next year and Kerslake got a move to Tottenham. So there was my chance and I took it.

Nick played 39 of the 46 matches that season. The play-offs were intensely dramatic. Swindon had lost their last two matches of the regular season and appeared to have gone off the boil badly but they started their home-leg play-off semi-final against fourth placed Tranmere with a bang. After less than a minute, Summerbee put in a wicked cross which the Tranmere central defender Vickers nodded past Eric Nixon, his own goalkeeper. Sixty seconds later, Nixon spilled a shot from MacLaren and Dave Mitchell put Swindon two up. With less than half an hour gone, the Aussie striker scored again and even though Tranmere put up some resistance, particularly in the second leg at Prenton Park, Swindon hung on for a merited 5–4 aggregate victory. Leicester City crushed the unfortunate Portsmouth who had finished in third place during the regular season to set up one of the classic Wembley finals of all time.

Nick had been there as a spectator in 1990 on the previous ill-fated occasion but this time he was a first-team regular and he knew he would be playing. He acquired tickets for Mike and Tina; the seats turned out to be so high up in the stands that they needed binoculars just to see the pitch. For Mike, it was a wonderful feeling to see his son walking out at Wembley, even playing down the same furrow he had ploughed for City and England. He couldn't help thinking of George and the contrast between their lives. George had been to Wembley three times with Preston and Portsmouth and never played. He had died before seeing his younger and less fancied son win the FA Cup, the League Cup and playing for his country there.

Now Mike had the chance to watch his own son at the home of legends which now boasted the largest urine lake in any European football ground.

The game matched the occasion, which tends to happen more often in play-off finals than in FA Cup finals. It gave Nick a special incentive to be facing Leicester City who had denied him a YTS place six years earlier. He had also taken particular pleasure in playing well at Norwich and proving that their decision to release him after two weeks was equally misguided. The game couldn't have started better for Swindon who, led from the back by Glenn Hoddle, raced into a 3–0 lead eight minutes into the second half. It was at this point that Nick started gesturing to his friends in the stands that they would be going out for a few drinks later.

Incredibly, Leicester hauled themselves back into the game scoring three times in 12 minutes to equalise. The pendulum had swung back with such force that it looked destined to keep Swindon out of the Premier League yet again. Stalwart forward Steve White came on as a substitute with just over ten minutes to go and won it for them six minutes later when a perfect 50-yard pass from Hoddle dropped into his stride. His somewhat theatrical tumble under challenge in the penalty area convinced David Elleray but not the Leicester manager, Brian Little. It was an emotionally draining 4–3 victory in one of the great Wembley finals of all time.

The celebrations were predictably fervent but again touched with anxiety. Glenn Hoddle, who had masterminded the campaign and proved himself to be the coming manager, was seen after the game in whispered conversation with Ken Bates. It was known that Bates wanted to replace Dave Webb as manager of Chelsea. Just as the party of 1990 had been destroyed, so the joy of Swindon's greatest footballing moment was soured when it was announced three days later that Hoddle would be taking over at Stamford Bridge. The Swindon players were greatly upset. It wasn't that they didn't like John

Gorman; indeed, he was a charming and sensitive man whom everyone liked, but he was known as a trainer not a manager. In the cynical competitive world of Premier League football, Swindon would have found it tough going even if Hoddle had stayed. Without him, they were doomed before the new season kicked off.

Nick was losing not just a manager but also a mentor. For all his early seeming lack of confidence in him, Glenn Hoddle handled Nick especially well. He turned him into a right wing-back because he liked to play in the continental fashion with three at the back and wing-backs to get up and down the field. He recognised that Nick could make a unique contribution in this position and it was no surprise when Nick started to win England Under-21 caps.

The Premier League season for Swindon Town was a nightmare. They won just four games all year. There was no money to strengthen the side and despite fighting valiantly, never escaped the relegation zone all season. When they went to Maine Road in February 1994, they were aware that City were playing badly enough under Brian Horton to accompany them. A couple of weeks earlier, Francis Lee and Colin Barlow had formed a consortium that had finally forced out the dreaded Peter Swales. The fans were high on the emotion aroused by Swales's departure. Nothing in his public life became him so much as the way he left the club – in a swirl of threats and demonstrations, alleged attacks on his 90-year-old mother and bitter outpourings in the press. With the end of Swales and the arrival of the folk hero Francis Lee, it was fondly believed that the good times were due to roll again at Maine Road.

It was almost a family occasion when Mike and Tina went to Maine Road to see Nick take the field in Swindon Town's colours. Nick had given interviews to the papers in which it was revealed that Mike would be strictly neutral but Tina would be cheering on Swindon. Tina was, awkwardly, the guest of Francis and Jill Lee. Francis Lee had known Nicholas since the day of his birth. You can see how, when it all went wrong later, this was the most complex of emotional situations because even on that day in February 1994 Tina confesses to being incredibly nervous, her emotions constantly on edge. In fact it turned out to be the (almost) perfect result. City won 2–1 and Nick had a blinder.

For many of us, it was a first proper look at Buzzer Junior and we liked what we saw. He ran Terry Phelan ragged (admittedly, he was neither the first nor the last opposing winger to do that) but above all he never stopped running and working for the good of his team in what became an unlucky losing cause. He looked a lot like Mike with his strong angular features and he ran up and down that right wing for 90 minutes in the inimitable Summerbee style. Everyone said the same thing afterwards – 'We've got to have him at Maine Road.' It was his destiny and ours too.

After the game, Nick took most of the Swindon players to a wedding celebration at Mottram Hall. Peter Cobb, the City supporter who had patiently withstood years of jibes from the little kid next door in the United shirt, was unable to go to the match because his elder daughter was getting married that day. Mike and Tina, of course, couldn't go to the church being otherwise engaged that afternoon, but when they all met up at the reception after the game there was nothing but good cheer and congratulations. Nick was a Manchester boy and it was about time he came home. Letters in the local Manchester press and letters to the chairman and the manager in the days that followed confirmed the feeling.

The fact that he was man of the match that day and, indeed, played better and better as the season progressed despite results constantly going against Swindon, cut no ice with the beleaguered Swindon supporters. They read constantly that Summerbee was going to be on his way at the end of the season. They were going to be relegated but that wasn't the issue. It is a point of honour with supporters that nobody leaves or talks of leaving until their fate is sealed. Nick could hardly prevent the newspapers speculating. In Manchester, we knew it was just a matter of time.

It is interesting to note that in the 4–2 defeat by Wimbledon at the County Ground, the match that officially relegated Swindon Town back to the Endsleigh League Division One, Nick Summerbee was by common consent the star player. The parallel with Mike's final performances for Swindon in 1965 was overwhelming. Nick Summerbee was made of the right stuff. He had the right name and he was in the right place at the right time. He was 22 years old, the same age his father had been when he made the journey from Swindon to Manchester.

After relegation, the first phone call Nick received was not from someone at Manchester City but from Bryan Robson.

Middlesbrough were still at Ayresome Park and in the First Division. Bryan Robson was away in Barbados but he phoned Dad up and said, 'We'll have Nick.' Middlesbrough have this jet, sponsored by ICI, and they flew me up there when Robson was back and he told me all about what it was going to be like, the new stadium. The ideas were fantastic. I met the chairman too, but I just had no interest in them. Middlesbrough kept on at me, made me feel dead welcome, couldn't do enough for me. But there was only one thing on my mind – I wanted to go to City. If there was a place where I was going to do it, that was the place. I just wanted to sign for City but nothing was happening there.

Blackburn Rovers too expressed an interest although looking at the squad that Kenny Dalglish was building up with the help of Jack Walker's money, Nick could see that he would never be anything more than a fringe player at Ewood Park. Blackburn went on to win the championship that year but that doesn't invalidate Nick's reasoning.

Another manager who was sure that the one place Nick should not go was Manchester City was Frank Clark, then successfully managing Nottingham Forest. He heard about the proposed deal from Adrian Whitbread, one of Nick's flatmates in Swindon, who had played under Clark at Orient.

Adrian rang me round about the time Nicky was going to move, and I said, 'Whatever you do, don't let him go to Manchester City. It's the wrong club for him, because of his father. He's never going to be the same kind of player as his father. Whether he's as good as his father is irrelevant. He's a different type of player. It wouldn't be the right move for him.' His father was a hero as a player and he's a hero from twenty-five years ago so he's a better player now than he was when he played. That was always going to be held against Nicky.

There were different points of view in the Summerbee household. Like Frank Clark, Tina instantly saw the downside, that if things went badly for City, Nick would be the first to suffer just because of his name. Mike wasn't greatly impressed by Bryan Robson but Tina was. She liked his style of doing things, the private jet, the managerial concern, the ambition and the promises, but it was Nick's decision to come home. It is true that home itself was an incentive, as was the presence on the City playing staff of his old Swindon YTS friend Fitzroy Simpson. It was Simpson who pointed out that playing for Manchester City offered more than the chance to turn out in front of the heap of rubble which was all that was left of the old Kippax Stand.

I used to come up to Manchester with Fitz and there wasn't a bird in sight; then I ended up signing for City and suddenly there were birds everywhere. Fitz says to me, 'Remember what it was like at Swindon? You couldn't get a bird anywhere.'

For all the superficial attraction of instantly available female company, there is no doubt that the main reason for Nick's decision to join City was that he saw City under Francis Lee and Brian Horton as a club that was going places. He was right about the momentum, of course. His only error was in predicting its direction.

He had some indication of City's way of doing things at the start. He knew that Horton was interested in signing him and he knew too that his prospective new chairman, for obvious reasons, could not be seen to be leading the stampede for his signature. Nevertheless, it seemed like ages before he received a call; certainly it was a long time after Robson and Dalglish had shown an interest. Then Nick and his agent, who at that time was Jon Holmes, were asked to meet Brian Horton and the secretary of Manchester City, Bernard Holford, at a hotel in Buxton – 'Probably not our strongest strike force,' concedes Francis Lee. Nick was deeply underwhelmed by their marked lack of enthusiasm for him, certainly compared with what he was still experiencing from Bryan Robson.

'That meeting was hard work and I kept thinking, "Hang on a minute. I want to sign but they don't seem to want me." I didn't understand. They were supposed to make me feel wanted.'

Eventually the deal was done and Nick signed for a transfer fee of £1.5 million. Mike was delighted. Like the rest of us, he shared the dream of a new Summerbee coming to south Manchester to show the faithful the way to the promised land.

Dad said City was a fantastic club and if you did well there you could get whatever you wanted in Manchester. People will always look after you. Just get your head

down and get on with it. But it was my decision to come
to City, not Dad's. Dad was helpful up to a point but
when we started talking wages he didn't have a clue. He
was used to playing for five pounds a week and a packet
of pork scratchings.

Actually, that was George. Mike was used to £40 a week and
he got to keep the car coat after the photoshoot. But this was
the Premiership. The days of Joe Mercer and his pocketed
teaspoon were history. The money and fame were on tap now
in Cottonopolis. Across town, the other lot had just picked up
the double, courtesy of David Elleray's awarding of two
dubious penalties in the Cup final against Chelsea. At City,
Francis Lee's arrival as chairman in place of the thankfully
departed Peter Swales, Mike Summerbee's return to work in
the commercial department at Maine Road, the presence of
Colin Bell and Tony Book on the staff, and the signing of
Nicky Summerbee, all seemed to suggest that a second version
of the glory years for City and their supporters was just around
the corner. Manchester would soon echo to the sound of rival
chants as the two clubs battled for the status of top dog in the
town. Only the wise Tina Summerbee had the foresight to
dismiss all this as nothing but the fantasies of vainglorious
men. Of course, by her own admission, she was a woman who
knew absolutely nothing about the game.

CHAPTER FOURTEEN

Manchester – the Inglorious Years

When Mike arrived at City at the start of the 1965 season, the team went undefeated in their first seven matches and lost just one of the first dozen. Nick's first match in 1994 was at Highbury. Uwe Rosler was sent off, Arsenal were a goal up inside two minutes, scored three and could have doubled the total. Fortunately, matters improved somewhat with two convincing home victories over West Ham United and Everton in the next seven days.

Indeed, apart from the occasional reverse, the first few months of the season led Tina to believe that her fears were unfounded. Nick scored his first goal in City's colours in a highly entertaining 4–3 win at Queens Park Rangers in the League Cup. It was a stunning volley into the roof of the net from outside the penalty area but Nick scarcely acknowledged the fact or the delirium of the travelling supporters. He simply turned round and trotted back to the centre circle. Personally, I found the modesty to be refreshing. Nothing betokens professional respect more than an old-fashioned handshake or a ruffle of the hair or, perhaps, in order to express extreme emotion, a manly grope of the buttocks. It is certainly to be preferred to the absurd posturing of so many players after they have scored a goal. Pardon me, but isn't that what they are there for? Isn't scoring goals part of their job description?

What I didn't realise then was that Nick's self-contained reaction was going to get him into big trouble with a crowd that doesn't believe a player wants to play for a club unless he kisses the badge of the shirt he is wearing in some ludicrous mediaeval ritual of fealty. Not even Mike Doyle could be found in front of the Stretford End taunting United supporters by cocking an ear to the crowd. He didn't need to do that. The United fans knew exactly what Mike Doyle was thinking and feeling every time City scored against them. He'd told them all the previous night in the *Manchester Evening News*.

In between two victories at Loftus Road in the middle of October 1994 came a scintillating 5–2 win at home over Tottenham Hotspur, which evoked from John Motson a parallel with the famous 4–1 ballet on ice victory of December 1967 that presaged Mike's championship glory. By this time, Tina was revelling in her son's choice of club. Everything Mike and Nick had talked about appeared to be coming true. The bearded Midlander Brian Horton with the mad staring eyes didn't sound like warm and witty Joe Mercer but you couldn't argue with results. Then came Old Trafford.

Manchester United are always the litmus test for the season. Even a relegation struggle is acceptable if we win the derby matches – something we did twice in the 1980s and not at all in the 1990s. For some time the club had been hanging on to the talismanic 5–1 victory achieved over United in September 1989. For all the derby draws and narrow derby defeats that followed, the well-publicised troubles in the boardroom and United's long slow march to glory, City supporters could always refer to that extraordinary day and reduce any United supporter to quivering speechless frustration.

It worried me that the game took place on a Thursday night. When was a derby match ever played on a Thursday night? Whoever devised this particularly stupid schedule clearly had no respect for this precious institution. Which Jew among us was surprised when Real Madrid knocked United out of the

European Cup in April 2000? UEFA had arranged the match for Seder Night, the first night of Passover and as the Jews of Manchester United celebrated in the dining room and thanked in prayer the Lord Our God for leading us out of Egypt, on the television set in the living room Alex Ferguson was leading them straight back into the House of Bondage. You mess with history at your peril. Just ask Moses.

Suffice to say that the torments of Nicholas Summerbee began that night and lasted for exactly three years. City lost the derby 5–0 to a rampant United who gloried in removing the stain of their 5–1 drubbing from living memory. For some blinkered City fans that was the worst part of the evening. For those of us who watched with both eyes open it revealed that too many players didn't much care whether they lost 1–0, 3–0 or 5–0; indeed, they appeared not to care whether they lost or won.

It was at this time that the rumour of Nick's being a United supporter began to gain credence. It was true of course, but it was difficult, if not impossible, to convince anyone that its origin lay in a teddy bear called Jimmy Greenhoff. Nick had gone so far as to admit the fact early on in a press interview but in a way designed to prove that although he had supported United as a boy he was now committed to the City cause. After that 5–0 reverse, there was a groundswell of belief that Nick couldn't play well for City because he was a United supporter.

It was nonsense. Steve McManaman stood on the terraces at Goodison Park but nobody attributed his sometimes disengaged performances for Liverpool to his Evertonian childhood. Peter Reid, by contrast, was an Anfield stalwart as a kid but nobody who ever saw him battling away in midfield against Souness and McMahon ever doubted for a moment that he wasn't completely committed to ensuring an Everton win in their derby matches.

Every professional footballer is a fan at first. Apparently, Robbie Earle of Wimbledon and Lee Dixon of Arsenal were

City supporters in their youth but I don't remember ever seeing them doing us a favour on the pitch. Professional footballers, especially these days, may pretend an affection that they don't genuinely feel for the club that pays their wages. Next week for a larger pay cheque they can be seen protesting their love of another set of fans. You can justifiably accuse them of being mercenaries, of caring for their own careers above the long-term emotional well-being of the fans for whom they display their talents, but you cannot accuse them of playing poorly on purpose against the side they supported as a boy. A footballer who 'cheats' for whatever reason is soon made aware that his manager, coaches and fellow players are on to him. Nick Summerbee had any number of poor games for City – it would be disingenuous of me to pretend otherwise – but not one of them was influenced by his early passion for Jimmy Greenhoff and Norman Whiteside.

Nick's time of torment was about to begin although for those of us who paid to see him in action it felt as though our suffering exceeded his. As Tina had foretold, when the Kippax Street Stand that housed the expectations of the City fans metaphorically collapsed, the rubble buried everyone alive.

The second half of the 1994–95 season was a familiar story for Nick – a relentless battle against relegation. As the tape spooled faster and faster nearing the end, I wondered where on earth the victories would come from. Inevitably, they came from the two games written off as unlikely to yield a single point.

Nick scored the first goal in an improbable 2–1 home win over Liverpool on Good Friday, a fixture that traditionally brought nothing but a 4–0 pasting. On Easter Monday, Sky Television covered the City game at Blackburn Rovers who were preparing to lift the championship from Manchester United. Mike Summerbee was the studio guest; his earnest protestations that City were going to win 'no problem' were ascribed by everyone, including me, to blind loyalty. What was he doing in the studio anyway when City were in trouble on the pitch? Already I was thinking that he should tear the shirt out of Nick's hands and put it on himself, despite his 52 years. It was a common fantasy among supporters of my generation.

When Shearer scored early on, I left the living room and went upstairs to work on a television script. I was brought clattering down the stairs again by a shout from my son who had decided to sacrifice A-level revision in favour of 90 minutes of self-flagellation. Quinn had been tugged back by Ian Pearce and Curle equalised from the penalty spot. Further goals from Rosler and Walsh brought an entirely unexpected but hugely significant victory and a relieved City ended the season in a disappointing but adequate 17th place. This was not the scenario Nick had been fantasising about a year before. He had had an undistinguished first season but the club was still in the Premier League and United had won nothing in 1995; the jury was still out on his performance. Life in Manchester had its compensations.

> I loved living in Manchester that year, absolutely loved it.
> I got a buzz just driving home after training. Dad was
> dead right about that. You were meeting people all the
> time who knew who you were and they just couldn't do
> enough for you. The night life was great, there were birds
> everywhere.

City had lost the last match of the season 3–2 at home to Queens Park Rangers. It offered Francis Lee the chance to remove Brian Horton and install his own man at the helm. Although the fans sympathised with Horton who had suffered from the inevitable instability during the protracted take-over saga, we all welcomed the chance for Francis to show us the true nature of his ambition for the club and happily speculated on the imminent arrival of Franz Beckenbauer. Like the mythical Russian soldiers who had been spied in Britain

during 1914 with 'snow on their boots', Beckenbauer was
projected to be arriving at Manchester Piccadilly station
almost every day throughout that glorious summer. We
believed only Richard Branson's incompetent running of the
newly privatised west coast trains was holding up the arrival
of der Kaiser von Maine Road.

The players couldn't help but be excited at the prospect of
working with one of Europe's top coaches. Francis had
promised us the known world and all the gold we could eat.
The club and its supporters deserved it and everyone knew
how much he wanted to deliver. Now that his hands were free
of the last remnants of the disgraced Swales regime, the Red
hordes would soon be trembling at the prospect of a true Blue
revival. As the days of summer lengthened, we started to
wonder a little uneasily why the Messiah had not yet managed
to find a taxi from Piccadilly station?

Eventually the first night arrived. The orchestra was tuning
up in the pit, the audience sat expectantly in the stalls, the
curtain rose and to the surprise of everyone who had bought
tickets for the show, the character on the stage turned out to be
a short red-haired man in a flat cap wearing a shell suit. Nick
and the other players were as unimpressed as the fans.

We all respected what Alan Ball did as a player, but as a
manager your job is to encourage players and he rarely
did. He could have helped us, used his experience, but he
was always talking about the old Brazilian teams. If you
made a mistake in training . . . We'd start a game and
after a few minutes he'd stop it and say, 'Hey, you,
c'mere! What are you? Brain dead? Or can you just not
play football?' No wonder we didn't get a win till
November.

Even more humiliating for the players was the unwelcome
presence of Mrs Ball.

'Did you know Alan Ball's missus used to come and watch us training? One day she said to Keith Curle, "You should have been tighter at the back . . ." '

If Nick's first year in Manchester had been disappointing, his second year was an undiluted disaster. For his first signing, Ball addressed the urgent matter of a goalkeeper. City had always prided themselves on their tradition of having great goalkeepers, from Frank Swift and Bert Trautmann to Joe Corrigan and the recently retired Tony Coton. Alan Ball's idea of a great goalkeeper was the VfB Stuttgart player, Eike Immel. Nick was horrified.

Eike Immel had slightly cross eyes. He looked at you with eyes pointing in different directions. Doesn't exactly inspire confidence in the defence when the new goalkeeper looks cross-eyed.

Fortunately, Immel's vision was strong enough to enable him to pick the ball out of the net, which he did on far too many occasions that year.

The other newcomer to the team was the controversial Georgi Kinkladze, the most gifted individual to play for the club since the great Scottish forward of the 1950s, Bobby Johnstone. Nick and Georgi became good friends although the elevation of Kinkladze to god-like status didn't do much for the rest of the team.

Bally loved Georgi. Georgi could do no wrong. I get on very well with Georgi and we weren't jealous because we could all see how talented he was, but some hated Alan Ball for doing that – except Georgi because he loved all the praise. You went into the souvenir shop and it was like the Georgi Kinkladze Road Show. Then it seemed that Georgi was getting a bit big-headed because when he should have been performing at his best, he wasn't doing it any more. People buttered him up too much.

The problem was that even with the great Georgian in the team, the results were terrible. At the end of October, City had the grand total of two points. Both derby matches were lost and in the space of four days the team conceded ten goals in two games at Anfield which Alan Ball had the temerity to claim that he enjoyed. It was a solitary pleasure. Alarm bells were ringing. Kinkladze was to be the key to salvation. This dogma was believed by almost everyone – the manager, the chairman, the fans and, to an extent, the players who saw the midfield genius's skill in evidence every day on the training pitch. The problem was that in order to accommodate those skills, significant compromises had to be made.

The problem with Georgi was you couldn't play 4–4–2 because to get the best out of him you wouldn't want him playing a conventional running midfield game. If there are two men wide, that leaves only one in midfield. He left me out for a bit and I played in the reserves. He changed the formation all the time – a sure sign he didn't know what he was doing. If you believe in 4–4–2, you stick with it.

Lomas and Flitcroft were effectively being asked to do Kinkladze's running for him. Ball seemed to believe that the senior players in particular were overpaid. Niall Quinn was the first to suffer from this conviction. With the success of Uwe Rosler and Paul Walsh it was believed that Quinn was surplus to requirements; plus they wanted him off the payroll. Quinn, a likeable articulate Irishman, had been awarded the status of a local folk hero when he had gone in goal during a match against Derby County after Tony Coton had been sent off for a foul, and saved the resultant penalty. Lee was keen to sell him to Sporting Lisbon but Quinn didn't want to leave. When he turned down the move, Quinn felt his face didn't fit at Maine Road for the remaining 12 months of what until that time had been a happy stay.

Under the pressure of bad results, managerial castigation and fan dissatisfaction, the dressing room spirit was starting to drop. With half a dozen games to go and City's Premier League status in the balance, Lee and Ball chose to sell Garry Flitcroft to Blackburn Rovers for £3 million. They were gambling that they could bank the money and avoid relegation. They couldn't. Quinn believes that it was the sale of Flitcroft, who by common consent of the fans had been the heart of the City side that year for all Kinkladze's pyrotechnics, that told the players that the management had lost it. Already the skilful and inventive Paul Walsh had been exchanged for Gerry Creaney, whom we thought overweight and useless, and the now notorious policy of replacing good players with bad ones was under way.

Relegation came on the last day of the season in the game against Liverpool. The timing was bad for the Anfield side, who seemed more interested in preserving their fitness than winning – they were playing in the FA Cup final against Manchester United in six days' time. They need not have worried – City's incompetence finally won out. An own goal, a mishit shot by Ian Rush, and Alan Ball believing inaccurate crowd rumours that Coventry, City's rivals for the drop, were losing, combined to complete a season that had begun in tragedy and concluded in high farce.

Niall Quinn had the decency to go on *Match of the Day* and apologise for letting down the supporters but we all knew he had played his last match for the club. Steve Lomas, who had joined City from Northern Ireland as a boy, kicked the boundary boards in frustration but from the others there was no sign of contrition. The crowd turned its anger on Alan Ball.

'He got what he deserved because he slated people,' says Nick. 'All he had to do was to make people feel good. If he slated Georgi all day long, he wouldn't have got much out of him.'

Nick had endured a season as miserable for him as it had been for the fans. After Lee and Ball, he was probably number three on the list of public enemies. He had bought a house in Sale in which he had installed his sister Rachel, newly returned from the west country with her certificates in looking after horses, as housekeeper. As the older sister, Rachel had always been protective of her little brother but now she was confronted with the problem on a daily basis.

> I was working at River Island, a men's clothing shop. You had City and United fans there and there was a bit of banter going on. But then it all went sour. People started telling me, 'Nick's really crap, he's really bad and it's all got worse since Francis Lee moved in.' It wasn't just Nick. It was the Francis Lee thing as well.

Mike and Tina were suffering the torture of the damned. Mike was Francis Lee's good and loyal friend but he was also Nick's dad. He was also, unlike Tina, well known in Manchester and, again unlike Tina, not known for shutting up when provoked. Even Francis, who wasn't short of a word or two as a player, knew you couldn't win when fans started attacking you. Although he was inclined to defend himself vehemently in open forums such as the increasingly fractious AGMs over which he presided, he would never respond to the taunts of the crowd at matches. Mike, on the other hand, could and frequently did have arguments with fans seated near him in the Main Stand. He could keep two or three of them going simultaneously with people who were sitting in different sections of the stand. No matter what he thought of Nick's performance, nobody was going to slag off his son in public without getting an earful back.

As the dreams of Lee and Summerbee for the club they once graced fell apart at the seams, the intrusion into their family lives intensified. Rachel, who had lived in the shadow of football all her life, started to resent it all bitterly. She was six when her father left City as a player, and ten when Mike retired. As a teenager, she discovered that potential boyfriends were more interested in talking to her father about football than in taking her out, but it wasn't until her brother returned to Manchester that she found the obsession with football almost impossible to handle.

I got fed up with it. Instead of anyone asking how I was doing, it was just about football. I got into trouble to draw attention to myself. I used to get into debt and pile it all on Dad. They weren't interested in horses, which was fair enough, but it was just the football thing all the time. Nobody was interested in me or in what I was doing. All the trouble I've caused them was through trying to get their attention.

Rachel fought hard for her interest in horses to be taken seriously at home, but she was helpless in the face of the overwhelming obsession with football. Tina had never been a horsey girl although her daughter was from the start. Neither she nor Mike was attracted by the prospect of a day spent in a muddy field watching eventing or show jumping. When Nick came back to Manchester and Mike went back to work at City, Tina was inevitably caught up in events at Maine Road.

The horses cost them a lot of money. It was part of the attention-seeking – 'Hey, I'm here. I'm alive!' It annoyed me that they never came to see me. I had good days and brought a few trophies home but nobody was interested. That did me in.

Just before relegation from the Premier League, an incident occurred at the stables where Rachel was working which typified her general experience that year.

They were just about to be relegated. One of the kids went past shouting 'Summerbee, Summerbee, Summerbee!' at me. City had a big game later that day. A guy there had a City shirt on and he looked at me and said, 'Who are you?' I said, 'It doesn't matter who I am.' He said again, 'Who are you?' So I said, 'I'm Rachel.' 'Rachel who?' 'Rachel Summerbee.' 'Are you any relation to that ****?' So I said to him, 'Can you not use that kind of language? This is a family area,' and he said, 'I don't give a ****. Your brother's shit.' I said, 'There's no point being aggressive towards me,' but he was going on. 'He's got no idea what he's doing out there. He thinks he's your father but he's not. He's just crap!' I said, 'Excuse me, this has got nothing to do with me at all,' and I asked him to leave the yard but he wouldn't. He was becoming quite loud and abusive – it was just pure emotion, no alcohol or anything. In the end, Tom, the yard manager, had to take him away because he was getting quite nasty. I wanted to kill the guy. It was all getting so personal.

However semi-detached Rachel felt from the world of football, once Nick was back in Manchester and City had begun their downward spiral, she was involved whether she liked it or not and she soon saw the effect it had on her brother.

I'd get the score relayed to me. They used to make a big thing of it. 'You got hammered again. Whaaaaaay!' That's how you find out. If I was in the shop, I wouldn't buy the Pink. After a bad defeat he wouldn't come home. He'd just go out and get drunk, or some of the lads'd come back and they'd have a big party, but at times he was really down.

Tina hated these times, too. On match days she would usually be the guest of Gill and Francis Lee for lunch in the boardroom before the game started. Mike would rarely join them. His job invariably took him to the other side of the ground into the hospitality boxes where the corporate entertaining was going on at the top of the new Kippax Street Stand. When things started to go wrong for City and for Nick, it became an excruciating experience for Tina.

> If I could get out of it I would. Gill wanted me to go with her but I started making excuses. I stopped getting the *Manchester Evening News*. The things that were being written about Francis were awful. Had Nick not been involved in that situation I might have been able to help them more but I was tangled up in what was happening to Nick and they were caught up in what was happening to the club. Francis would criticise the players and that would make me defensive because my son was one of them. I had lost my priorities at that stage. I usually know what I'm doing but I didn't in that situation. It could have led to the destruction of the friendship but in the end it didn't. I don't know how we all kept it bubbling along like that.

As the wife of Mike Summerbee, Tina had led a charmed life. Mike never brought his problems home with him and besides, by the time she met him he was already famous, popular and successful. It had all looked so effortless to her; the only negative experience she had was the occasional barbed comment in the butcher's shop about Mike being a dirty player – usually the ill-informed comment of an ill-informed United fan which could be treated like the joint of lamb that was currently being hacked with the meat cleaver. She turned to Dulcie for advice as the vitriol being hurled at her son increased.

> Now I can understand much more what Dulcie's always said to me over the years because it's come out like that for me with Nicholas. I didn't appreciate it when Mike was playing because he just went out to work in the morning. I'm much more wary now. It hurts so much hearing someone you love being criticised like that. I just want to be in the middle of nowhere to get away from it. That's how it makes me feel. I find it very difficult.

Nick has inherited some of Tina's Christian Science philosophy and responded to the abuse of the fans, and relegation to the First Division, as he responded to John Trollope's comments. To the crowd it seemed as if he didn't care. They thought he was lazy and arrogant, typical of the mercenaries who came to City in those benighted times, took their money, i.e the supporters' money, and didn't give a toss about the club, i.e the supporters. You could never accuse Mike of not trying or not caring. He wore his heart on his sleeve and everyone respected him for it. However, Rachel had inherited this temperament, not Nick. Mike can walk into a roomful of strangers and amuse them for an hour. He must have picked up something from his friendships with Michael Crawford, who stayed at the house for six months, and from other showbusiness luminaries like Jimmy Tarbuck. Nick has never been able to do that. He's a quiet lad although his appearances on the front pages of the popular press wouldn't necessarily have convinced a sceptical Manchester public of the fact. He never asked to be compared to his father, but only his mother foresaw the danger that the comparison would be regularly made – and that it wouldn't benefit Nick.

Occasionally, it had its amusing side. Peter and Mary Cobb

were with Mike and Nick when a young autograph hunter, sent over by his parents who stood 20 yards away, proferred his book for signature to Nick. As Nick took the pen, the father bellowed in dismay, 'Not him, the other one!' and the mother called out helpfully, 'The father, not the son!' The Holy Ghost of hubris looked on and smiled.

Nick's experiences of the tabloids provide a striking parallel with Mike's times as a lad about town with George Best in the 1960s. Mike is, to outward appearances at least, a gregarious man, and he revelled in the attention that came his way when he and George were the epitome of fashion and popular culture in Manchester. He never pretended that he was teetotal or that he went home every night and was in bed by ten o'clock with a good book. But the journalists who wrote about football in the 1960s and 1970s wrote about the game. They had no interest in exposing his social life. Besides, if Mike went out drinking, it was usually on the back of a great victory, and since Malcolm Allison also revelled in this public champagne lifestyle there was nothing to expose.

More to the point, City were a terrific side and Mike was a significant component of its success. Nobody ever saw Mike the worse for wear during training, let alone during the match. Like Bobby Moore, whatever time he had gone to bed the night before, he was always on the training ground next day ready to display that consummate professionalism that distinguished them both. Unlike Best, he could tell the difference between a genuine friend and a hanger-on and, also unlike Best, he married at 26 and settled down. Best effectively left the game at 26 whereas Mike played for another 11 years.

Nick has been unfortunate in that his propensity to behave like every other footballer with a liking for a drink and the company of attractive women has landed him in trouble. The newspapers now regard footballers' activities off the pitch as legitimate areas of so-called public interest. Nick's first major excursion into the world of the tabloids was a sharp eye-opener for both him and his sister. Nick's seven years at Swindon had not prepared him for the goldfish bowl of Mancunian celebrity. He began a brief relationship with a girl who lived round the corner from his house in Sale. Rachel recalls the night they went out together.

> There was myself, this girl, her friend, John Sharpe, Lee's brother, because he was living with us at the time, Garry Flitcroft's brother and his friend who was the goalkeeper for Gillingham. We all went out in my car to a disco in Alderley Edge. The following week, this girl went to the papers with a story saying that all of them had had sex with her. I was out with them all that night and I knew exactly what went on. I got really stroppy with her over that.
>
> All the blokes I worked with started saying Nick was a typical bloody footballer with his brains in his pants. I got protective then because people had no idea what they were talking about.

In March 1996, the *News of the World* gave over its front page to a story headlined 'Soccer Stars in Drugs and Sex Orgy Shame'. This was six months after an alleged incident involving a teenaged blonde:

> A teenage blonde told last night how two soccer idols tried to lure her into depraved sex orgies. Pretty Lindsay Pendo, 18, had already suffered humiliation at the hands of Nicky Summerbee, the Manchester City star.

Apparently, this young woman was kindly helping the socially responsible newspaper with its in-depth investigation of Manchester's evil drugs scene when she suddenly remembered a 'night of shame' chez Summerbee the previous September.

She went on to describe in explicit detail the moment when she suddenly realised that making love with the right-winger had turned into a theatrical performance for his friends, one of whom she thought 'looked like Frankenstein's monster'. (Perhaps it was Jaap Stam in town for an early shopping trip to the United Megastore?)

The other soccer star in the story was Lee Sharpe. He allegedly persuaded this same cutie and her friend, who turned out to be a *News of the World* reporter, to invite him to her hotel bedroom where he unwisely expounded on the prospect of a retirement spent in a cannabis-induced haze on a yacht in the Caribbean, though there was no suggestion of any drugs being taken. When told that the tabloid paper had them both bang to rights, Nick replied to the effect that he had never met the girl. Presumably an avid City fan, President Clinton initially tried this approach the following year when asked about his relationship with the White House intern, Monica Lewinsky. Lee Sharpe's response, according to the newspaper, was less politically astute – 'You've got me by the b****cks. I'd better have a word with the gaffer.' Mr Sharpe was shortly afterwards to be found plying his trade in west Yorkshire.

As with so many of these tabloid tales, the truth is both more complex and less dramatic. In March 1996, Mike and Tina had sold the house in Hatherlow and were living with Nick and Rachel in Sale while they waited to move into a smaller house outside Wilmslow. Tina overheard Nick answering the phone.

I heard Nick say, 'Yeah, we can all meet you, that's fine. I'll bring some of the lads.' And I remember when he put the phone down he said, 'There's something fishy about that.' It was this girl they'd had a bit of a party with before at the house. Apparently, she was suggesting they do it again and she would bring some of her friends. She was asking what sort of girls they like and Nick said ones with big tits.

Right at the end, she asked, 'What about drugs?' Nick said, 'Oh yeah, I can get hold of that.' Then she said, 'Let's meet in town at Johnson's Bar. We're staying in a hotel and we can go back and have the party there.'

Nick thought it was strange that the girl didn't want to come back to the house and he thought it might be a set-up. So, having fixed it up, he rang the other players back to say it was off. Tina continues the story.

The girl went to the bar with some others. She'd been recording Nick when she was on the phone to him and one of the women she was with was from the *News of the World*. Who does she see in the bar but Lee Sharpe – he was in the papers quite a bit then – and when the lads didn't turn up, she made a beeline for him. Lee Sharpe had gone out, minding his own business, but he went back to the hotel with the girls and he's spouting off about how when he retires he's going to get a yacht and just party and, of course, it was all being recorded.

The result was acute embarrassment all round, particularly for Tina.

We knew it was going to be in the paper because when the team got back to Manchester Airport after a match one Saturday night, the press were there waiting for them. It didn't come as a surprise but I didn't like to see 'Nicky Summerbee in sex and drugs scandal'. I talked to Dulcie and my mother and tried to protect the grandparents. I was heartbroken reading all that stuff. I never thought I'd see a son of mine in the papers like that. I found I was getting invitations to go places and I'm sure it was because people were embarrassed for me. Everyone knows your business. It's very humiliating.

The following week the alleged sexual proclivities of the then Nottingham Forest striker Kevin Campbell were revealed to the nation over its Sunday breakfast. The moving finger writes and having writ tittle tattle moves on to the next Premier League club.

Nick had a girlfriend called Claire during his time in Manchester but unfortunately, according to Rachel, she wasn't much help to Nick when times became difficult.

> They ended up throwing things at each other but if you tried to explain to her, 'Look, he's under enormous pressure,' she didn't seem bothered about that. She made it awful for me, too. She'd be ringing me at one in the morning, two, three o'clock saying, 'Is Nick in yet?' and I didn't know. She wasn't the right sort of person for him at the time. She added to the pressure. He didn't need that.

He didn't need his private life to be exposed in the *News of the World* either. Of course, the 'revelation' merely confirmed what all the fans had already suspected, that Nicholas Summerbee was a self-indulgent, debauched, overpaid hedonist and this sort of behaviour was the root cause of City's problems on the field. The unfavourable comparisons with Mike increased and the pressure on Rachel intensified.

> Nick is Nick. He's not my dad. I'd hear, 'Oh your dad was a far better footballer. He knew what he was doing but your brother doesn't. His dick's bigger than his brain,' and this kind of crap. 'He thinks he's a really good footballer and he's not, he's a lazy git. All you see of him in the papers is 'cos he's shagging women.' Now that's personal, that's not about football at all. I was never involved with football because it's not my kind of thing, but when I was living with Nick I couldn't help

but be involved with it. If I went home and spoke to Nick about it he'd just say, 'Oh, ignore them.' It looked like water off a duck's back but I knew that underneath it was bothering him. He doesn't open up to anyone; the only time was when he got absolutely leathered. He could hear what the fans thought of him and he could read it in the Pink.

What the Pink had to say on its features and letters pages was inevitably influenced by what appeared on its front page. After relegation from the Premier League, City lost two of their first three matches in the First Division. To the sound of cheering fans, Alan Ball fell on his sword with a high-pitched squeak. Some of the players were not sorry to see him go. Unfortunately, Ball's departure was the prelude to further public embarrassment as the last three months of 1996 produced five managers. Manchester City became a synonym for incompetence and the butt of widespread jokes. The only thing less funny than these jokes was having to support the team and listen to them.

Asa Hartford took over temporarily until the right man was identified. This turned out to be Steve Coppell who lasted exactly 33 days. His health deteriorated at Maine Road to such an extent that he was forced, under doctor's orders, to return to London and manage Crystal Palace until he recovered. Phil Neal took over on an even more temporary basis; he demanded that the board back him or sack him and quickly found himself the proud possessor of a spanking new P45. It was during Phil Neal's stewardship that Nick's career sank to a new record low.

I had a tough time when Phil Neal was manager. I think it was in the League Cup game against Lincoln when he took me off and the crowd was cheering when I was substituted. I went up to him and said, 'Don't ever fucking do that again!' Sometimes when you're having a bad time you just need to tough it out but I got a standing ovation when he took me off.

Sometimes the crowd didn't wait till he was substituted to demonstrate what they thought of him.

They used to boo me before we'd even kicked off – 'Number seven Nicky Summerbee' and they all booed. That's great for your confidence, isn't it? It was out of order what they did when my family was there.

A few days after Christmas 1996, the lugubrious Frank Clark arrived from Nottingham Forest where he had fallen foul of crowd expectations and problems in the boardroom. Unbelievably, things soon took a turn for the better. Kinkladze and Rosler in particular were revitalised and the goals started to flow again. Nick was the recipient of one piece of sage advice from Clark, who knew all about the troubles Nick had had with the crowd and who sympathised with his predicament. He had been the butt of the crowd's displeasure many times during his 13 years as Newcastle United's left-back.

When I first got there it was disastrous. A month or so before I arrived, he had reacted angrily to some abuse from the crowd so they were really on to him, even worse than normal. I had to resolve that. I got Nicky in very early on because I'd heard about this fracas with the crowd and I said, 'Listen, it's all water under the bridge as far as I'm concerned, but if you ever do that again it'll be two weeks' wages because we've all been through it. Once you react, you're dead. You've got to win them over.' And to his credit, he did. He was terrific for me. I ran for balls at Newcastle that I hadn't a hope of catching but just because I'd run for it, it lifted the crowd. Nicky is a totally different character from his father. He can be a bit surly, I think, very moody, and sometimes out there on the pitch he gives the impression of being uninterested. Perception is everything. I told him to chase around and throw himself into the game.

Unfortunately, it was not a piece of advice that fell upon receptive ears. Nick didn't take kindly to being told how to deal with this particular problem.

I'm not saying I won't listen but I'll find my own way out of the problems with the crowd. It's like someone telling you to go over to the crowd and kiss the badge when you score a goal, but I'm not like that. You are what you are. I understood what he was saying but that wasn't the way out for me.

In fact the problem became briefly irrelevant. Clark's arrival seemed to settle the team and results improved so dramatically that within weeks the fans who had been staring with open-mouthed horror at the prospect of relegation to Division Two for the first time in the club's history were, inevitably I suppose, speculating on a last-gasp play-off victory and Premiership football. My friend David Green, with whom I had been going to City matches since 1962, told me in his office in March 1997 that City were definitely going up under Clark the following year. We haven't spoken much since then.

The season concluded with City in 14th place and the memory of a Cup run that finished in the fifth round when Middlesbrough literally elbowed them aside. Nick had scored the only goal that won them the tricky away tie at Brentford in the postponed third round and under Clark he, like the rest of the side, looked like a different player. They were going to be leaving that horrible Division One the following season. Everyone from Francis Lee to David Green was absolutely sure.

Then they bought Lee Bradbury. In one way it was good news for Nick. City had splurged a club record fee of £3 million on a very ordinary Portsmouth striker who in turn became the focus of all the expectation in the blue three-quarters of Manchester. A combination of Albert Einstein, Albert Schweitzer and Albert Quixall could not have fulfilled those expectations. Albert Tatlock wouldn't have helped and Lee Bradbury had much the same impact.

Before the end of the 1996–97 season, Nick was offered a new contract. According to Frank Clark:

He was adamant that at the end of that season when his contract was up he wouldn't sign another one. Under Bosman we had to get him to sign another contract but he said, 'I'm not staying here.' I talked to Nicky and his agent and I soon realised that Francis was never going to agree to what the wages in the new contract would have to be to get Nicky to sign it. It was going to be a case of us having to sell him before he walked out for nothing.

But Nicky did sign a new three-year contract at the start of the ill-fated 1997–98 season. For his mother this was a mixed blessing.

'I remember when he re-signed his contract at City, he and his agent Scotty rang me from a wine bar in Hale and he told me he'd re-signed and my first reaction was brilliant, and then I was churned up.'

Frank Clark liked Nick as a player despite coach Richard Money complaining about his surliness. Nick had skills that enabled him to play as an orthodox right-winger, a right-sided midfielder or a full-back in a 4–4–2 formation. He could also play as a right wing-back in a 3–5–2 formation. His skills were undeniable, his versatility was more than useful but Clark bought Ged Brannan and dropped Summerbee. Now Nick couldn't even get into the team. You might think this was a blessing in disguise in that he would be spared the calumny of the crowd but you would be wrong; the professional footballer lives to play football in the first team. Every Saturday afternoon at 3 p.m. (Sky Sports notwithstanding) there exists the chance for personal redemption. Being dropped means that the chance is denied, but Clark had a problem.

> When I bought Bradbury, I tried to get him, Rosler and Kinkladze playing together. I didn't think I could play Nicky as well, although Bradbury and Rosler together would have been a terrific front two for Nicky because he's a great crosser of the ball – he's a better crosser of the ball than his father. He's got the knack of crossing it without having to beat the full-back.

Nick had finished the previous season believing, along with his friend Georgi Kinkladze and the rest of us, that a couple of good summer purchases and City would certainly be challenging for promotion. But it didn't work out that way and Nick was puzzled.

> The next season when we came back it was like the manager was a different bloke. He signed me to a new contract, then he dropped me for Ged Brannan. We all thought he could turn it round if he bought a couple of good players but he bought Brannan and Bradbury.

Dropped for Ged Brannan, Nick's life started to plummet again. Rachel remembers the atmosphere in the house becoming extremely bleak.

> He just used to sit there looking really miserable. Sometimes he wouldn't even acknowledge I was there apart from saying, 'I'm going out now. Make sure you do this or do that before I get back.' He got bossy. He used to

spend his money on clothes – obscene amounts of clothes. The washing basket would be full of clothes that he'd worn for maybe an hour.

He was George Summerbee's grandson all right.

Then came the infamous car crash on Princess Parkway that landed him and Kinkladze in court. A week after one of those buttock-clenching 1–0 home defeats (this one by Stoke) that so disfigured the second half of the 1990s, and three days after City had revealed their ineptitude to the hundreds of people watching them on Sky Sports 2 as they lost 2–0 at Queens Park Rangers, Nick and Georgi, in their separate high-performance cars, turned out of the Four Seasons Hotel in south Manchester on to the main road. According to Nick, Kinkladze put his foot down on the accelerator too soon and lost control of his 335GT Ferrari Testarossa which raced past him out of control, somersaulted and threw the midfield genius out of the car through the sun roof.

Nick could see Georgi was in trouble and followed him in his BMW to find that the Ferrari had finished upside down in the middle of the road. For Nick, it was a simple case of a powerful car getting away from an inexperienced driver but for both of them what followed was another lesson in the downside of celebrity. Initial news reports didn't even mention Nick but as reporters went digging, a story suddenly emerged. Summerbee and Kinkladze had been racing their cars and turning Princess Parkway into the Wythenshawe 500.

We got prosecuted for racing but it was just the biggest joke. It was a farce. One guy said he came out of the Four Seasons Hotel and saw these two cars, a Ferrari and a BMW, and he thought what fantastic cars they were and the next minute he could hear the tyres screeching as they raced off into the distance. Someone else said, 'As they drove past, they were going so fast that me and my girlfriend had to throw ourselves into the bushes.'

The case made headlines of course, and Nick and Georgi were prosecuted for dangerous driving.

> We went to court and they adjourned it. We had all these people lined up to give evidence for us. I had to hire a QC because I could have got banned from driving and yet I'd done nothing. We had these people to pay on a daily and an hourly basis. Georgi was flying in from Ajax. Then the case was delayed and we didn't get into court till nearly one o'clock and we'd been there since nine. They said they were going to adjourn it again and it was costing us a fortune. Georgi couldn't keep coming back from Amsterdam or Georgia so we asked what was the easiest way to clear the whole thing up. The result was that Georgi pleaded guilty and was banned from driving in England for a year. I got away with it but it cost me seven grand and it cost Georgi nine.

Meanwhile, the team had stumbled from the inept to the indescribable. Manchester City had become the equivalent of a huge cruise liner heading inexorably for the rocks. On the bridge, the captain and the first lieutenant were yanking at the steering wheel, which eventually came off in their hands. The passengers downstairs were complaining loudly that they were supposed to be on the beach in St Lucia at this point on the itinerary. Through the starboard window, they could see their sister ship, HMS Manchester United, steaming blithely on to the New World, the passengers from Scandinavia and China tucking into caviar and canapes in the dining room while below deck the ship's officers ran their American Express cards through the 2,000 credit-card machines they had winched on board with a crane.

It was a nightmare for Mike and Tina, an unwinnable situation. Nick was out of the team and miserable. Mike wasn't running the club; he wasn't a director although many people thought he was. He was a brilliant former player who, like Francis Lee and Alan Ball, watched the players on the pitch and was unable to reconcile what they did there and what they got paid for it with what they themselves had done and what they had been paid. People who stopped Mike to chat about football and City found it difficult to avoid mentioning what was happening to Nick, but what could Mike do about it? Indeed, out of the team as he was, there wasn't much that Nick could do about it, either. Mike could only rage internally in impotent fury. Then, just as City slipped into the relegation zone, Rachel discovered she was pregnant.

CHAPTER FIFTEEN

Sunderland – Paradise Lost

Peter Reid came into Nick's life like a ministering angel and left it like an avenging one. He had taken Sunderland into the Premier League at the same time as Alan Ball was skilfully guiding City out of it. Unfortunately, once there, Sunderland found it difficult to remain and they slid out even as the finishing touches were being applied to the new Stadium of Light. Peter Reid swore colourfully for a BBC documentary series called *Premier Passions* which followed the club's doomed enterprise, but by the start of the 1997–98 season, Sunderland and Manchester City were sharing tenancy of the Nationwide First Division.

During that summer of Bradbury, Frank Clark had tried to sign Sunderland's 23-year-old Jarrow-born forward Craig Russell, but he failed his medical examination at Maine Road. Learning that Russell's subsequent cartilage operation had been successful, Clark renewed his interest at the beginning of November. Reid was now more interested in reaching an agreement because he wanted someone City had – Nicky Summerbee. He had a potent strike force in Niall Quinn and Kevin Phillips whom he had recently signed from Watford for £650,000. He needed someone who could supply the ammunition for them and Summerbee was his man.

Interestingly, City wanted Russell more than Nick wanted to

go to Wearside. He still clung doggedly to the dream that he could make it in Manchester with City but the dream had begun to defy logic many months before. Still, his reluctance to leave gave him the edge in the negotiations that were to follow. He had another two and a half years left on his new contract and he hadn't asked to move.

My agent [Scott McGarvey, the ex-Manchester United player] phoned up Francis Lee and said Nick Summerbee is a Manchester lad and he doesn't want to go and live in the north east. You owe him a hundred and seventy thousand pounds. The agent did a good deal for me up there so he said, 'If I get you seventy grand of what City owe you, will you be happy?' I said yes. So he said to Francis Lee, 'You've got to make it worth his while – give him seventy grand and he'll sign the deal.' Lee said no, so the agent said, 'Well, give him all the money you owe him but pay him over three years,' and he said yes to that.

No. I don't understand the mathematics either.

Tina, who is not given to saying 'I told you so', breathed a huge sigh of relief when the transfer went through.

It was just easier all round. He was away then. When you don't know what the kids are doing, it's actually easier. When they're around in Manchester it's so much harder. There's so much temptation here. The drink's here, the hospitality, the girls are all lovely but you've got to stay focused and it's difficult. I don't know why I should be saying this. I mean he's twenty-nine for God's sake.

Rachel wasn't quite so delighted. For a start, Nick had to sell the house which meant that she was now both pregnant and homeless. Her parents were not thrilled.

It was difficult because I didn't know who I could speak to. Mum and Dad were so wrapped up in everything that was going on with Nick and the club, I didn't tell them. My parents don't really agree with me about anything, but after Nick left I had to move back with them. It wouldn't have been practical for me to stay with the baby so I had to look for somewhere else to live. It wasn't right for us all to be in the same place. At the time it was such a shock. Mum had an idea of what was going on. She was just waiting for me to make the confession. I was thirty-two weeks gone when I told them.

Rachel had been going out with Mark, the father, on and off for six or seven years but she didn't feel comfortable telling him either and tried to ignore her condition for as long as she possibly could.

I was still working full-time at the Atlas café on Deansgate. I didn't tell anyone. Mark didn't know. I just went to my local GP because I used to teach his son. I got sent over to Wythenshawe Hospital because nobody had any idea how far gone I was. I was still riding [horses] and doing everything like that.

Samuel Summerbee, fourth in the line descended from Charles Edward Summerbee of Winchester, was born at the end of April 1998 just as his grandfather's employer was facing relegation to the Second Division and his uncle was about to experience the drama of the First Division play-offs. The boy's destiny is already laid out for him.

Two weeks after the car crash on Princess Parkway, in November 1997, after ten goals in 156 appearances, Nicholas Summerbee left Manchester City and signed for Sunderland in a straight swap with Craig Russell, each player being valued at around one million pounds. As usual, City got the raw end of the deal. Nick didn't like being pushed out but Frank Clark wasn't exactly begging him to stay and Peter Reid had dealt with him honestly. 'I hear you like a drink,' he said when they first met. 'You keep putting that ball on Niall Quinn's head and I'm buying.' Nick thought Peter Reid was the bee's knees and for the next two years the feeling was mutual despite an early sticky patch.

I was left out soon after I arrived and then I really got stuck in and I played all the time after that. When I was dropped, I thought, 'Oh no, here we go again,' but he brought me back and I scored against Tranmere and that was it. I was in. It was like a kick up the backside.

Thereafter, it was moonlight and roses. He had scored on his debut in a 4–1 win at Portsmouth and he added another two goals in his 25 appearances as the team lost only three games between November and the end of the season. There was that surreal return to Maine Road described in the first chapter and a frantic but unavailing pursuit of Nottingham Forest and Middlesbrough who finished just one point ahead of Sunderland having scored fewer goals. They girded their loins for the play-offs and eventually slipped past a tired Sheffield United when a 2–0 win at the Stadium of Light overturned a surprising 2–1 defeat in the first leg at Bramall Lane. It was Nick's second Wembley play-off final in five years and it was even more dramatic than the 1993 occasion but with a less happy conclusion. Charlton were not expected to trouble greatly the free-scoring Sunderland but Alan Curbishley's underrated team matched their opponents goal for goal.

We were the clear favourites to beat Charlton but when the whistle blew for the start we were rubbish. I think we were too confident. They were the underdogs and they had nothing to lose. We thought that all we had to do was to turn up and play and we'd beat them. We really played poorly that first half.

Clive Mendonca's 23rd-minute goal separated the sides at half-time but following the traditional volley of abuse from Peter Reid, Summerbee crossed for Niall Quinn to equalise five minutes after the restart. Kevin Phillips put Sunderland ahead but Mendonca pulled his side level again two minutes before Quinn scored his second. With five minutes left and both defences tiring rapidly, the Sunderland goalkeeper Perez made a mistake and Richard Rufus sent the game into extra time.

Mike and Tina hadn't gone to Wembley this time. They were watching the match with Peter and Mary Cobb in Hatherlow. Great were the celebrations in that corner of Cheshire when in the ninth minute of extra time Nick chose the appropriate moment to make himself a hero with the Sunderland fans by scoring what everyone believed would be the winner. Three minutes later, Mendonca completed his hat-trick and the question of which club would play in the Premier League the following year had to be settled by penalties.

Peter Reid asked me to take one and I said yes. Some of them didn't fancy it. I was confident because I'd just scored in open play so I took the first one. I thought if I place it and the keeper saves it I'll always be gutted; if I smash it and he saves it there would be nothing I could do about it. So I ran up and blasted it and I hit it perfectly.

Successful penalty followed successful penalty as nerves that were absurdly taut to begin with were stretched even tighter. Somebody had to miss. It was just a question of who was going to be known for the rest of his life as the man who cost his team promotion with one kick. With the score at 7–6 on penalties, the England left-back Mickey Gray shot tamely and Ilic, the giant Charlton goalkeeper, saved it. The world disintegrated.

'At the time, Mickey Gray was just devastated,' says Nick. 'No matter what you say to him in that situation, he's going to feel worse. "Oh don't worry about it" – that's not going to help much, is it?'

In Hatherlow, the planned celebration was cancelled. There wasn't much to celebrate for Manchester City, either. In February 1998, Frank Clark had gone and been replaced by Joe Royle. In March, Francis Lee had relinquished the role of chairman after a particularly humiliating 2–1 defeat at Port Vale that brought out the vitriol in the fans in the same quantity as was poured over Peter Swales. Three weeks before Nick's appearance at Wembley, Mancheser City were relegated to the third tier of professional football for the first time in their history.

Nick and the players were drained by the emotions they had expended and devastated by the ultimate defeat.

Reidy handled the media brilliantly. He wished Charlton all the best, said he felt sorry for Mickey and that we'd be back next year. We were supposed to stop at Peterborough on the way back up the A1 for a champagne reception. When we arrived we could see them wheeling the champagne out of the hotel and putting it back in the van. The place was all done up for the party but there was nobody there. Everyone was so devastated. We shot off soon afterwards. We went home, packed up, flew off to Benidorm and tried to forget about it all till pre-season training.

The following season was a triumphal procession. Sunderland started well and never looked back. This time their tag of favourites was not a burden as they strode through the First Division laying waste their opponents and amassing a record number of points. Summerbee sent over the crosses for Niall Quinn and Kevin Phillips to score, just as Reid had requested the day he persuaded Nick to sign for him.

'I thought Reid was great because he was straight. If you're good enough, you play in the team, and if you're not good enough, you get dropped. Simple as that.'

Unfortunately, nothing in football is as simple as that, as Nick was eventually to discover for himself.

It went funny that season with one lad, Andy Melville, but the time it really happened was with the left-winger Alan Johnston. Apparently, he agreed to sign a new contract but then decided against it. After that, Reid didn't play him for a whole year. Then he said that Michael Bridges wanted to go, but if you want to keep a player you keep him, don't you?

So by the start of the 1999–2000 season, back in the Premier League, Peter Reid seemed to have fallen out with two of his most effective forwards. It was particularly important that the team stay in the Premiership this time. One relegation in the first year back is unfortunate, two looks like carelessness, which means a sacking. The first match was a difficult-looking fixture at Stamford Bridge. Poyet ran riot and Chelsea crushed them 4–0.

I knew it would be hard in the Premiership because we'd bought very few players – only Stefan Schwarz and Steve Bould, but he was quite old, and Gavin McCann. We didn't have a left-winger because of that trouble with Johnston so there was more for me to do. I was the only winger. But it worked, except for that first game at Chelsea. I think we all felt, 'Oh no, here we go,' and I thought if we finished fourth from bottom we'd have done fantastically well.

Fortunately, the capricious mistress of a fixture computer gave them a first home game against the previous season's fortunate play-off winners, Watford. Kevin Phillips scored a penalty and a magnificent 20 yard goal and Sunderland recorded a precious 2–0 win. On the Saturday, Reid packed the side with defenders and they ground out a dull but important scoreless draw against Arsenal. Four points from three games gave them the platform they required. Thereafter, Sunderland embarked on their best run since the mid 1930s when Nick's grandfather was at Preston, and Sunderland, Arsenal, Preston and Manchester City were the powers in the land. Happy days!

After a narrow defeat at Elland Road, Sunderland went to St James' Park where, on a wild and stormy night, goals by Quinn and Phillips beat the local enemy Newcastle United and brought a thankful end to the reign of the Toon Army's version of Alan Ball, the dreadlocked Dutch manager who had dropped some of his best players. Sunderland won six of the next eight matches, losing only at Liverpool.

At the start of October, Sunderland rose to third in the Premiership, and when the presents were opened on Christmas morning they were still there, defying gravity without visible means of support, way beyond the fondest hopes of their fans and way beyond the expectations of the players.

Whatever he was doing, it was working. We were going to places and just knowing that we weren't going to lose. That was a totally fantastic feeling to have. I'd never had that at City. There, it was more a case of how are we ever going to win one? You have to give Reid the credit for getting the winning habit going here.

The bond between manager and players seemed unbreakable.

At the end of October, Sunderland entertained Tottenham. The night before the game, Nick was violently ill. He didn't think he could get to the ground to report in sick but he was persuaded to do so by Chris Makin. He dragged himself to the stadium, believing he would be back in bed within the hour.

> I went into Peter Reid's office and told him and he said, 'Just do me a favour.' I said, 'I can't play. I've never been like this.' He said, 'We can stuff you with tablets. I need you to play. Do us a favour.' I played ninety minutes for him that day.

Respected by the management, Nick Summerbee was also a crowd favourite. They sang his name and recognised his vital contribution as Kevin Phillips set the Premier League alight. Nick had liked the Stadium of Light from the moment he stepped on to its turf when he came on as a substitute for Manchester City, who had the good grace to lose there 3–1 in the first match of the 1997–98 season. He had suffered the slings and arrows of outrageous fortune at the County Ground, the whips and scorns of his time at Maine Road, now he was finally playing in a good team, riding high and was one of the darlings of the crowd. He even scored in a 4–0 battering of Bradford City at Valley Parade. It doesn't get much better than this; but then it doesn't last.

On 20 December Everton tore them apart at Goodison Park, scoring five times without reply.

> Everton were really up for it that day – they'd have beaten Manchester United. But that was a sign of respect for us. It showed they regarded it as a big game. We were third in the League and they wanted to show us. We knew we didn't have much strength in depth in the squad, and we knew that at some point we were going to get

absolutely battered. It was an indication of how far we'd come that we were getting all that respect from other teams.

In a televised match shortly after Christmas, Sunderland snapped back, racing into an early two-goal lead at home to Manchester United. It appeared that Reid's team had the fortitude to recover well from the mauling they had taken at Everton, but then the 20th century ended and Summerbee's torment began afresh with the new millennium.

On 3 January, Sunderland lost unluckily to Wimbledon. Defender Ben Thatcher was seen in close-up on *Match of the Day* elbowing Nick in the neck. It won him national sympathy. I asked Nick if, in the tradition of the honest journeyman footballer, he was planning on taking his revenge. He affirmed that he might but it would take some time and he would leave Thatcher to worry about when retribution might be exacted. I told Mike that I thought this was a shrewd tactic. Mike just smiled. Clearly he thought that not many defenders would be lying in bed and worrying the night before they were due to face his son.

The next week, in an FA Cup tie against Tranmere, Reid struggled to compose himself as the referee, Rob Harris, showed the red card to a Tranmere player and then permitted a substitute on to the field; Tranmere knocked Sunderland out of the FA Cup with 11 men, despite having had a player sent off. Wimbledon had already knocked them out of the Worthington Cup in the third round so what with their experience at Chelsea, trips to London had been a problem for Reid. Even he couldn't have anticipated the aftermath of their next game, away at Arsenal.

It was another bad defeat, this time by 4–1. Steve Bould, on his return to Highbury at the age of 37, was run ragged by the pace of Thierry Henry. Nick was substituted by the recent signing from West Brom, Kevin Kilbane. The last five games had now brought four bad defeats and a 2–2 draw against United. The players and management all started to feel the pressure. At the end of away matches, players have the option of returning with the team or staying overnight and making their own arrangements to return the following day. It is not normally a bone of contention.

After the match at Highbury, Nick joined the full-backs Chris Makin and Mickey Gray for a night on the town. In 'London's plush Met Bar' they encountered, according to the following Monday's edition of the *Sun*, 'fun-loving telly babe' Melanie Sykes. Apparently, a good time was had by all. The alcohol flowed, the music played and the conversation no doubt sparkled to a positively Shavian dimension. As they were getting ready to move on elsewhere, Melanie Sykes disappeared briefly. On emerging from the bar, she and the players were dazzled by a rat pack of photographers. The following day, Ms Sykes was interviewed on Radio 1 by Jamie Theakston during the course of which she announced that she had had 'a naughty time with three Premiership footballers', which raises the obvious question. Had the players trapped in the glare of the camera lights been playing for Leyton Orient or Hartlepool United, would the fun-loving telly babe have been so instantly taken with them? Was this the purpose of the Premier League when it broke away from the Football League?

In the changing room on the Monday morning, the other Sunderland players gave a round of applause to the three gay cavaliers (old-style gay cavaliers). Page 13 of their daily reading had revealed the full extent of their colleagues' Saturday night fever. The players' paper of choice informed its public that Chris Makin was a married dad of two and that he had been out with Ms Sykes again on Sunday night 'at a Trafalgar Square' bar. In fact, Makin was separated from his wife and sharing a flat with Nicky in Durham.

Ms Sykes, clearly a woman of considerable physical

dexterity, had also spent Saturday 'flirting all night' with Mickey Gray although she subsequently admitted 'we didn't go the whole nine yards', which is presumably 'fun-loving telly babe' language for having sex. Additionally, the *Sun* added helpfully that Mickey Gray, apart from recently making his international debut for England, had also 'been fined £200 for urinating in a shop doorway after a Christmas bender'. The phrase 'completely irrelevant' flashes across the inward eye which is the bliss of solitude.

Things went from bad to worse for Nick. The following Friday, the team was preparing for the Sunday afternoon match against Leeds. Nick takes up the story.

The reserve team plays in the style of our next opponents. It gives the first team the chance to get used to the tactics and formation we're going to use the next day. The manager read out the first team and I wasn't in it. Then he read out the reserve team and again there was no mention of me. Chris Makin and I were both dropped for this game against Leeds, but Mickey Gray was in. Anyway, they got hammered by Leeds and it was all down their left-hand side – Jason Wilcox scored two goals that day. The manager brought us back for the next league game at home to Newcastle and I thought that was it, it was all over. We'd served our punishment, the point was proved.

Having played all the first 22 games, Nicky found himself in and out of the team for the rest of the season, starting only seven of the last 16. Sunderland won just five of the games they played after the 5–0 drubbing at Everton in December and, significantly, Nicky was in the team for three of them.

It clearly wasn't just the infamous incident with Melanie Sykes that caused Nick Summerbee to move from being an ever-present in the side to a less regular selection that season.

The bad result at Arsenal may have had an impact, but there were other frictions, too.

> I'd had a couple of arguments in the dressing room with Reid. It was nothing major, just sticking up for myself after a game at Southampton. [Sunderland won 2–1.] The assistant manager [Bobby Saxton] seemed to be having a go at me all game, screaming on the touchline he was and he had another go at me in the dressing room. I just took my shirt off and threw it at him. I thought then that it would be the last time I'd ever play for them.

It nearly was. He was dropped for the next four matches, making a return for the last three. The left-footed Mickey Gray who survived Reid's wrath was picked at one point to play on the right wing instead of Nick. Makin, who had also been restored to Reid's good graces more quickly than his flatmate, finished the season as captain of the side.

Nick was one of the few unmarried men in the side. He heard a story that the management did not like the fact that Makin had left his wife and was now living a bachelor existence with the outlaw Summerbee, though clearly Makin remained in favour. Sporting managements like their players to be married and domestically settled. The theory is it helps to keep them focused. Keith Fletcher, the captain of Essex, was famously of the opinion that getting married helped Derek Pringle to stop overstepping the crease and giving away needless runs from no-balls. As sporting psychology goes, it is not exactly foolproof but perhaps Nick's bachelor lifestyle was a cause of some suspicion.

It was particularly unfortunate that Leonie, Nick's regular girlfriend and then his fiancée, was working in Australia just as everything started to go wrong at Sunderland. Leonie is an intriguing contrast to the previous women in the lives of the

Summerbee footballers. Dulcie was a straight, honest Lancashire lass who worked nearly every day of her life until she was 70. Tina, the well-educated daughter of a prosperous Lancashire businessman, was a beautiful blonde air hostess and model, the perfect realisation of the aspirational 1960s as far as her husband was concerned. Leonie is a survivor of a background that belongs on *The Oprah Winfrey Show*.

Her maternal grandfather was born in a small town outside Nairobi. Memorably, he had a bullet wound in the centre of his forehead. On a night out in Manchester, he met a girl from an Irish family living in Burnley. Together they had two boys and six girls of whom Leonie's troubled mother was the youngest. Two of those children turned out to be white – it is presumed as a consequence of certain indiscretions during the time Leonie's grandfather was away at sea. The family was always dysfunctional as her grandfather was an alcoholic. Leonie's mother grew up very close to one of her black brothers, Kevin, a strong young man who unfortunately died of a heroin overdose when she was 19. The family history sounds like a charge sheet.

> Mum had me when she was seventeen. Then she started taking heroin. She was in love with my father who was half Irish and also from Burnley. He was close to his father but he was stabbed to death by a Pakistani in a dispute over the children.
>
> Both my parents were heroin addicts. My father died of heroin when I was five. I remember him very well because I used to go and visit him in Strangeways prison with my mum. When he got out, my mum had already started seeing somebody else. He didn't turn up for my sixth birthday party and that was when we learned that he was dead.

The tragedy accelerated the slide into the lower depths.

I ended up going to live with her best friend's mum, Winnie; then she got cancer and there was no one left to look after me. I was in and out of care from the time I was three.

That Leonie survived such a traumatic childhood at all is a miracle, but she emerged as a young woman who was shrewd and brave enough to give up her job to study for further GCSEs. That she and Nick should have begun a serious relationship is an interesting variation on the changes in British society since Nick's grandmother met his grandfather on the upper deck of a bus going past Deepdale. Nick was brought up short by the events of the first five months of the new century. All Leonie could do was listen to Nick's increasingly worried phone calls and hope things improved when she returned to England in the summer of 2000.

Nick knew that some of the backroom staff didn't greatly care for him but he had one year left on his contract and, after consultation with his father, he decided that his best course of action was to throw himself into pre-season training and prove Reid wrong as he had proved John Trollope and others wrong before. He loved the Stadium and its atmosphere, the fans and their loyalty. The worst that could happen was he'd play in the reserves; time was on his side because after a year he would be out of contract and free to leave on a Bosman. Just as pre-season was starting, he was the subject of an offer from Bradford City.

All of a sudden the phone rings and I'm told that Bradford are interested and Sunderland have already said yes to it. So obviously they aren't going to give me the chance to prove the manager wrong. They want to get rid of me. Reid just wants me to go.

Turning down Bradford City was a calculated gamble. Nick was not chosen for any of the pre-season games which help to make players match fit. When his team-mates left to go on tour, Nick felt like a naughty boy who is sent to his room to think about the consequences of pouring his dad's lager into the cat's saucer of milk.

The first match of the season was at home to Arsenal. Two days before, the manager wandered over to Nick on the training pitch and asked him if he felt fit enough to play against Arsenal on the Saturday. Nick was surprised to say the least; he had no idea he was even featuring in Peter Reid's plans. He hadn't played in any matches apart from a couple against local amateur teams and he knew the Arsenal game would be both high profile and high tempo. He wasn't match fit and much as he desperately wanted to play in the first team, to do so and not do himself justice would have been foolish. The crowd still loved him and he didn't want them to see him turn in a sluggish performance. More to the point, if the club was still determined to sell him, he didn't want prospective purchasers to see him under-performing. He confessed his lack of fitness to the manager who nodded and wandered away.

He doesn't say a lot. He's very distant. He doesn't say much during the week, only on the day of the game. The training's done with Bobby Saxton and Adrian Heath. They've done me no favours. They'll have their come-uppance one day.

The team, without Nicky, beat Arsenal 1–0 in a bad-tempered affair in which Vieira was sent off and the normally unflappable Arsene Wenger was sufficiently incensed by his treatment to incur a 12 match touchline ban from the FA. The next match was a return to Maine Road but this wasn't the Maine Road of Chapter 1; this was a New City and a hat-trick from Paulo Wanchope brought them a merited 4–2 win. Sunderland's season stalled. A couple of weeks later during a disappointing

1–1 draw at home to West Ham, the crowd started singing Nick Summerbee's name.

Nick and Leonie were sitting up in the stands. Leonie was a little surprised to hear Nick say to her uncertainly, 'I must be a good player. The crowd wouldn't sing my name if I wasn't.' She hadn't realised how the experience of the previous months had drained the self-confidence out of him. Nick was immensely grateful to the crowd for voicing their appreciation of his efforts but, as he suspected it might, it had a negative effect. The manager didn't care to have his team selection criticised and set to music.

Before the next match, away to Manchester United, the papers reported Reid as saying that Nick Summerbee had told him he didn't want to play for Sunderland Football Club in the match against Arsenal. Nick said:

> It's a fantastic stadium here. When I go out there I've got forty thousand people on my side. But one man, the manager, has decided I'm not good enough. 'Go out there and do well,' he used to say and I did and now he's taken it all away from me. I sit there and watch and I know that I'm the best right-winger they've got at Sunderland Football Club. He's the one who can make or break me and in my case he's chosen to break me. I would have run through a brick wall for him.

Throughout the autumn of 2000, Nick trained with the youth team, going through much the same experience as Mike had when Ron Saunders took a dislike to him. On Fridays, he would be reminded of his status as an untouchable as the reserve side and first team was announced and would trot off to the far side of the training ground to play their rehearsal match for the important Premier League fixture the next day. Nick would help to pick up the cones and wonder how much longer this would last.

> I don't feel part of it now in the dressing room. They're a great bunch of lads and I get on really well with them, but when you're not playing it's all different. You feel distant. They're doing different things.

In November, he was told that his presence on the training ground was no longer required. In fact, he felt as if he had been banned from the north east of England so he and Leonie trailed home to Manchester to house-sit for his parents for a week.

The year 2000 was the blackest of Nick Summerbee's life. Evicted from the club he had thought was his salvation, he knew he would never kick a ball again in the Premiership until the end of the 2000–01 season. If a Premiership club were to make an enquiry, Sunderland could easily put a price on his head that would kill the prospect of a deal at birth. The only thing he could do was to sit tight and wait until his contract expired, at which point he would become a free agent and clubs would be interested again.

The prospect of over twelve months without playing in a single match was a nightmare, however positive he and his family tried to remain. Tina clung to her Christian Science background to help her through yet another crisis in the turbulent career of her very mild-mannered son.

'I just have to be positive and believe that the next club he goes to will be brilliant because Nicholas lives for playing football, he just lives for Saturday afternoons. It's all he ever did as a little boy – play football.'

Mike's attitude towards Sunderland and its manager became considerably more agitated, as you would expect of an ex-player who once got himself sent off for punching an opponent during a testimonial game.

In January 2001, the telephone finally rang with the best possible news. Sam Allardyce, the manager of Bolton Wanderers, wanted to take Nick on loan until the end of the season with a view to a permanent move in the summer. Bolton would take over the contract Nick had with Sunderland, pay him exactly the same wage and the contract would finish, as before, on 30 June, 2001. He would be off Sunderland's payroll with immediate effect and free to negotiate with Bolton from a position of strength provided things went well for both player and club over the next four months.

Initially, that is exactly what happened. Although ten points behind Fulham, Bolton then occupied the other automatic promotion place. At the very least they were guaranteed a play-off slot, and a return to the Premiership with a fourth different club loomed large for the relieved Nick. In particular, he relished the prospect of a return to the Stadium of Light to show the crowd on the pitch that Peter Reid had made a grievous error.

Nick immediately repaid Sam Allardyce's faith in him. Within half an hour of his first start, in the FA Cup fourth round tie at home to Scunthorpe United, Nick placed two perfect crosses onto the head of Dean Holdsworth and Bolton went on to win 5–1. In the league he made his debut at Hillsborough, coming off the bench to help secure a 3–0 win.

He fought for the first team shirt and won it as of right when he scored in a 2–0 win at Crystal Palace. Having made nine first team appearances in the number seven shirt, and added three more as a substitute, out of a possible 16, he was a hero in Lancashire again. He saw with grim irony the real possibility of exchanging places in the top division with his father, as Manchester City slid ominously into the relegation zone.

Unfortunately, Bolton's form during that period in the closing weeks of the season was patchy, while that of their neighbour, a resurgent Blackburn Rovers, was irresistible. In the space of ten days at the end of February they hammered Bolton 4–1 at the Reebok Stadium in the league and then dumped them out of the FA Cup as well. As Bolton stuttered with five draws in six matches in March and April, Blackburn seized second place and held onto it, relegating Bolton to the uncertainty of the play-offs. By this time, however, Nick Summerbee was no longer involved.

A shoulder injury, sustained in a 1–0 win at Barnsley at the end of April, ruled him out of the last matches of the regular season. Although he was fit by the time the play-offs began in the middle of May, he was no longer Allardyce's first choice. He retained some hopes that the manager would regard his experience as a crucial factor in team selection. After all, he had been an integral member of the successful Swindon Town team in 1993 and the traumatised Sunderland in 1998 when they had faced similar pressures.

Ultimately, however, Allardyce was not motivated by such thoughts and Nick sat glumly in the stand to watch Bolton dispose of West Bromwich Albion in the semi-finals by a comfortable aggregate score of 5–2 and a young, vibrant Preston North End side in the final at the Millennium Stadium in Cardiff. The sense of unhappiness that had clouded his life for nearly eighteen months overwhelmed him. He felt little affinity with this Bolton team now and couldn't wait to leave. He was getting married in a country house hotel outside Chester the following Sunday. He did not feel the need to celebrate the triumph of a promotion that had been achieved largely without him.

His absence, however, was noticed and he believes it was a factor in Bolton's decision not to offer him a new contract. In retrospect he concedes that he made an error of judgement. It was all the stranger for the fact that he had never previously shown himself to be averse to a drink or two, especially with team-mates. His father, of course, had travelled to Australia in 1970 with a broken leg just to be with his City team-mates. Mike was under no obligation to do so, but the prospect of Francis Lee enjoying himself at the club's expense on the other side of the world was too overwhelming. He hauled himself onto the plane on crutches. Mercer and Allison who knew a thing or two about Summerbee's contribution to the team's morale were delighted to have him along. What a contrast to events 31 years later.

The spectacular wedding ceremony was arranged in impeccable taste by Leonie, now three months pregnant. Nicholas got an unfortunate but enormous laugh during the otherwise solemn exchange of vows when he promised to be faithful and forswear all others. While those guests of a certain vintage gave vent to a full-throated chorus of 'Sha-la-la-la Summerbee' and 'Hi ho, Hi ho it's off to Mexico' when the bridegroom's father got up to speak. Dulcie did not attend.

Nick and Leonie left to honeymoon in the United States in good heart. At this stage, the consequences of his failure to attend the promotion celebrations had not yet manifested themselves. He knew he was a Bosman free agent in less than a month and he had been part of yet another club's rise to the Premiership. He was confident that if things didn't work out with Bolton, his agent could always find him another club.

On his return he soon learned the bad news from Bolton, but pre-season training had only just started. There was still time to get fixed up with another club. His agent Scott McGarvey proved unable to do so and was released. Agents always need to maintain a good working relationship with their clients' potential employers, which can lead a client to undue fears that they are lower in importance than they would like to be.

Over the next few nightmare months Nicholas spoke to no fewer than five different agents. The answer came back in the negative from every club they approached. They didn't 'fancy' him; his temperament was suspect; his commitment was questioned. Nick was barely 30 years old and hadn't played regular first team football since he was 28 when he was regarded, along with Beckham, as the best crosser of the ball in the Premier League. Now even First Division clubs refused to take a chance on him. It wasn't the ideal start to married life and it contrasted strongly with Mike and the European Cup tie which abutted his own wedding. Nick was in danger of turning into another George.

Ironically, Bradford City showed some interest in him. It was Nick's refusal to move to Valley Parade a year previously, because he suspected they would be relegated, which had accelerated his decline. Bradford had duly been relegated along with Manchester City and Coventry. He played a match for the reserves on a school pitch, the like of which he had not experienced since his days on the YTS scheme. It was not a success. Out of the blue, or perhaps as a result of Mike's proximity, Kevin Keegan offered Nick a possible solution. He could come and train at Maine Road again, there would a contract of sorts, but the money would be minimal. Nick seized the chance eagerly.

It was great to be back with some of his old mates – Kevin Horlock, Paul Dickov, Richard Edghill and Jeff Whitley – who all remembered the bad times under Ball and Clark. However, City had experienced back-to-back promotions since then and, despite a disappointing end to their first season in the Premiership since 1995–96 and the dismissal of Joe Royle, Manchester City were, for them, a relatively stable club. Mike and Tina's friends were sure that this time it would work out. Nick was no callow youth but an experienced professional who had demonstrated his qualities in the Premiership with Sunderland. He was back home and Keegan had offered everyone at Maine Road the chance to start afresh. Maybe this time . . .

In Manchester at large there was a more muted welcome. The fans were suspicious of Nick as they were suspicious of Keegan. Their past histories suggested that neither would stick at it, but Nick was delighted to get the chance to show them what a good player he was. Jeff Whitley had sustained a bad injury, Terry Cooke seemed permanently out of favour whoever the manager was and Alfie Haaland hadn't played since the start of the season which ostensibly created a vacancy for a right wing-back or a right-sided midfielder. This was Nick's chance, or so he thought, but the opportunity to play in the first team never came.

Dave Jones, the manager of Wolverhampton Wanderers, contacted one of Nick's agents and offered him a week's trial. With Keegan's permission, which he thought a little ominous, Nick roared off down the M6 to Molineux. His trial was indecisive. Jones wanted three further weeks to look at him. After all, he had just bought Shaun Newton from Charlton for the same position. He had to be absolutely sure that Nick was a better proposition, but Nick thought that Wolves were confronting him with exactly the same position that he was in at City and he retained a touchingly naïve belief that Maine Road was still his destiny.

It wasn't. On his return to Manchester City, and after just two reserve team games, Nick was told in that wonderfully euphemistic manner that every profession adopts that 'it wasn't working out'. It wasn't exactly the same as that dreadful moment at Norwich when the shouting coach had told him, in effect, that he wasn't good enough to make a professional footballer but the rejection had potentially similarly dire consequences. It wasn't so much that he would never have a career as a player as much as the dawning realisation that perhaps it was all over. After all, who would want him now?

Nick accepts that he didn't reveal everything he could do in two reserve team matches, but it is impossible to replicate the first team match atmosphere. This, however, was Glenn Hoddle's flawed and fatal reasoning for refusing to practise penalties before the World Cup match against Argentina. The fact is, Keegan and his staff wanted to see Nick hurtling around the practice match like a crazed thing. It has never been Nicholas Summerbee's style and, just as when he turned down Frank Clark's advice to chase hopeless balls, he paid a heavy price. For Tina, Nick's misfortunes at Maine Road, whether self-inflicted or not, simply confirmed her long-held belief that her son and the club were fated never to be together.

After he left City in the autumn of 2001 Nick plunged into that nightmare world of players who are out of contract. This should have been his peak earning time – his last big four-year contract to ease him through to a comfortable retirement. After all, though he was, by most working men's standards, well paid at Sunderland his contract had been negotiated when they were a First Division club. He hadn't been on Premiership wages since City were relegated in 1996. Now, he was out of work and so desperate he would agree to play for no wages at all. He just wanted a chance to get a foot back onto the first team ladder.

For weeks the answers were a succession of 'no's. Anyone who rang Sunderland to ask for an assessment was unlikely to be given a paean of praise. By the time November came, Nick and Leonie had discussed the stark realisation that his career was over. It had been nearly two years since he had played regular first team football. He was out of contract, there was no transfer fee, he would not be asking for high wages, he was scarcely 30 years old, he had a Premiership pedigree – yet nobody wanted to hire him. It seemed to them, and to Mike and Tina, that his career was over and that he'd better do something else.

He bought a house in south Manchester, did it up and re-sold it at a profit. It wasn't as satisfying as beating a full back and crossing for Quinny to nod it home to the acclaim of a 47,000 full house, but it was a living and a living was the one thing football certainly wasn't offering him. He thought about a pub, not in the way George might have thought about a pub as a retirement occupation, but as another possible property development business. Then the phone rang.

Paul Hart, who had been the brains behind the emergence of the exciting Leeds United youth team (for which he has received little public credit), was now the manager of the financially ailing Nottingham Forest. David Platt had spent what little money Forest had before rejoining his former mentor Sven-Goran Eriksson as the manager of the England Under-21 side. Hart, of course, was the son of Johnny Hart who had been the City trainer during Mike's golden years in Manchester and who had briefly and unhappily succeeded Malcolm Allison as the manager in 1973 before giving way to Ron Saunders. Football can be a small world and the importance of personal relationships cannot be over-estimated.

Nick liked Paul Hart immediately and the feeling was mutual. Hart was honest and straightforward. He explained that there was little money, and not even the chance of a contract in the near future, but if he worked hard he'd get a chance in the first team and he'd be in the shop window. It was all he needed to hear and everything he wanted to hear. Working hard at his fitness levels, which had inevitably dropped, he demonstrated to Hart and the Forest coaching staff that he retained his hunger for the game. Hart was as good as his word and at the end of November 2001 Nicholas Summerbee took the field as a Nottingham Forest first team player.

The Forest fans were delighted to see him and he soon repaid their generous welcome by revealing the touches which had so enthused the Sunderland supporters when he had first arrived on Wearside. He gave the under-strength Forest team width and speed, and began to send over those devastating crosses that defenders hate and forwards adore. Unfortunately, Forest had no predatory strikers of the calibre of Quinn or Phillips but everyone could see what Summerbee was capable of offering. The long-suffering Forest fans knew their club was losing thousands of pounds a week, and that Nick was only playing for them so he could place himself in the shop window, but their fear was that he would be snapped up before he could help Forest to safety. For them, as for Paul Hart, the arrival of a free Nicky Summerbee was manna from heaven. He told the

313

local paper that all he wanted was first team football and the chance to earn a permanent contract somewhere. He hoped the Forest supporters would not believe the unfounded rumours about his previous behaviour. Most Forest fans hadn't the faintest idea what he was referring to, for which Nick was duly grateful. Within weeks of his first game for Forest, he began to hear more pleasant rumours of clubs being interested in him again.

In the middle of December Nick returned to south Manchester to be with Leonie as she went into labour. Mike was not impressed. His son had a game against Wimbledon on the Sunday, what was he doing messing about in a maternity ward three days before the match? Tina smiled. She remembered Mike's performance in similar circumstances. Just before Rachel was born, Mike got talking to a new father in the waiting room. He had arrived on the bus and Mike was not going to let him return home that way on such a special day. Wishing Tina a breezy farewell, he set off with his new friend in the car. By the time he had returned Rachel Summerbee had made her appearance.

Two years later they were back in the same Altrincham maternity hospital. This time Mike had been persuaded to see it through in the same room as his wife, but very shortly got chatting to a pretty nurse even as the new baby's head was engaged in the birth canal. With the sort of words Mike had previously heard only from referees he was sent from the delivery room to continue his conversation elsewhere. Tina gave birth without the aid of her sociable husband.

Late on Thursday 13 December, two days before his grandfather's 59th birthday, the latest Summerbee boy, Harley, arrived in the world. It was a fortunate piece of timing because Nicholas easily made it back to Selhurst Park in time to take the field in front of the traditional 5,000 Wimbledon faithful and the local ITV audience. For all his protestations of commitment, Nick had the sort of game City fans remembered

314

only too well – off the pace and totally disengaged. Five minutes before the end he was substituted. He had a reasonable excuse, of course, and he would hardly be the first new father to lose form temporarily. It occurred to me, watching him struggle, that after his wedding Mike lost form for seven months and after the birth of his first child history threatened to repeat itself until Dulcie took a hand. Would Dulcie, even after a triple bypass operation at the end of 2000, still have to drive over to Paul Hart's house and offer her usual blunt words of advice?

After the death of her second husband in 1984 Dulcie moved back to the north from her exile in Devon, back to the land of her birth which she had left so full of trepidation with George and the two little boys back in the summer of 1950. Now, in her little cottage in the Peak District, having survived major heart surgery, Dulcie sits and watches television in a state of constant trepidation, worrying what will happen to her grandson now. She worries if Nicholas has been picked for the first team, she worries if he's going to lose, she worries that he might never get another contract, she worries that a bad result or a bad injury or a change of manager will finish his career.

'I hate Saturday afternoons. I do now with Nicholas. I have it on Sky all the time waiting for the results to come through. I hate it.'

Dulcie first became a great-grandmother with the birth of Rachel's son, Samuel. She never liked football much as a young girl despite the fact that she lived next door to Deepdale when Preston were playing some of the brightest football in their history. She married a footballer and liked it even less as she saw at first hand the way it destroyed lives and people. To Dulcie, football is a malignant destructive force. It killed her husband even before the Addison's Disease attacked his vital functions and though her son and grandson have found fame and fortune it has always been at a price.

For Nick and Leonie there seems an inevitability about the

profession their son will follow. Already there is talk in the family of four-year-old Samuel who is showing outstanding hand–eye co-ordination. His grandfather recognises the signs of incipient footballing greatness. His great-grandmother shudders. Don't talk to her about 'the beautiful game' and the prospect of either of her great-grandsons becoming embroiled in it. Let her comment on the prospect be the last.

'I hope to God they don't become footballers. I hope I die first. Well I shall, I shall be dead then, shan't I?'

Coda

Those of us who fall in love with football tend to do so at an early age. For my generation and those before me, it was through playing in the street outside the house or in the park for hours at a time. We played because there was nothing in the world that we enjoyed doing more. We supported our teams because they somehow embodied all our heroic aspirations. Even in bad teams, children can find one hero, if only by default, or seize on the occasional victory to reinforce their dreams.

Until recent times, the media was more interested in how footballers played football than in how they lived their lives off the pitch. We all conspired to create an idealised world of football. As spectators we wanted heroes, the clubs wanted to tell their supporters they were employing heroes and the footballers wanted to be heroes. That's why they became footballers; they were influenced by the same propaganda as the rest of us.

There was no essential difference between George Summerbee, the teenage wing-half in the Hampshire League, desperate to attract the attention of his local professional club Aldershot Town, and Michael Summerbee, the teenager who played for Baker Street YMCA in Cheltenham, knowing that unless somebody spotted him he would be destined for a life of soul-destroying routine at Dowty Equipment Ltd. It may be that Nicholas Summerbee, growing up in relative affluence in the rural comfort of a large detached house in Cheshire, had the advantage of nurturing those same dreams, secure in the comfort that his father's reputation would give him access to that desired world of professional achievement. If so, crying down a pay phone as a rejected 15-year-old at Norwich City soon destroyed the fantasy.

Many are called but few are chosen yet nobody starts on the road in the belief that he is anything other than one of the few. George Summerbee left Winchester railway station that cold January morning in 1935 convinced that he was on his way to fame and fortune. He died 20 years later a deeply unhappy, disappointed man, his life broken by the very sport he had loved so passionately. If Cecil Green had not stopped in Cheltenham that day in 1958 and watched a youth-team match, who knows what might have become of Mike Summerbee?

Mike was lucky. He will be the first to admit the fact. The public parks are full of clever skilful footballers who will never grace professional grounds. Yet even Mike's combination of skill and luck did not seem so potent in the summer of 1965 with Swindon relegated and seemingly nobody interested in taking him elsewhere. Who knew what kind of concoction the blend of Joe Mercer's recent illness and Malcolm Allison was going to produce? Maybe the other managers were right. Maybe he didn't have what it took to be a successful professional footballer.

The sleazy stories of footballers and their various nefarious off-field activities fuelled by too much money and too few brains has in no way slowed the rush of boys who want to follow in their footsteps. The media's apparently insatiable interest in them, the emergence of football as social chic, the increase in the number of people who should know better but who feel it necessary to affect an interest in the game, the seemingly unstoppable torrent of money being tipped into football as if off the back of a lorry, all have resulted in keeping the game's profile high. In the opinion of many of us, it is too high and it is doing the game no service. It would be nice to blame Manchester United exclusively for this state of affairs but the social historian in me keeps clamping his hand over the mouth of the Manchester City supporter.

If you talk to the older players and ask them what was the satisfaction they gained from playing the game, none of them ever mentions the medals or the glory or any of the things that first fired their enthusiasm as boys. Sitting in the bath after a hard-fought victory, knowing you had pitted yourself against an opponent and won, comes up a lot. Mike, who won a lot of games and medals and glory, is even more to the point.

'I've met lots of successful people in all walks of life and all of them would have changed their lives for mine. I made a living out of the game.'

And that's why the dream still persists and would persist even if the money drains out of football. None of the Summerbees ever went into it for the money. George never earned more than £8 a week. Mike never earned more than £350 a week. Nick's done all right because the peak of his career coincided with this obscene rise in players' wages at the top of the game, but when he is sitting at home on a Saturday afternoon because the manager isn't playing him any more, all the ISAs and TESSAs and pension plans and all the Range Rovers and holidays in Dubai are no compensation for the fact that somebody else is wearing his shirt and playing instead of him. David Niven once remarked of Errol Flynn, 'You can always rely on Errol. He'll always let you down.' At some level, football is the Errol Flynn in the lives of too many young men.

Don't put your daughter on the stage, Mrs Worthington, and think very carefully before you encourage your son to become a professional footballer. Behind the fantasy world of glamour and wealth beyond the dreams of avarice created by the unholy alliance of greedy football people and rapacious media jackals, lies another world, one that is distinguished by crushed dreams, broken relationships and financial penury. We call it real life.

THE WAY IT WAS
My Autobiography

STANLEY MATTHEWS

The number one bestseller from football's
greatest hero.

Sir Stanley Matthews was a legend, the first superstar
of world football. In this, his long-awaited and
definitive autobiography, completed just before his
death in February 2000, he recalls the untold stories
about many of football's most famous characters and
games. The camaraderie, humour and tragedy are all
revealed in this remarkable memoir from a man who
was loved and respected around the world.

'A fascinating and amusing insight into the inner
workings of football during its golden era'
Daily Telegraph

'A ticket to a different era, when the game wasn't
saturated with money and men like Sir Stanley upheld
sporting ideals' *The Times*

'Brings vividly to life some of the greatest games of the
time and features his perceptive analysis of the
characters who illuminated the age' *Independent*

NON-FICTION / AUTOBIOGRAPHY 0 7472 6427 9

PSYCHO
The Autobiography

STUART PEARCE

The bestselling football autobiography of 2000

With the whole nation willing him on, Stuart Pearce took two famous penalties – and no one can forget what happened next. But what was it like for the man in the middle of it all? In *Psycho*, Pearce reveals all. Not just about those penalties, but about life at the top over the past two decades. This is a remarkable story from one of the most popular and charismatic footballers of our time. Packed with brilliant anecdotes, this updated edition will fascinate and inspire all who read it.

'Unputdownable . . . Pearce's honesty shines through' Sarah Edworthy, *Daily Telegraph*

NON-FICTION / AUTOBIOGRAPHY 0 7472 6482 1

More Non-fiction from Headline

JOHN BARNES:
THE AUTOBIOGRAPHY

JOHN BARNES

'Marvellous . . . only a work of literary beauty coud do
justice to this man's playing career. And it does'
Total Football

'A highly readable account of a life spent quietly kicking
against stereotypes and prejudices' *Independent*

John Barnes' story is much more than a tale of English
football over the past two decades. It describes how he rose
to the highest level with Liverpool and England, battling
against racism and the England establishment's mistrust
of genuine flair.

In this updated edition of his bestselling autobiography, he
reviews his first taste of management at Celtic. He talks
revealingly about his innovative views on football and
reflects on the characters he has met over the years,
from Paul Gascoigne to Nelson Mandela. He recalls the
horror of Hillsborough and that mesmerising dribble
through Brazil's defence in Rio, arguably the greatest goal
ever scored by an Englishman.

The result is a thoughtful book that will appeal not just to
football followers everywhere but to those simply interested
in the varied life of a unique, very intelligent man.

NON-FICTION / AUTOBIOGRAPHY 0 7472 6007 9

Now you can buy any of these other bestselling non-fiction titles from your bookshop or *direct from the publisher*.